Value Making in International Economic Law and Regulation

This book examines the contemporary production of economic value in today's financial economies. Much of the regulatory response to the global financial crisis has been based on the assumption that curbing the speculative 'excesses' of the financial sphere is a necessary and sufficient condition for restoring a healthy economic system, endowed with real values, as distinct from those produced by financial markets. How, though, can the 'intrinsic' value of goods and services produced in the sphere of the so-called real economy be disentangled from the 'artificial' value engineered within the financial sphere?

Examining current projects of international legal regulation, this book questions the regulation of the financial sphere insofar as its excesses are juxtaposed to some notion of economic normality. Given the problem of neatly distinguishing these domains – and so, more generally, between economy and society, and production and social reproduction – it considers the limits of our current conceptualization of value production and measurement, with specific reference to arrangements in the areas of finance, trade and labour. Drawing on a range of innovative work in the social sciences, and attentive to the spatial and temporal connections that make the global economy as well as the racial, gender and class articulations of the social reproductive field within it, it further asks: what alternative arrangements might be able to affect, and indeed alter, the value-making processes that underlie our current international regulatory framework?

Donatella Alessandrini is Reader in Law at the Kent Law School. Her research interests are in the areas of critical development studies, trade theory and practice, and feminist political economy.

Value Making in International Economic Law and Regulation

Alternative Possibilities

Donatella Alessandrini

Routledge
Taylor & Francis Group

LONDON AND NEW YORK

First published 2016
by Routledge

2 Park Square, Milton Park, Abingdon, Oxfordshire OX14 4RN
711 Third Avenue, New York, NY 10017

Routledge is an imprint of the Taylor & Francis Group, an informa business

First issued in paperback 2017

British Library Cataloguing in Publication Data
A catalogue record for this book is available from the British Library

Library of Congress Cataloging-in-Publication Data
Alessandrini, Donatella, author.
Value making in international economic law and regulation : alternative possibilities / Donatella Alessandrini.
ISBN 978-1-138-93674-4 (hbk) -- ISBN 978-1-315-67665-4 (ebk) 1. Trade regulation. 2. Foreign trade regulation. 3. Value. 4. Profit. 5. Surplus value. 6. Economics--Political aspects. 7. Financial risk management. 8. Derivative securities--Valuation. 9. Labor theory of value. I. Title.
K3840.A94 2016
338.5'21--dc23
2015030058

ISBN: 978-1-138-93674-4 (hbk)
ISBN: 978-1-138-56549-4 (pbk)

Typeset in Garamond by
Servis Filmsetting Ltd, Stockport, Cheshire

For Maria

Contents

Acknowledgements

Among the friends and colleagues who have made this book possible with their ideas, questions, images and readings, I would like to thank Paddy Ireland, Stacy Douglas, Hyo Yoon Kang, Rosemary Hunter, Nick Piska, Davina Cooper, Maria Drakopoulou, Jasper van Doreen, Serena Natile, Jose Bellido, Didi Herman, Sally Sheldon, Iain Ramsay, Emma Dowling, Ann Stewart, Rosie Harding, Connal Parsley, Ruth Fletcher, Ntina Tsouvala, Sarah Slowe, Vicky Conway, Irene Leon, Magdalena Leon, Rhadika Desai, Asta Zoykatite, Luis Eslava, Laura Binger, Simone Wong, Thanos Zartaloudis, Helen Carr, Mairead Enright, Sinead Ring and Will Mbioh; and in particular Emily Haslam, Maria Tsoukala, Anastasios Gaitanidis and Anisa de Jong.

I am grateful to the British Academy and Kent Law School for their financial support, and to the post-graduate research community at Kent for our weekly study group and the thought-provoking discussions that have sustained me in the final stage of writing.

I would also like to thank Iain Frame, Judy Fudge, Fiona Allon, Lisa Adkins, Anne Kovaleinen, Emilie Cloatre and Martyn Pickersgill for their generous feedback on portions of the book and earlier versions of the arguments; Amanda Perry-Kessaris and Luis Eslava for their wonderful help with the cover image of the book; Colin Perrin, Laura Muir, Glynis Dyson and Abigail Pukaniuk for their editorial advice and support; and Marie Selwood for her assistance with the final draft.

Special thanks to Fiona Macmillan, Toni Williams, Lorenzo Corsini and Suhraiya Jivraj for helping me work out ideas and arguments, and for their incredible support; to Kate Bedford, whose incisive feedback and wonderful friendship have been vital to the development of this project; to Brenna Bhandar for the many conversations within and outside our reading group, and for pushing me with crucial questions; and to Emily Grabham for engaging so generously and critically with the whole book. I cannot thank you enough for your encouragement, friendship, time and labour. I have not been able to do justice to all your comments but the book is much improved as a result of your feedback.

And finally I would like to thank Silvia Federici and Antonella Picchio, whose work has been a source of profound inspiration for this book, among other things.

List of abbreviations

ALBA	Bolivarian Alternative for our Peoples of the Americas
BIS	Bank for International Settlements
ELR	Employer of Last Resort
EMH	Efficient Market Hypothesis
FCC	Federal Communication Commission
GATS	General Agreement on Trade in Services of the World Trade Organisation
GATT	General Agreement on Tariffs and Trade
GDP	Gross Domestic Product
IPRs	intellectual property rights
LANDS	Law and New Developmental State
LIBOR	London Interbank Offered Rate
NPED	New Political Economy of Development
OTC	over-the-counter
RMA	Regional Monetary Agreement
SSF	social studies of finance
STS	science and technology studies
SUCRE	Unified System for Regional Compensation
UN	United Nations
WTO	World Trade Organization

Introduction

This book is about value. Its idea emerges from a series of reflections concerning shifting public and regulatory debates about the US subprime mortgage, turned financial, turned (world) economic crisis, and the place of value making within these debates. At stake is the missed opportunity for change that the international community was presented with in the period 2007–2010: that of radically affecting the economy–society nexus. Whereas previous financial crises were thought to be limited to certain regions in terms of both their effects and causes,[1] *this* crisis was seen as striking at the heart of a system, the Anglo-American one, which had been praised for its 'efficiency', 'depth' and capacity for 'financial innovation' around the world. Between 2008 and 2009, alongside the emphasis on reforming the international financial system, questions about the relationship between the process of financialisation and the economy were increasingly raised which challenged the sustainability as well as desirability of financialised models of growth.[2] A year later, however, the crisis had become, in the UK as well as in many other European countries, a fiscal one and the breadth of this debate was reduced to the question of the extent to which public spending needed to be cut in order to regain the confidence of financial investors. Fiscal imperatives came to replace earlier reformist agendas and questions about the role of finance were removed from public debate. Austerity had become the dominant discourse and policy prescription.

The factors that have contributed to this sudden change in 2010 are complex and would require much more careful and detailed exploration than I am able to undertake in this book. There is, however, one particular aspect of the debate that I think constrained, since the very beginning, the possibility of imagining alternative and more creative responses to the crisis and this has to do with the way in which value making is conceptualised in international economic regulation. Much of the regulatory response to the crisis was predicated on a belief that what had happened represented an excess, an anomaly within the realm of finance which had thrown the

economic system off balance. The assumption was that curbing the speculative 'excesses' of the financial sphere through appropriate regulation of
risky innovations was a necessary and sufficient condition for restoring a
healthy productive system endowed with 'real' values separate from the
ones produced by financial markets. From this perspective, I would argue,
the transition to austerity was not as radical a departure: its acceptance was
possible, at least in part, because the belief in financial excess as the antithesis of economic normality has been to a large extent internalised. Rather
than viewing it as the manifestation of a particular normality, that is of a
specific system of norms and values that regulate, discipline and arrange
the economy–society nexus, the crisis has been understood as an anomalous
situation brought about by irresponsible consumers, borrowers and lend-
ers, and by regulatory oversight. The implication of this line of argument
is the belief that once the irresponsible borrower *par excellence*, that is the
state, is disciplined, normality, purged from the excess that has given rise
to the anomaly, can be restored.

Why, then, talk about value making in this context? Because normality
thus understood, that is as a situation where the economic system ought
to be purged from the excess of financial speculation, relies on a pervasive
and problematic understanding of economic value that is common to both
advocates and critics of financial markets. For the advocates, value is that
which is produced in the sphere of the so-called real economy, that is the
sphere within which goods and services are produced, but which financial
markets are able to measure accurately. For the critics, financial markets
distort economic value, by creating a financial value which for the most
part bears no sound relationship with the economic value of the asset measured. For both, therefore, the idea is that there exists a real economic value
which is either reflected in or distorted by financial markets. This position
was evident in the debate concerning the regulation of financial derivatives that took place between 2008 and 2010. Much of the discussion then
was premised on the assumption that a distinction could and should be
made between a 'real', productive sphere of the economy that needed to
be re-appropriated and stimulated and a purely speculative, unproductive
one that needed to be tamed, with financial innovations belonging to the
latter. This kind of framing characterised not only financial commentaries (Jenkins, 2008; Ishikawa, 2009) and reform proposals (US and EU in
particular) but also a certain position in the social sciences which, even as
it recognised that speculation is inherent in capitalism, saw derivatives
as violent financial innovations whose threat had and could be eradicated
through more stringent regulation (Lipuma and Lee, 2004; Dodd, 2005).

The problem with this position, however, is that significant work has
called into question exactly such assumptions. To start with, we have
learnt that the financial sphere is coterminous with the sphere of the real

economy: indeed most profits made by manufacturing and services companies derive from their financial sectors (Krippner, 2005; Bayliss, 2014). What this implies is that finance not only provides the means for economic activities meant to realise profits, it has also become a direct source of profits. At the same time, we have come to appreciate how difficult it is, conceptually and empirically, to disentangle real from financial values. For instance, studies on financial derivatives have demonstrated how their trading can affect the value of the assets they are supposed to be based on and shown how, save their banning, regulation can limit but not eliminate the effects of such value making processes (Pérez Caldentey and Vernengo, 2010).[3] The most practical and immediate consequence is that faith in regulation as the means for curbing the excesses of the financial sphere is misplaced. This is not to say that regulation is irrelevant. As I argue in Chapter 1, there are limitations to what it can achieve. Specifically, regulation juxtaposes financial excess to economic normality while leaving intact the arrangements through which the production–finance nexus is currently organised. More fundamentally at stake, however, there are questions about the way we conceptualise the relationship between the real and the financial spheres of the economy and of value production and its measurement at their intersection. What if the normality we have to work with contemplates the difficulty, even the impossibility, of neatly distinguishing between the real and the financial spheres of the economy? What does it mean to acknowledge that value is produced at their intersection? How can we act then?

This book is an attempt to think about these questions in three realms of international economic regulation. I have drawn on previously published work which, relying on case studies conducted between 2010 and 2014, shares a commitment to thinking in a particular way about the contingency of value making processes as well as our ability to contest them;[4] and chosen to focus on finance, trade and labour as examples of the many spheres that constitute the nexus between economy and society, a nexus which is the very stuff of political economy.[5] Focusing on how value is produced and circulates within different spheres enables us to see how the various attempts made to conceive of and act upon them as neatly separate domains are deeply problematic. This is because such separations do not attend to the complex ways in which these spheres co-produce, and not merely exist alongside, one another; this is not just the case with the financial regulatory debate, which remains premised on a neat distinction between a real and a financial sphere. The current austerity debate is also predicated on, while actually effecting, a very problematic separation between the productive and reproductive spheres of life that does specific political economic work, that of generating more (economic) value from the very terrain on which life is reproduced.[6] Taking into account such work, I ask whether alternative institutional arrangements can provide a better appreciation of the co-production of these different spheres, and by doing so, whether they can enable other values to inform action, thereby arranging the economy–society nexus otherwise. The book therefore addresses two main questions: first, taking into account the difficulty of neatly distinguishing between the real and the financial spheres of the economy, and between real and financial values, how do we conceptualise value production and measurement? And second, what institutional arrangements can we think of that are able to affect current value making processes?

I return in the last section to the theme of institutional arrangements and the particular way I envisage them. In the meantime, if the ability to contest the arrangements that intervene in current value making processes is one recurrent theme of this book, the other, with which contestability is inextricably connected, is our ability to think value's contingency. Thus, while the book aims to show the limitations that regulatory frameworks place on our ability to think differently about international economic action, it does so by exploring the complementarities and important differences between three currents of thought which I have grouped together as constructivist approaches to economic value. These are the performativity of economics approach, and within it the social studies of finance (SSF) school (Callon, 1998; MacKenzie, Muniesa and Siu, 2008); and two particular traditions of Italian thought, the post-workerists turned immaterial labour scholars (Hardt and Negri, 2001; Vercellone, 2006, 2009; Virno, 2004) and those feminist scholars who are associated with the 'Wages for/against Housework' campaign in the Anglo-American world (Dalla Costa and James, 1972; Fortunati, 1981; Federici, 2004). The reason I consider them together despite their important differences is that they all share an understanding of the nexus between economy and society that is much more nuanced than regulatory accounts assume. At the same time their different understanding of value's contingency, a concept which has attracted quite a lot of attention in the social sciences, provides crucial resources for thinking about how to contest and therefore intervene in processes of value making.

Value's contingency and contestability

What makes a product valuable today? The question of where economic value comes from has a long history in economic thought. Although notions of use value and exchange value go back to Aristotle and Aquinas – limiting one's analysis to Western philosophy – the shift in thinking about the source of economic value is often presented as one from objective, intrinsic to subjective, extrinsic accounts. The former identifies value as pertaining to the sphere of production, with the Physiocrats seeing land as the source of value and agriculture as the productive activity *par excellence*; and classical political economists identifying labour and industry as its source and productive activity respectively. The subjective approach to value places it instead in the sphere of exchange, with neoclassical economists introducing the idea of 'marginal utility' according to which economic value is determined exclusively by the wants and desires of consumers. For the marginalists, there is no intrinsic value as such; no property or substance that bestows value upon goods but only consumers' preferences. Economic sociologists have acknowledged the limits of this approach in that it does not explain how preferences are formed and how they change over time. While agreeing that value is an effect of the desire of potential purchasers, Beckert and Aspers (2011:11) for instance argue that 'the valuation of goods and changes of these valuations need to focus on the *meanings* that goods obtain for actors and on the social and institutional structure of markets'.

The position I take in this book is somewhat different: I agree that a focus on the activities constituting value requires us to pay attention to processes, including meaning making activities, rather than on a predetermined substance – whether an objective source such as land or labour or a subjective one such as consumers' preferences. However, as I argue in Chapter 2 through a re-reading of Smith's and Marx's work on value, and Federici's engagement with the latter in particular, I think that the 'substance' thesis has been exaggerated. Foucault (1966) for instance argued that underlying both subjective and objective accounts is a preoccupation with source and origin which he saw as characteristic of all modern human sciences, including political economy, since the eighteenth century. From this perspective labour and preferences, however seemingly different, can both be seen to occupy the position of quasi-transcendentals, that is, of unquestionable sources of value. This reading, however, is possible only if these accounts are purified of all controversies which, as I hope my engagement with Smith and Marx will demonstrate, were already present in their works. What I therefore intend to show is that thinking about value's contingency has a history which is longer and more fraught than is often assumed, a history which has struggled with the question of how to think contingency, its qualifications, and its relationship together with the ability to contest powerful value making processes.

How to think this history has been the underlying question that has accompanied, albeit not always explicitly, my thinking around contingency. I approach this question by bringing the theoretical insights of feminist and critical political economy to bear on both the scholarship of the performativity of economics and on that of cognitive and immaterial labour. What I find interesting is the fact that, already in the 1970s, 'Wages for/against Housework' scholars had argued that value was neither subjective nor the effect of an irrefutable logic but the result of the complex dynamics of an economic system which is always bound up with other (non-economic) values. More recently, SSF have traced the complex ways in which economic models and financial innovations actively shape, rather than merely reflect, the economy (Callon, 1998; MacKenzie, Muniesa and Siu, 2008; Bryan and Rafferty, 2006). And post-workerists and cognitive labour scholars have reflected on the transformations that have occurred at both the level of the economy and that of subjectivity, thereby affecting the links between labour and value in post-Fordist economies (Hardt and Negri, 2001; Mezzadra and Neilson, 2013a; Lazzarato, 2014). On the one hand, my interest in considering these approaches together lies in exploring the extent to which they complement one another in theorising value production and measurement and, by doing so, are capable of opening up the debate on how to act in the face of financial and economic uncertainty. This is a question that concerns the possibility of arranging the economy–society nexus otherwise.

On the other hand, there is a more specific intervention that I aim to make by relying on the insights of critical and feminist political economists. I think their work brings two important qualifications to the contribution that both performativity scholars and post-workerists have made to the contingency debate, and these qualifications matter for analytical and political reasons. First, they have shown how seeing value as contingent and its measurement as a construct means acknowledging that there is not one natural or correct way for us to measure what we produce and exchange. This, however, is not the same as saying that value is today beyond measure. The latter is a claim post-workerist scholars often make when describing the shifting relationship between labour and value from Fordist to post-Fordist value production. I do not mean to deny that there are important differences in the ways in which both labour and value, as well as their relationship, are conceptualised, produced and organised in post-Fordist economies, as Mezzadra and Neilson's recent work has insightfully shown (2013a). However, as I argue in Chapter 1, the manner in which the rupture from Fordism to post-Fordism is posited, specifically by scholars of cognitive capitalism and immaterial labour, risks conferring a fixity – almost naturalness – to both these categories and their relationship that, as this feminist work has shown, particularly that of 'Wages for/ against Housework' scholars, was never there. Thus, to claim that value is today beyond measure is to disregard the fact that it is not that *socially necessary labour time* (particularly understood as clock time) once provided the accurate measure of value and today is no longer capable of doing so, but that the way in which value measurement is constantly instituted has important political consequences (De Angelis, 2005). The point is not to ignore the profound transformations that are taking place but to say that such transformations and the ways they affect, while being affected by, social relations have to be carefully traced rather than assumed so as to be able to see the many different ways in which measuring takes place (Harvie, 2005; Bryan, Rafferty and Jefferis, 2015). Acknowledging that measuring constantly takes place, and that measures are heterogeneous in character, also helps us unpack the assumption according to which considering value as contingent means that anything is possible. While contingency points to the fact that there is not one natural or 'correct way for a society to measure a commodity' (Mirowski, 1991:568), its measurement is instituted nonetheless. The consequences – the crystallisations this process of instituting enables – have to be taken into account when thinking about alternative value making processes, and this is why in Chapter 1 I emphasise the role derivatives have come to play in measuring bits of capital across the world, that of giving continuity to global production and accumulation (Bryan, Rafferty and Jefferies, 2006, 2013, 2015; Allon, 2015). If I keep a focus on the seemingly defunct 'law of value' as a powerful organising logic for economic and social relations (of which derivatives are a manifestation), this is not because I believe it to be ubiquitous or all-encompassing force but because, as Mezzadra and Neilson have pointed out, 'it is necessary to keep both the systematic and differentiating abilities of capitalism in view' in order to understand how (capitalist) value continues to be produced and measured despite the heterogeneity characterising forms of labour, production and regulation around the world (2013a:81, 86).

There is, however, a second qualification that this work, in particular that of 'Wages for/against Housework' scholars, brings to the contingency debate. This is the fact that, by engaging with classical political economists, not only have they shown that economic categories and the reality they described were more fluid and contested than is often assumed to be the case; they have also brought to the fore the crucial role that social reproduction plays in processes of value making, a role that both Smith and Marx disregarded as they thought *generally* about the totality of processes through which a socio-economic system reproduces itself; and the specificity of this role continues to be overlooked even by scholars who have moved past both objective and subjective accounts of value. As Rai, Hoskyns and Thomas (2010:3) have argued, social reproduction encompasses biological reproduction, including sexual, affective and emotional services; unpaid production of goods and services in the home and within the community; and the reproduction of culture and ideology, which can both stabilise and challenge dominant social relations. The link to processes of value making is evident since each of these activities contributes to processes of production, consumption and exchange.[7]

While this conceptualisation brings crucial (gender, sexual and racial) qualifications to the more general definition of social reproduction, there is something else to be gained by going back to the work of Dalla Costa,

Fortunati and Federici. For them, social reproduction has certainly to do with the way we collectively organise our living, the way we produce and reproduce life's conditions, and therefore also with the way economic value is constantly produced and measured. At the same time, by focusing their attention on the historic separation between production and reproduction, they have been able to trace the processes through which the latter, in as much as the former, is deeply entangled with processes of capital accumulation. Although it was by no means a universal case both within and outside Fordist economies, they saw unpaid housework in particular as providing the means through which the labouring population was reproduced and value was extracted. Today the sexual division of labour, as well as the prominence of wage labour, can no longer be assumed (Adkins, 2009). However, this does not mean that their contribution is no longer relevant. Indeed, despite their initial focus on domestic labour, their work soon highlighted both the enormous pool of unwaged labour that sustains the life process and the ways in which this pool generates value for capital, with the consequent problematisation of both the analytical and political privileging of wage labour. Similarly, despite the initial attention to the situation of women in Fordist economies, their analyses became gradually attentive to the spatial and temporal connections that make the global economy and the racial, gender, sexual and class articulations of the social reproductive field within it, and this I think remains a specific quality of their present work (Federici, 2011). This attention is what tends to be missing in accounts that privilege the immaterial or cognitive aspects of global production, thereby severing those crucial connections of which they are an integral part.

This work therefore offers the possibility of remaining attentive to both the articulations that make the social re/productive field on a global scale, and the relevance of other values, actually existent or not, that coexist with, even as they are obfuscated by, those informing current action (Gibson-Graham, 1996; Bedford, 2009; Spillman, 2012). Indeed social reproduction, seen as the production of the very conditions of life, is not just the realm on which capital relies to extract value but also the terrain on which to struggle for engendering alternative valorisation processes. At stake is the question of how otherwise to forge the nexus between economy and society. Latour and Lepinay (2009) have argued that the problem with current understandings of political economy, that is the nexus between economy and society, is the belief in an economic order regulated by natural laws that exist out there, which society has to discover and implement. This is the belief that this body of work has challenged since at least the 1970s, pointing to how categories, concepts and theories (including socially necessary labour time and the law of value) were not given but constructs whose validity and solidity were achieved and fabricated rather than natural. Understanding this process, which is both an epistemological and ontological one, is essential in order to intervene in it, that is, in order to format the nexus otherwise.

Institutions and alternative valorisation processes

It is from this perspective that I ask the question of what kind of institutional arrangements might be able to shift current value making processes. As Chapter 1 shows, although the crisis seemed to have presented the opportunity, even if briefly, to rethink the economy–society nexus, this possibility was hardly ever there since the debate has been limited to the regulatory realm, and even within this sphere it has been framed in terms of a very unhelpful juxtaposition between real (read industrial/manufacturing) and parasitical (read financial) values that does not pay attention to the complex ways in which finance and production are deeply imbricated. Lothian and Unger (2011:20), for instance, note how under 'the present arrangements of market economies, the production system is largely financed on the basis of the retained and reinvested earnings of private firms. Theoretically, the role of banks and stock markets is to finance production as well as consumption.' In actual fact they played a very minor role, despite the increase in financial activities, in the 'funding of long term investment [having] increasingly more to do with financing of asset trading and position taking by highly leveraged financial institutions' (2011:20).[8] This is not an issue of production pertaining to the real economy and of finance belonging to a fictitious, parasitical sphere, but of the kind of nexus that arranges the relationship between the two, equally real, spheres. Interestingly, they point to the fact that much of the response to the crisis is predicated on an unacknowledged anti-institutional bias which has characterised the history of English political economy after Smith, with the only exception to be found in Marx, and which consists of the belief that 'despite minor national variations, a market economy has a single natural and necessary institutional form' (2011:37). As they put it:

> It is remarkable that this idea of the inner legal logic of a market economy has maintained its ascendancy in the face of its deconstruction by a hundred and fifty years of legal analysis. No theme is more constant in the legal thought of this historical period than the step-by-step and often involuntary discovery of the multiplicity of alternative institutional forms, defined in legal detail, that a market economy can take, each form with different consequences for the distribution of advantage as well as for the organization of production and exchange.

Hence, as Chapter 2 argues, the importance of re-reading Smith and Marx's work consists not only of showing that they conceptualise, or at least can be read to conceive of, value in a much more fluid way than what is often presented by the literature that relegates them to substance or objective-like accounts. Their work is also important for the way in which it recognises the crucial role played by institutions in arranging the economy–society nexus and the way it can therefore suggest the always already present possibility of arranging it otherwise. To be sure, I do not see the role that institutions play in generating change as unidirectional. This is a point that has also emerged more recently in the context of a debate within the 'new institutionalist' school that has acknowledged the limits of an analysis which, in order to take account of institutions in explaining action, tends to regard them as 'overly "sticky"'.[9] The turn to what Vivien Schmidt (2008) has called 'Discursive Institutionalism' is meant to unstick institutions by treating them simultaneously 'as given (as the context within which agents think, speak and act) and as contingent (as the results of agents' thoughts, words, and actions)' (2008:314). The challenge that this brings is both 'ontological (about what institutions are and how they are created, maintained, and changed) and epistemological (about what we can know about institutions and what makes them continue or change with regard to interests and norms)' (2008:313). While this debate resonates with the premise of the constructivist approaches to value that I engage with, my interest in institutions is different. I take institutions to be both constitutive of and constituted by action; but whereas Schmidt's interest lies in understanding what kind of processes makes institutions change or remain the same over time – and the role specifically played by ideas and discourse – mine is in thinking of specific institutional arrangements as provocations, that is as attempts to engender value making processes which are different from the ones that are currently formatting the economy–society nexus.

There are two points I wish to make in this respect. First, I talk of institutional arrangements to both highlight the dynamic nature of the nexus to which the arrangement aims to contribute, while also being shaped by it, and to own the 'perspectival seeing' from which I am making the intervention. This makes clear, as the reference to Nietzsche in Chapter 2 indicates, that what is at stake is a struggle over the 'hierarchy of values'. Chapters 3 and 4 give three such examples in the areas of finance, trade and labour: the Regional Monetary Agreement (RMA) proposed but not adopted by Ecuador; the Boliviarian Alternative for the Peoples of our America of which Ecuador is also a member; and the recent proposal by feminist economists and post-Keynesians for the state to become an Employer of Last Resort. As institutional arrangements, these examples are potential experiments that aim to 'infuse' institutions with *values* different from the ones that dominate current arrangements and simultaneously they are attempts to transform the *processes of valuation* that underlie such arrangements.

This might seem at odds with the theoretical tradition I have drawn upon for thinking about value making and its measurement, and which has focused on processes of self-valorisation conducted at a distance from both the state and wage labour. From this perspective, thinking about institutional arrangements at the international level may appear a contradictory and self-defeating project. However, as I argue in Chapter 4, this does not necessarily need to be the case. Indeed, the second point I make is that the work of 'Wages for/against Housework' scholars can be read to show that engaging with institutions can take provocative forms. That is why I conceive of these arrangements as provocations, and am proposing to think of institutional arrangements more generally as provocations, in this tradition of feminist thought: not as blueprints for action but as forms of intervention in the economy capable of provoking alternative valorisation processes. I maintain a focus on action even though I acknowledge that the reality provoked by these interventions might be very different from what 'we' envisage through such interventions. I am also aware that whatever the 'goals' we aim to achieve, the act of rearranging markets and with them the economy–society nexus will always involve exclusions, some of them more problematic that others depending on one's 'perspectival seeing'. With these qualifications, I hope to move past what I see as the impasse of some constructivist approaches to value. As I argue in Chapter 3, particularly those which have been influenced by science and technology studies (STS), have made an important contribution to our understanding of the complex workings of markets in general and financial innovations in particular. There is, however, one important limitation that has emerged when the question of how to act in the midst of such complexity has come to the fore; while opening up many 'black boxes' of financial practices, STS-inflected SSF have up until now refrained from thinking about how to 'format' markets, and arrange the economy–society nexus, otherwise. In conceiving of value as both contingent (albeit with important qualifications) and contestable and of institutional arrangements as provocations, I hope to open such a debate. This is where I think lies the potential for collaboration among constructivist approaches to political economy that share a commitment to complexity, contingency and contestability.

Outline of chapters

I begin, in Chapter 1, with financial derivatives. Analysing derivatives is important because it illustrates how value making is a contingent process (Bryan and Rafferty, 2006), and it also shows how such contingency implies neither that value is beyond measure nor that regulating mechanisms are non-existent or ineffectual. Chapter 1 reflects on the blurring of boundaries between the real and financial spheres of the economy and the problematic nature of accounts that resort to substance-like explanations of value to justify intervention in the economy, usually through the means of regulation. As the chapter argues, derivatives are powerful technologies through which bits of capital are commensurated across time and space and this commensuration has important consequences for production and labour processes around the world. Understanding how the measurement of value is instituted in the midst of financial and economic uncertainty is therefore crucial in order to intervene in the production–finance nexus, which in turn entails affecting the relationship between production and social reproduction. Although Chapter 4 deals with this relationship in more depth, Chapter 1 introduces 'Wages for/against Housework' scholars and the contribution they have made to our understanding of value as a specifically contingent process, one made of spatio-temporal connections that arrange the productive–reproductive fields on a global scale. This chapter therefore shows the limits of regulatory approaches that have dominated the post-2007 debate, while also introducing important qualifications to arguments that cast the 'contingency of value' as a recent and novel phenomenon (eg Hardt and Negri, 2001, 2009).

Chapter 2 addresses the apparent 'newness' of arguments about value's contingency. By going back to Smith's *Wealth of Nations* and Marx's *Capital* we can see how objective or substance-like accounts of value can be posited as unequivocal only by filtering the many controversies that troubled the existence of such substance in the first place. I argue that Smith's work can be read as an attempt to introduce in the emergent field of classical political economy a theory or model able to actively format the economy–society nexus. This point is not new: it has been made by Poovey (1998) in relation to Smith's approach to numbers and quantification. It has, however, a particular relevance for the argument I make, and which seeks to qualify value's contingency, in that it brings to light how value measurement is always *instituted*. I read Marx's work as an attempt to denaturalise and therefore politicise this model whilst taking seriously its material effects. In this respect I see Marx's positioning of the figure of *labour* not as a quasi-transcendental, as Foucault (1966) for instance has done, but as the historical form that relations take when (capitalist) value becomes a powerful organising principle of social activity. Seeing value not as a natural attribute or substance of things but as a process which is constantly enacted enables a focus on the hierarchy of values investing socioeconomic relations. The chapter concludes with a reflection on the 'perspectival seeing' Nietzsche (1887) advocates in *On the Genealogy of Morals*, in a different context albeit around the same time as Marx, for struggling over the current hierarchy of values. Focusing on both aspects (ie the current hierarchy of values and the struggle from a specific 'perspectival seeing') enables me to introduce the way in which Chapters 3 and 4 conceive of specific institutional arrangements as *provocations* (Weeks, 2011). I use this concept in the tradition of 'Wages for/against Housework', that is, as an attempt to intervene in current value making processes not on the premise that they are unreal, inaccurate or beyond measure, but that they are deeply undesirable from a perspective that pays attention to the relationship between value production and socially reproductive activities. As the chapter also shows, the inattentiveness to this crucial relationship has a long history, one which, as Federici (2004) has argued in *Caliban and the Witch*, relies on the constant production of separations and divisions for the generation of (capitalist) value.

Chapter 3 takes Ecuador's RMA as a *provocative* attempt in the area of the transnational management of exchange rates' derivatives. I ask whether, by implicitly considering the economic and financial spheres as co-constitutive, and therefore real, such a form of intervention provides an opportunity for enacting values which are different from the ones populating the current hierarchy, starting with the individualisation of risks and precarisation of life promoted by financial markets (Fumagalli and Mezzadra, 2009), and for acknowledging the crucial role played by social reproductive activities. I then explore a similar question in another area of international economic regulation, that of multilateral trade law and negotiations. Whereas the two-decades-long existence of the World Trade Organization (WTO) has shed serious doubts over the presumed universally beneficial impact of trade liberalisation, I show how entrenched and pervasive the value of global competitiveness has become, even in critical trade and development debates. I turn to the Bolivarian Alternative for our Peoples of the America (ALBA) and ask whether it should be dismissed as an ineffectual attempt to challenge the current trade and development value hierarchy; or whether it can be understood as an opportunity to think differently about multilateral trade relations.

In a sense, these are very odd instances for thinking about alternative valorisation processes as they are forms of macroeconomic intervention that sit uncomfortably with the experiments from which I have drawn inspiration for thinking *provocatively* about institutional arrangements. Chapter 4 returns to the crucial contribution feminists have made to our understanding of the economy–society nexus, a nexus which is traversed by a problematic separation between production and social reproduction (ie Picchio, 1992; Federici, 2004). It enables me to expand on the argument I have introduced in Chapter 1, that is that the contingency of value thesis takes on analytical and political salience only if we pay attention to the spatio-temporal connections that arrange the productive–reproductive fields on a global scale, and in particular to the racial, gender, sexual and class articulations through which such fields are constituted. I do this by revisiting a vexed feminist debate, that concerning the possibility of engaging with the state and wage labour, and examining it in light of the 'Wages for/against Housework' campaign launched in the 1970s. By reflecting on the way in which scholars and activists behind this campaign promoted experiments at a distance from the state while also demanding that reproductive labour be recognised as productive of (capitalist) value, I ask whether current attempts by feminist economists to join the post-Keynesian call for the state to become an Employer of Last Resort (ELR) are anachronistic and self-defeating political experiments or whether they can offer an opportunity to transform the meaning of work and productive activities.

This book then intends to show, and move beyond, the limitations that current regulatory frameworks place on our ability to think differently about international economic action. International economic lawyers have troubled the boundaries through which the discipline is organised, for instance, by bringing to light the historic and institutional separation with which the economic realm of the international order was insulated from political concerns, particularly after decolonisation (Macmillan, 2004; Anghie, 2007; Pahuja, 2013). This book contributes to these efforts by showing how current dichotomies, such as the real/financial economy one, continue to insulate 'economic' matters from 'political' life – for example, by neatly dividing the 'field' between the finance, trade and labour realms. By examining the porosity of such boundaries through the prism of value, it argues that these spheres are constantly produced through processes of value making and measurement; and that these processes include, although are not limited to, institutional arrangements. In other words, institutional arrangements do matter and this book is an attempt to think of alternative possibilities in international economic law and regulation. At the same time it is an attempt to think what international economic action would look like if we acknowledged value's contingency but moved past the 'immeasurability' of value thesis: if value is, and has always been, contingent, our ability to contest it is inextricably linked with the ability to see the power of measurement and measuring devices. And 'perspectival seeing' can inform international economic action even as we acknowledge that the world our action contributes to is not all of our making, a point to which I return in the concluding chapter.

Notes

1 Most financial crises which occurred in the 1990s were attributed to the improper implementation of sound economic policies. Laura Hyun Yi Kang, for instance, looks at the debate that emerged after the 'Asian crisis', showing how it was explained in terms of Asian 'cronyism' (2012:411–436).

2 For instance, the rise of household debt was scrutinised in the light of the unequal income distribution that, since the 1990s, has led to insufficient demand at the global level (Seguino, 2010:181). And wealth concentration, the other side of income inequality, was identified as one crucial factor leading to the growth of the markets for assets-backed securities (Lysandrou, 2011:232). I understand financialisation not merely as 'the increasing role of financial motives, financial markets, financial actors and financial institutions' (Epstein, 2005:3), but as the restructuring of the relations between production and reproduction: one manifestation of such restructuring, for instance, is that the reproduction of labour power starts with credit, rather than commodities; another is the introduction of general economic calculus and enterprise as the organising principles of household 'management' (Bryan, Martin and Rafferty, 2009; Allon, 2011).

3 As Chapter 1 will argue, this is because alongside allowing for speculation, derivatives also enable firms and governments to hedge, that is to protect themselves, against the risks of price volatility and other sources of financial uncertainty.

4 Chapter 1 draws on and substantively reworks two articles: 'Regulating Financial Derivatives? Risks, Contested Values and Uncertain Futures' (2011) 20:4 *Social and Legal Studies* 1–22 and 'Immaterial Labour and Alternative Valorisation Processes in Italian Feminist Debates: (Re)exploring the "Commons" of Re-production' (2012) 1:2 *feminists@ law* 1–28. Chapter 3 bridges between and significantly expands on two pieces: 'Financial Derivatives and the Challenge of Performation: Where Contingency Meets Contestability' in E. Cloatre and M. Pickersgill (eds), *Knowledge, Technology and Law: At the Intersection of Socio-Legal and Science and Technology Studies* (Routledge, 2015); and 'WTO at a Crossroads: The Crisis of Multilateral Trade and the Political Economy of the Flexibility Debate' (2013b) 5:2 *Law, Trade and Development* 256–285. Some ideas in Chapter 4 regarding the ELR proposal were explored in 'A Social Provisioning Employer of Last Resort: Post-Keynesianism Meets Feminist Economics' (2013a) 4:2 *World Review of Political Economy* 230–254.

5 I use the term 'nexus' instead of 'relationship' to put the accent on the dynamic nature of the entanglements that implicate one sphere with another, whether we are talking of the 'real' and the financial spheres of the economy, economy and society, or production and reproduction.

6 Living conditions are being squeezed through cuts to social welfare in many European countries. As the Women's Budget Group (2013) has pointed out, for instance, in England between 2010 and 2015 the largest cuts have been in social housing (33.8%); higher, further and adult education (32.6%); social care (23.4%); early years education and care

(19%); and schools (10.9%). What we are partly witnessing through austerity programmes is the reduction of the costs of social reproduction, some of which were previously incurred by states, at the same time as states allegedly attempt to stimulate 'production'. Indeed, the reduction of the costs of social reproductive activities is seen as the precondition for the growth of 'productive' activities.

7 This conceptualisation comes close to what some feminist economists have defined as the social provisioning approach to the study of economics, which is not an adjunct to economic analysis but a different starting point, one which considers the interconnectedness and mutual constitution of the productive and reproductive spheres (Power, 2004:7).

8 Greta Krippner's work (2005) has been particularly important in emphasising the increasing role that investment in financial instruments by non-financial companies has played in the generation of these companies' profits. One example is General Motors, which, in 2004, reported that 66% of its profits came from GMAC, its financial arm dealing with insurance, banking and commercial finance.

9 I thank Toni Williams for pointing me in the direction of Schmidt's work.

Chapter 1

Of value and its measurement: derivatives and the challenge of financial uncertainty

... if theories of value cannot incorporate finance in a central role, then they are disengaged from the frontiers of capital accumulation

(Bryan, Rafferty and Jefferis, 2015:308)

The generalization of affective labour, i.e., its dispersal over every form of work, takes us back to a pre-feminist situation, where not only the specificity but the very existence of women's reproductive work and the struggle women are making on this terrain become invisible again

(Federici, 2011:67–68)

Financial derivatives raise crucial questions about value production and its measurement in today's financialised economies. As such, they provide a very helpful lens through which to explore the real/financial economy debate. Since capital controls have been lifted and exchange rates were made to fluctuate in the market in the 1970s and 1980s, derivatives have become an important tool to manage the risks of global investing. They provide firms and governments with the means to hedge, that is, to protect themselves against the risks of price fluctuations, for instance, those deriving from floating exchange and interest rates. However, as derivatives are instruments whose value relates to that of the underlying asset, they have also given rise to speculation, and this latter aspect has gained prominence in the context of the financial crisis of 2008. The consensus among international policymakers at that time was that their regulation was necessary to curb their speculative excesses while preserving their hedging purpose. This consensus relied on the assumption that a distinction could and should be made between a so-called real, productive sphere of the economy that needed to be re-appropriated and stimulated and a purely speculative, unproductive one that needed to be tamed, with financial derivatives belonging to the latter sphere. This kind of framing characterised not only financial commentaries (Jenkins, 2008; Ishikawa, 2009) and reform proposals (US and EU in particular) but also the position in the social sciences which, even as it recognised that speculation is inherent in capitalism, saw derivatives as violent financial innovations whose threat needs to and can be eradicated, usually through more stringent regulation (Lipuma and Lee, 2004; Dodd, 2005).

While the violence that financial derivatives, and more generally financial capitalism, entail has been widely investigated (eg McNally, 2009; Marazzi, 2010; Harvey, 2010), my interest lies in exploring what is missing in a perspective that views financial derivatives as an excess that can be done away with. This position, I intend to show, underestimates two crucial aspects of derivatives' trading: first, the extreme difficulty, if not impossibility, of neatly distinguishing between the hedging and the speculation they allow. Second, and importantly, is the fact that, contrary to what derivatives claim to be doing, they do not merely derive their value from that of the underlying asset but also participate in the making of that value. Taken together, these two aspects challenge the assumption according to which the speculative 'excesses' of financial derivatives can be easily curbed in order to restore an otherwise healthy system of production, usually the industrial/manufacturing one, endowed with a 'real' value separate from that produced by financial markets.

Focusing on the technology of financial derivatives allows us to complicate the real/financial economy distinction underlying the regulatory response to financial innovations. In turn, this shows how blurred the boundaries between the two spheres are (de Goede, 2015).[1] What is at stake in recognising this blurring is not only the challenge to the regulatory response to the crisis but also the problematisation of the 'return to the real economy' argument insofar as it presupposes the possibility of disentangling financial from real values. The significance of derivatives, I argue, is that they show the complexity of such a task by bringing to the fore the uncertainty and contestability of value – both financial and real value. Reflecting on the technology of financial derivatives enables us to start confronting the first question with which this book is concerned, namely *how to conceive of* economic value at the intersection between production and finance, and between economy and society. While the merit of the literature I have grouped together under the umbrella of 'constructivist approaches to value' is to have brought the focus back on value's contingency and contestability, my argument, further developed in subsequent chapters, is two-fold.

First, that value has long been a contested concept: this is certainly the case with classical political economy despite the fact that most interpretations tend to emphasise the substance-like approach of its value theories. As Graeber (2005:57) has argued, for most classical political economists, thinking about value meant thinking about the relation of the parts to the whole. Whereas such a relation can, and as I argue should, be reconceptualised as the tracing of the connections that make up our (common) world (economy), the importance we attribute to our meaning-giving action cannot be underestimated. This includes the meaning enacted through institutional arrangements such as those which, as Chapter 3 shows, have led to the privatisation of risks and uncertainty and the precarisation of life.

The second, interconnected, argument is that claiming that value is beyond measure, as some of the scholars adhering to the 'contingency of value' thesis do – particularly those focusing on the paradigmatic shift in value production brought about by the ascendancy of 'immaterial labour' (eg Hardt and Negri, 2009) – does not help us understand how measuring is *instituted* (Mirowski, 1990, 1991). This appreciation is crucial to address the second question of the book, namely *how to act* once we accept the blurring of these boundaries; not only those between the real and the financial spheres of the economy, but also those between economy and society and, as this chapter goes on to argue, those between productive and social reproductive activities. To this end, the second section of this chapter introduces the work of Italian 'Wages for/against Housework' scholars who, by focusing on the crucial if shifting relationship between 'productive' and 'unproductive' labour, have made an important contribution to our understanding of value as neither subjective nor the effect of an irrefutable logic but as the result of the complex dynamics of an economic system (Dalla Costa and James, 1972; Fortunati, 1981; Federici and Fortunati, 1984). While showing the limits of regulatory discourses that have dominated the post-2007 debate, this chapter therefore introduces important qualifications to arguments that cast the 'contingency of value' as a recent and novel phenomenon, and one which has dispensed with measurement altogether. It argues that while value is contingent and contestable, the ways in which measurement is instituted has important consequences (Mirowski, 1991), and it is such measurement that we need to confront to promote alternative valorisation processes.

Valuing derivatives

Derivatives have acquired the centre stage in the course of the financial crisis that started in the US and spread quickly to other (mainly Western) financialised economies. Despite the different interpretations of the underlying factors (McNally, 2009; Gowan, 2009; Bellamy Foster and Magdoff, 2009), the consensus was that the unregulated proliferation of financial derivatives has been one of its most important triggers, particularly since the 'miscalculation' of their risks emerged fully in 2008, sending shock waves through the international financial system first and the global economy later. The fact that the notional amount outstanding for over-the-counter

(OTC) derivatives, that is derivatives not traded on formal exchanges, was estimated by the Bank for International Settlements (BIS) at US$615 trillion (BIS, 2010) and led many to wonder exactly what kind of financial instruments derivatives are, what kind of value they express and what type of relationship they have with the so-called real economy.

Addressing these questions, however, is not an easy task. The standard definition of derivatives in finance textbooks is that of contracts whose value is derived from the value of an underlying asset, an asset being a commodity or a financial asset, such as interest rates and exchange rates (see eg Goss, 1976; Gordon, 1986). However, to talk about derivatives in an undifferentiated manner is problematic since they refer to different things as well as different values. For instance, futures and options, which are the simplest forms of derivatives, are different contracts. Generally speaking, futures are contracts where two parties commit to buy or sell a certain asset at a future date and at an agreed price, whereas options are contracts that confer the right to buy or sell a particular asset at a certain date and at a certain price. Not only are they different things, they also refer to different values. With futures we are talking about the value the asset is supposed to have at a future date, whereas with options at issue is the value of the right to buy or sell the underlying asset at a certain price. It is sufficient to think about the various other types of derivatives that are today in circulation – forward, swaps, credit default swaps, collaterised debt obligations, etc – to appreciate that any comprehensive definition is unsatisfactory.

Thus, one way of approaching the question of what they are is to look at what they do. Historically their realm has been that of commodities, in particular agricultural commodities, and they have been important in ensuring continuity to the production cycle by allowing farmers, for instance, to hedge their operations against the risks of price fluctuations. Hence, the official purpose they serve is that of hedging against the risk of price volatility. However, as finance textbooks clearly indicate, speculation is also built in and this is because there will always be discrepancies at any time between the demand and offer of hedging opportunities (Goss, 1976; Yamey et al., 1985; Gordon, 1986). These markets need, in other words, speculators to take on the risks, and this applies to both commodity and financial derivatives.

In addition to this form of 'necessary' speculation, however, it has become apparent that there exists a less 'honourable' one associated with manipulation and gambling. Debates about the legitimacy of trading practices on financial exchanges in general and futures and options in particular date back at least to the nineteenth century, when derivatives concerned predominantly commodities and had as their underlying assets storable goods (de Goede, 2005:48–85). Indeed, the role of speculation in commodity prices has been and still is the object of intense controversy (Wray, 2008).

However, since capital controls have been removed, exchange rates made to fluctuate and financial markets liberalised, derivatives based on financial assets have increased exponentially and so have reports about their speculative excesses. In the past two decades they have repeatedly made headlines because of the financial disasters with which they have been involved, so that today they are mainly associated with gambling and speculation. Indeed, their most common characterisation is that of a mature form of 'casino capitalism' (Strange, 1997), with the very term 'casino' 'suggesting an economy of chance completely separate from the fundamentals of "real economy"' (Lipuma and Lee, 2004:85). Writing before the financial crisis, Lipuma and Lee had already argued that 'technologically driven derivatives detach the value, cost and price of money – manifest in exchange and interest rates – from the fundamentals of the economy, particularly the state of production, the social welfare of the producers, and the political needs of citizens' (2004:2). And when the crisis erupted, scholars started to focus on the complex relationship between the rate of foreclosures on housing in low income areas in the US, the highly rated, turned-toxic mortgage-backed securities held by banks and investors around the world, and the increasing rate of worldwide unemployment (Harvey, 2010:4).

While it is clear that financial derivatives can compromise social welfare, the nature of their relationship with the so-called real economy is less apparent. Indeed, this account of financial derivatives as representatives of a speculative capital that remains distinct or distinguishable from the 'fundamentals' of the real economy requires further scrutiny as it relies on two assumptions about derivatives that have been called into question by the reality of their trading. This has implications for both the possibility of effectively controlling derivatives so as to eradicate the threat of unnecessary speculation and that of drawing neat boundaries between the financial and the real spheres of the economy. The latter aspect in particular opens a series of crucial questions about the way in which 'real' and 'financial' values are made today as well as the kind of 'worthy' investments in the 'real' economy we advocate. While the remainder of this section focuses on the challenge that trading practices have brought to the two main assumptions about derivatives, the next section brings these insights to bear on the broader real/financial economy debate.

The first assumption underlying regulatory debates concerns the possibility of effectively distinguishing between hedging, on the one hand, and speculation, on the other, so that by curtailing the excesses of the latter, derivatives can be kept in line. Thus, the argument made is that it is necessary to curb the excesses of speculation so as to preserve the otherwise healthy purpose that derivatives serve in hedging against risks, thereby giving continuity to production on a global scale. As Bryan and Rafferty (2006:202) have argued, however, the fundamental problem with this position is that in actual markets the behavioural differences between the two types of market participants – hedgers and speculators – as well as between necessary speculation and arbitrage, ie the practice of making profits by trading on the price differences between markets, are difficult to establish: 'studies have not only found a range of reasons for (or types of) both hedging and speculation, but also that, at any point in time, market participants may be engaged in both speculative-type and hedging-type activities'. Thus it seems to be virtually impossible to distinguish *a priori* between these categories.

The second assumption is that it is possible to differentiate between the value of the underlying asset and that of a derivative. However, contrary to what most finance textbooks argue, the value of a financial derivative does not derive from the value of the underlying asset, but from the *trend* of that value in the market. This is an important point since the trend in market prices can be influenced by the same market players, which means that the mechanisms that determine the value of the derivative are not linear. That is to say that the derivative affects the value of the underlying asset on which it is supposed to be merely based. There are indeed empirical studies showing that derivatives affect prices in spot markets, ie markets in which the underlying assets are traded (see Garbade and Silber, 1983; Stoll and Whaley, 1990; Vrolijk, 1997). In particular, and significantly for the argument I make in Chapter 3 when I look at alternative institutional arrangements, futures currencies have long been shown to be important determinants of spot exchange rates (Maldonado and Saunders, 1983; Jabbour, 1994; Chatrath et al., 1996). The point emerging from these empirical studies is that these agreements represent events the market cannot ignore. In very basic terms, to know that two players have agreed on a certain price means to know that at a certain date there will be people prepared to exchange that underlying asset at that particular price.

Bryan and Rafferty make a similar point when they talk about the 'blending' and 'binding' functions of these instruments. Financial derivatives, and in particular swaps, have the capacity of blending different sorts of assets together: 'It is possible, for example, to forward sell (or purchase) an asset so that future price rises (or falls) can have the opposite effects on a firm's profitability to that which would be expected from on balance sheet positions' (2006:184). This is possible because with swaps the underlying asset does not need to change hands. And, they point out, 'the capacity to change the appearance of an asset is important in cases in which there is a need to distinguish between different kinds of capital such as in the case of capital controls' (2006:184), which they therefore consider difficult to enforce. The other important function they see derivatives playing is the '"binding" of the future price of an asset to its price in the present or of the price in one place with those in another', such as in the case of exchange rates' derivatives (2006:183). The collapse of Bretton Woods and the move towards floating exchange rates, coupled with the lifting of capital controls and the proliferation of contractual outsourcing, has resulted in the increase of old risks such as counterparty and interest rates risks, and the emergence of new ones, such as currency and 'socio-political' risks: without the 'binding' function derivatives provide, global production would be affected considerably. This is why they argue that dismissing derivatives as 'unproductive' fails to recognise that, by bridging the spatio-temporal gaps or discontinuities in the international financial system, these contracts give continuity to global accumulation. The discontinuities they talk about are not simply disequilibriums in the financial market that disappear with arbitrage or larger volume of trade (they show that these are not disappearing despite the fact that the volume of transactions is increasing); rather, discontinuities suggest a constant need of commensuration of both present and future values and values denominated in different currencies (Bryan et al., 2000:2). Thus, they conclude, derivatives trade exactly on the *contestability* of such values (Bryan and Rafferty, 2006:37).

Financial derivatives are therefore contracts through which by anticipating or speculating on the value of an asset, one also affects that very value. The fact that the derivative makes the value of, as much as it derives value from, the underlying asset creates a strange circularity which raises important questions about the way in which value is conceived of and determined within trading systems such as derivative markets. Saying that derivatives affect the value of a 'real' asset may seem nonsensical from a perspective that upholds the distinction between prices, pertaining to the level of circulation, and values, pertaining to the level of production and deriving from those labouring activities which are able to produce 'surplus value'. Yet, if Bryan and Rafferty's analysis of the blending and binding function of derivatives is taken seriously, and the function that derivatives serve in providing continuity to global accumulation is duly acknowledged, then we cannot but recognise that derivatives indirectly affect 'surplus value' as they have a direct impact on productive processes around the world. This point I think is crucial to a Marxist theory of value, the primary analytical and political contribution of which is not to explain why prices are what they are and how they correspond (or not) to the labour time spent to produce the actual commodities, but to shed light on how labour processes come to be organised around the world and on the political consequences deriving from this constant re-organisation (Elson, 1979), a point to which I return in the next section.

To sum up, the difficulty of distinguishing between hedging and speculation as well as between the value of the derivative and that of the underlying asset points to both practical and conceptual problems with the regulatory response to financial derivatives. First, their speculative dimension cannot be completely controlled so as to eliminate 'unhealthy' excesses without banning derivatives altogether, and therefore without doing away with the hedging function they perform. Second, this response presupposes a clear demarcation line between the real sphere of the economy, that within which goods and services are produced and endowed with an 'intrinsic' value, and a financial sphere which is supposed to be based on the values produced in the real one. However, by participating in the making of the asset's value, derivatives show the contestability of such value, thereby complicating any unidirectional reading of the relationship between the two spheres.

Speculating on 'fundamental' values

One observation needs to be made at this point with respect to the circularity described above: the fact that expectations (and therefore a degree of speculation about the future) play a role in the price formation of financial assets is not new.[2] Fundamentals analysts at the beginning of the twentieth century posited that each financial asset had an 'intrinsic' or 'fundamental' value which reflected the present expected value of future payoffs (see Pérez Caldentey and Vernengo, 2010:71). In their 1940 *Security Analysis*, Graham and Dodd argued that the value of stocks and other securities was 'justified by the facts, e.g., the assets, earnings, dividends, definitive prospects, as distinct, let us say, from market quotations established by artificial manipulation or distorted by psychological excesses' (Graham and Dodd, 1940:20–21, in MacKenzie, 2008:76–77). Thus, although such value always involves a degree of indeterminacy, which is inherent in forecasting dividends, they believed that they could point to instances in which market prices differed from plausible estimates of fundamental values, plausible because grounded in the economic position of the firm which, for instance, could be evinced from its balance sheets, income statements and cash flows (MacKenzie, 2008:76–77).

The Efficient Market Hypothesis (EMH) formulated by Fama in 1964, and which has come to inform finance theory ever since, does not reject the view that assets' prices reflect the health of the corporation issuing them, and this includes expectations of future profits, but posits that market prices are the most efficient indicators of such value since they 'always "fully reflect" available information' (Fama, 1970:383, in MacKenzie, 2008:77). To put it differently, atomistic rational agents constantly bring different (although incomplete) information about the value of the asset to the market, which then metabolises it and transforms it into market or equilibrium price. Thus, both fundamentals' analysis and the EMH contemplate a role for expectations in affecting the value of assets. Whether because of the invisible hand of the all-knowing organism that is the market or the scrutiny of agents who carefully assess the health of the company, expectations about the future payoffs affect today's value so that the future is always already brought to bear on the present value of financial assets.

However, there are also crucial differences between the two approaches. A number of assumptions characterising the EMH have been challenged, and this long before the 2007 financial crisis, particularly the belief that 'no opportunities are left open for consistent speculative profit, that technical trading (using patterns in past prices to forecast future ones) cannot be profitable except by luck, that temporary price overreactions – bubbles and crashes – reflect rational changes in assets' valuations ... and that indices of trading volume and price volatility are not serially correlated in any way' (Arthur et al., 1996:1). Thus, despite the fact that the EMH continues to hold its authority in the academic discipline, it is today widely recognised that speculation takes place. And this is not just an issue of the single agent being smart enough to beat the market, à la Warren Buffet (Pérez Caldentey and Vernengo, 2010:71). What is becoming increasingly evident is the fact that 'In [today's] asset markets, agents' forecasts create the world agents are trying to forecast.' In other words 'markets have a reflexive nature in that prices are generated by traders' expectations, but these expectations are formed on the basis of anticipations of *others'* expectations (Arthur et al., 1996:21, original emphasis). This is a different scenario from the one depicted by the EMH where market prices reflect the health of the corporation issuing the asset: market prices today depend on agents' anticipation of others' expectations. We might consider this as the first degree of abstraction from fundamental values operated at the level of expectations.

The circularity described with respect to financial derivatives in the previous section adds another layer to the reflexivity or self-referential character of expectations in financial markets, and therefore a second degree of abstraction. Financial derivatives intensify the process by which the future is brought to bear on the present because of their role in the determination of the value of the underlying asset and the fact that the latter has already been subjected to the first degree of abstraction. In other words, they make expectations exponentially productive since they are financial entities relating to other financial underlying assets. As argued in Chapter 3, scholars working on the performativity of economics have pointed to the referential character of financial entities (Callon, 1998; Muniesa and Callon, 2007:166–168). For instance, in discussing the mathematical model of Black-Scholes-Merton on the pricing of options, MacKenzie shows that the model created the reality it had posited, even if only until the crash of 1987, rather than describing a reality existing 'out there' (MacKenzie, 2008:54–81).

This is what derivatives do to the value on which they are supposed to be based: rather than simply deriving their value from the equilibrium price or fundamental value of the underlying asset, they participate in its actual construction. The self-referential character of expectations thus challenges, if not discards altogether, the EMH, and particularly the idea of equilibrium prices reflecting fundamental values. It is therefore understandable why many scholars critical of financial markets have argued in favour of an analysis of fundamentals that grounds expectations firmly in the economic situation of the firm: that would be the argument that finance has to be grounded in, or brought back to, the real economy (Pérez Caldentey and Vernengo, 2010; Arthur et al., 1996). Indeed, it makes a difference whether expectations relate somehow to the health of the entity whose worth they are engaged in assessing and/or whether they end up being all there is to the determination of financial value. However, the difficulty the fundamentals' position is confronted with is that not only are prices today so distorted, but that firms' balance sheets and state accounting are so compromised that assessing the health of a company, let alone that of an economy as in the case of exchange rates, is an extremely arduous task (de Goede, 2015:356). In addition to this, the blending and binding functions of derivatives, together with the difficulty of drawing a clear distinction between hedging and speculation, add another layer of difficulty in accounting for the 'real' or fundamental value of an asset. Even attempts to distinguish between real (ie deriving from manufacturing/industrial activities) and financial profits are proving increasingly difficult. As Arrighi (2009:140) points out, referring to Greta Krippner's analysis of available data:

> not only had the share of total US corporate profits accounted for by finance, insurance, and real estate (FIRE) in the 1980s nearly caught up with and, in the 1990s, surpassed the share accounted for by manufacturing; more important, in the 1970s and 1980s, *non-financial firms themselves* sharply increased their investment in financial assets relative to that in plant and equipment, and became increasingly dependent on financial sources of revenue and profit relative to that earned from productive activities. Particularly significant is Krippner's finding that manufacturing not only dominates but *leads* this trend towards the 'financialization' of the non-financial economy. (original emphasis)

Indeed, what is distinctive about the relationship between manufacturing and financial activities of non-financial companies is the fact that financial activities permeate the whole production cycle rather than coming at the end of it. As Marazzi puts it: 'we are in an historic period in which the finances are *cosubstantial* to the very production of goods and services' (Marazzi, 2010:28–29). This clearly shows how disentangling financial from 'real' value is not a straightforward task and the significance of derivatives is that they bring to the fore exactly this difficulty. McNally argues that what was interesting and at the same time destabilising about the 2007 crisis is not only that financial institutions had lost or 'written down' so much money (US$300 billion only in 2008) but that it was not entirely clear how much exactly (2009:69–72). Thus, it might well be that, as Bryan, Rafferty, McNally and others have suggested, derivatives actually point to the crisis of value measurement, and therefore of capitalism.

This argument, however, raises a series of complex questions: what exactly does it mean to say that value measurement is in crisis? Is value beyond measure? Is this a recent phenomenon? These are crucial questions for thinking about how to act once we accept the blurring of the boundaries between the 'real' and the financial spheres of the economy. In order to address these questions, I engage with one particular strand of the post-Fordist literature which has become paradigmatic of the immensurability argument, that is, of the claim that value is beyond measure because of crucial shifts in the ways in which it is produced. I do not think that we can fully appreciate the significance of the argument these authors articulate – and this is particularly the case with Negri's work – without an understanding of their use of the concept of immaterial labour, a concept which has played a crucial role at least since the 1970s in Italian feminist debates. By referring to these debates I do not claim that Italian feminists were the first to think about immaterial labour. I focus on their work for two main reasons: first, because several authors who have become known as the theorists of immaterial labour and cognitive capitalism draw specifically, although problematically, on the work of these feminists; second, because the contribution the latter have made to our understanding of the relationship between labour and value has important implications for the ways in which the 'contingency' of value is articulated today, in the context of the financial uncertainty derivatives bring to the fore and beyond. This work has also important implications for thinking about the kind of arrangements that may be able to shift current value making processes. As the next section argues, its importance consists of having brought to light the arbitrary ways in which capitalist processes of valorisation produce particular oppositions, especially that between material and immaterial, manual and mental and ultimately productive and unproductive labour.

The argument I make is that, by selectively relying on this work while positing a radical rupture in the 1970s – this is the claim that immaterial labour has become paradigmatic of the post-Fordist mode of production, with value becoming immeasurable – arguments about the primacy of immaterial labour and the collapse of measurement end up reinforcing the existence of such oppositions, thereby undermining the important contribution this work has made. In the context of the discussion of financial derivatives, for instance, this contribution enables us to appreciate how the contingency of value that derivatives have 'revealed' is neither new nor has it dispensed with measures altogether; and that it is the struggle over measurement and the arrangements that institute it that is important for engendering alternative valorisation processes.

Value beyond measure?

There are two aspects emerging from the Italian literature on post-Fordism and cognitive capitalism that are relevant for thinking about financial uncertainty and more generally about the contestability of value that derivatives have brought to the fore. The first, with which this section is concerned, is that formal labour time can no longer provide the measure of value because the distinction between labour and leisure time (the time for production and reproduction respectively), as well as that between material and immaterial production, is becoming increasingly blurred (Codeluppi, 2008; Vercellone, 2009). The second point, which I will touch upon in the concluding section, is that, parallel to the loss of labour time as the determinate measure of value, what we have witnessed in the past two decades is financial markets becoming more and more the place where value is actually determined (Fumagalli and Mezzadra, 2009:211). These two points are connected: however, it is not possible to appreciate their significance without engaging with the argument about the paradigmatic shift brought about by the ascendancy of immaterial labour on the basis of which the immeasurability of value thesis rests.

Hardt and Negri argue that our common wealth is not limited to the material world, such as water, air, soil, forests and all nature's bounty, which classical European political texts refer to as the common inheritance of humankind. It also, and more importantly, includes 'those results of social production that are necessary for social interaction and further production, such as knowledges, languages, codes, information, affects and so on' (Hardt and Negri, 2009:viii). Their argument is that with the shift from Fordist to post-Fordist capitalism, 'production has become first and foremost production of knowledge and subjectivity', in other words biopolitical production (Hardt and Negri, 2009:131). If, they argue, what produces value today is above all 'human faculties, competences and knowledges' (Hardt and Negri, 2009:132), then this means that capital operates outside directly productive processes and has become entirely parasitic; hence the possibility for the multitude of overcoming it through a common decision (Hardt and Negri, 2009:137). This is not an automatic process, of course, for biopolitical production implies 'new mechanisms of exploitation and capitalist control [... However, it also] grants labour increasing autonomy and provides the tools or weapons that could be wielded in a project of liberation' (Hardt and Negri, 2009:136–137). This project 'opens a new space for politics' in which to pursue the construction of a common world through creativity and cooperation (Hardt and Negri, 2009:ix).

This is a political project that Negri in particular has pursued for some time within the Operaist, or, as referred to in the Anglo-Saxon world, Workerist, movement. Now known as post-workerists, militants within this tradition have, since the 1960s, sought to engage with, and find alternatives to, what they see as the two major forms of modern oppression, namely the state and wage labour. One important concern of the movement has been the relationship between capitalist productivity and workers' struggles. Whereas Tronti (1966:89–95) for instance, has argued that the latter lead capitalists to constantly devise ways of increasing labour productivity in order to extract surplus value, so that capital always reacts to labour's inventiveness, others, such as Panzieri (1994:73–92), have seen this causality operating in the reverse direction, so that it is the capitalist reorganisation of production processes that, more often than not, is capable of originating new struggles.

This debate on the historical tendency of capitalist development and, within it, the relevance of Marx's labour theory of value has been central to the post-workerist debate and can be seen informing Hardt's and, particularly, Negri's work. For them, the continuous pressure that workers' struggles have put on capital since the 1960s has led not only to changes in the composition of the labour force, which has become more flexible and precarious and registered the ascendancy of the immaterial worker; but at the same time it has also generated changes in the composition of capital, with the proportion of value produced by (immaterial) labour increasingly higher than that produced by constant capital (Hardt and Negri, 2009:132). Thus, they claim, the tendency towards the hegemony of biopolitical production requires that we deal with 'the new conditions of the production of surplus value' – as value production invests all realms of life exceeding the confines of formal work time (2009:137) – so to be able to identify the new (post-Fordist) forms of exploitation.

But what is the concept of value Hardt and Negri use here? In pointing to the value produced in the immaterial sphere they seem to be referring to the income generated through the sale of services. However, income is not synonymous with value. Desai (2011), for instance, has argued that Hardt and Negri's misunderstanding of Marx's labour theory of value makes their argument about the importance of cognitive and biopolitical labour and production redundant. For her, Hardt and Negri confuse use value (which speaks of the usefulness of a thing) and exchange value (which refers to the commensurability of things on the market) and take the sphere of circulation (of prices) for that of production (of value). I would, however, suggest that Hardt and Negri's understanding of Marx's labour theory of value is much more nuanced than what it is presented here, not only in *Commonwealth* (2009) but also in *Empire* (2001) and *Multitude* (2004). They know very well that the object of Marx's labour theory 'is not to look for an explanation of why prices are what they are and find in it labour' (Elson, 1979:123). Put differently, the object of Marx's enquiry was never to theorise prices or account for 'the origin or cause of anything' (Elson, 1979:121), hence also the weakness of arguments according to which the category of value is inadequate to account for actual prices in the market (Elson, 1979:116). Rather as Elson, whom Hardt and Negri cite, argued, the object was to understand why 'labour takes the forms it does and what the political consequences are' (Elson, 1979: 123). Thus, it is clear to them that this is an issue of labour and its organisation: in their 1994 *Labour of Dionysus*, they point to the fact that Marx conceived of the labour theory of value from two perspectives. From one, which corresponds to the tradition of the classical political economy of Smith and Ricardo, value is the (socially necessary) labour time embodied in the commodity and the law of value explains the deployment of labour power among different sectors of social production; in other words the law of value tries to explain how coordination is achieved when there is no centralisation of production in the chaotic world of capitalist producers. But they also acknowledge that in Marx the labour theory of value is presented differently from classical political economy. Here labour is an antagonistic feature and its relationship to value is not unidirectional, although, as I argue in Chapter 2, this 'unidirectionality' should not be taken for granted in Smith's work either. From this perspective:

> the unity of value is primarily identified in its relation to 'necessary labour', which is not a fixed quantity but a dynamic element of the system. Necessary labour is historically determined by the struggles of the working class against waged labour in the effort of transforming labour itself. This means that although in the first theory value was fixed in the structures of capital, in the second theory labour and value are both variable elements. It is not sufficient to pose the economic structure of labour as the source of a cultural superstructure of value; this notion of base and superstructure must be overturned. If labour is the basis of value, then value is equally the basis of labour. What counts as labour, or value creating practices, always depends on the existing values of a given social and historic context; in other words ... [t]he definition of what practises comprise labour ... is not given or fixed, but rather historically and socially determined, and thus the definition itself constitutes a mobile site of social contestation.
>
> (Hardt and Negri, 1994:9)

What emerges from this second perspective is their acknowledgement that for Marx the law of value is not a transhistoric concept: it is rather a category meant to analyse the form of exploitation specific to capitalist production. Hence its contingency, and its constructed quality, is brought to full light. My point here is that Hardt and Negri know very well that the creation of value is a collective undertaking that has to do with the organisation of labour and production. They also know that it never made sense, except in capitalist terms, to conceive of commodities as things whose value was simply the product of factory work that could be measured on the basis of the clock time spent to produce them. Thus, they are not really saying anything new when they point to the growing importance of 'externalities' to show how value always exceeds measure. In *Commonwealth*, for instance, they refer to real estate values as an example of the impossibility of measuring value according to labour time or any other 'internal' factor:

> Contemporary real estate economists are fully aware, of course, that the value of an apartment or a building or land in a city is not represented exclusively by the intrinsic characteristics of the property, such as the quality and size of its construction, but it is also and even primarily determined by externalities – both negative externalities, such as pollution, traffic congestion, noisy neighbours, high levels of criminality, and the discotheque downstairs that makes it impossible to sleep on Saturday nights; and positive externalities, such as proximity to playground, dynamic local cultural relations, intellectual circuits of exchange and peaceful, stimulating social interaction.
>
> (Hardt and Negri, 2009:154–156)

Yet, when they say that the production of value of a commodity is *no longer* limited to the factory but is dispersed across society as a whole and that value has *become* immeasurable, they are positing this as a radical break, which is highly problematic, for two interconnected reasons. The first is that they contradict the insight deriving from the second perspective on the law of value they articulate in *Labour of Dionysus*, thereby reasserting the unidirectional (causal and transhistoric) link between labour and value even as, and exactly because, they state that this relationship has now been broken. How, then, to account for the difference between the second more nuanced conception of value in *Labour of Dionysus* and the more ambivalent one in their later work? At one level, this can be explained through the fascination post-workerists have had for some time with the section in *Grundrisse* where Marx points to a stage in which the increasingly 'scientific' nature of production processes will pave the way to a communist future where labour time will no longer provide the measure of value and exchange value will therefore collapse:

to the degree that large industry develops, the creation of real wealth comes to depend less on labor time and on the amount of labor employed than on the power of the agencies set in motion during labor time, whose 'powerful effectiveness' is itself in turn out of all proportion to the direct labor time spent on their production, but depends rather on the general state of science and on the progress of technology, or the application of this science to production ... As soon as labor in the direct form has ceased to be the great well-spring of wealth, labor time ceases and must cease to be its measure, and hence exchange value [must cease to be the measure] of use value. The *surplus labor of the mass* has ceased to be the condition for the development of general wealth, just as the *non-labor of the few*, for the development of the general powers of the human head. With that, production based on exchange value breaks down and the direct, material production process is stripped of the form of penury and antithesis.

(Marx, 1857–1858:704–706, original emphasis)

However, claiming that there is a tendency which has crystallised with the shift to post-Fordism and has led to the collapse of exchange value, the value that allows commodities to be commensurated on the market, is highly questionable: 20 years ago Caffentzis pointed to the parallel growth of 'labour intensive' and 'knowledge intensive' sectors and showed how:

an enormous amount of work must be produced and extracted from the Low sectors in order to be transformed to capital available for the High sector. In order to finance the new capitalist 'utopia' of 'high-tech,' venture-capital demanding industries in the energy, computer and genetic engineering areas, another capitalist 'utopia' must be created: a world of 'labor intensive', low waged, distracted and diffracted production. ... In this juncture, as always in capitalism's history, a leap in technology is financed out of the skins of the most technologically starved workers ...

(Caffentzis, 1992:249)

The fact that low tech and high tech sectors have grown in tandem thus casts serious doubts over whether or not this passage in *Grundrisse* can be relied upon to describe the current stage of capitalism. This does not mean to say that nothing has changed but that the nature of the transformation described must be carefully analysed. Caffentzis has made a similar point with regard to the conceptual and historic transformations on which Hardt and Negri rely to argue that value *has become* immeasurable. As already seen, their argument is that, as a result of the changes in the composition of capital generated by workers' struggles, socially necessary labour time is no longer able to provide the measure of value. It was an appropriate measure when capital had only formally subsumed society; in our current phase of real subsumption, however, such a measure, and measuring itself, becomes meaningless as value is created by immaterial labour which percolates across society.[3] This claim, Caffentzis argues, is problematic because it relies on a periodisation of Marx's categories of formal/real subsumption along Fordist and post-Fordist lines when for Marx they described phenomena which already coexisted in the mid-nineteenth century (Caffentzis, 2005:104). This takes us back to the point about the coexistence of low tech and high tech sectors around the world which complicates Hardt and Negri's argument about the primacy of 'immaterial labour' in value generating processes, a primacy which they claim has resulted in value *becoming* immeasurable.

The immeasurability claim is also based on their historic argument that the unilateral decoupling of the dollar from gold and the breaking down of Bretton Woods are paradigmatic of the arbitrariness in the measurement of value in post-Fordist capitalism. The prices of commodities, they point out, are given by so many elements woven together that there cannot be any 'economic determinant of last degree' such as socially necessary labor time; indeed, indexes such as currency exchange rates can 'only be defined on the basis of always contingent and purely conventional elements' (Hardt and Negri, 2001: 355; in Caffentzis, 2005:96). Whereas the analysis of derivatives carried out so far illustrates exactly the difficulty with retrieving any fundamental value or economic determinant of last degree, the problem with their argument is that this is neither a new phenomenon nor one that involves the disappearance of measurement.[4]

Again, this is not to say that things have remained the same but, on the contrary, that we need to appreciate how measuring has changed rather than dismissing measures and measuring altogether. Indeed, as Allon (2015:295–296) has argued, it is important to appreciate how the post-1972 monetary environment is one in which money has become a tradable commodity in its own right, which means that it can no longer claim its privileged measurement function. This is the case with other 'benchmarks' such as gold, London Interbank Offered Rate (LIBOR), government bonds and the US dollar which can no longer act as external anchors exactly because they are 'inside the process of risk calculation and commensuration' (Bryan and Rafferty, 2013:146, in Allon, 2015:296); that is why derivatives have become such crucial instruments of commensuration. At the same time, she argues, this is a hybrid monetary system where financial instruments have increasingly acquired 'the property of moneyness' in terms of the liquidity they allow (Allon, 2015:285). The consequences of this manifold process is that 'ordinary citizens are inserted into calculative dynamics (investment, speculation, pension funds)' (Allon, 2015:293).[5]

And according to Bryan, Rafferty and Jefferis (2015:317–318), this incorporation is exactly what is at stake in 'the emergent and distinctively capitalist' forms of finance: this is 'the real subsumption of labor to finance, in which households become directly subject to the calculative imperatives of capital' (see also Williams, 2007).[6]

If the mechanisms for measuring value are thus multifarious and ever-changing, this does not mean that they are non-existent. This is true of immaterial labour as much as of material labour. Leaving aside the problematic separation from its material dimension to which I return in the next section, immaterial labour seems today to be beyond capitalist measure precisely because, as De Angelis has pointed out, referring to Harvie's work on measurement:

> it is a form of social cooperation that is constituted by relational and communicational patterns defined by the doers themselves (hence measured by themselves) … [But in fact] the degree of autonomy of the doers has precise limits defined by the processes of capitalist measure … Nurses, doctors, teachers have a variety of degree of autonomy but are increasingly exposed to a measure which is posed *outside* them, which is heteronymous, which instructs them, *in a context of declining resources and number of staff*, to meet certain quality targets that relate in a way or in another to external benchmarks.
>
> (De Angelis, 2005:80–81, original emphasis)

The essential point here is that measures have changed but measuring takes place all the time. However, positing a radical break with Fordist value production not only refuses to attend to the important connections that form the global economy but also makes the more challenging analysis of the relationship between labour and value (as articulated in *Labour of Dionysus*) devoid of theoretical and political import, that is the challenge to capitalist value through the instantiation of other processes of valorisation.

This speaks directly to the second reason why I think the positioning of such a break is problematic, and this is because it undermines the important feminist work on value on which it relies.[7] Indeed, the most interesting insights regarding the relationship between labour and value derive from the feminist work they mention in passing. They acknowledge that certain lines of feminist enquiry and practice have brought into focus the different forms of 'affective labour, caring labour and kin work that have been traditionally defined as women's work' so that 'these studies have demonstrated the ways in which such forms of activity produce social networks and produce society itself' (Hardt and Negri, 1994:9). However, with the exception of Elson's work, to which they explicitly refer, they hardly explore the significance and implications of these studies. It is exactly this body of work that I turn to now to show how, despite being relied upon, its radical potential has been cut short by positing a moment of rupture between the 1970s and 1980s.

Immaterial labour in Italian feminist debates

In the early 1970s, Dalla Costa, Federici and Fortunati started to assess the capacity of Marxist concepts to explain women's position within the capitalist system, focusing in particular on the distinction between productive and unproductive labour and that between material and immaterial production (Dalla Costa and James, 1972; Dalla Costa and Fortunati, 1977; Federici, 1980; Fortunati, 1981).[8] While Marx saw the domestic sphere as unproductive (that is, from the point of view of commodity production), they instead claimed that the production of goods and services, including prostitution, was a crucial stage in the production of surplus value: reproductive labour produced and reproduced the commodity most precious for capital, that is, labour power (Fortunati, 2007:145). Fortunati's work in particular focused on the inadequacy of socially necessary labour time *qua* clock time to provide the measure of value of a commodity. This was because socially necessary labour time does not take into account the time necessary for reproducing labour power, which is not, in contrast to factory time, 'easily' calculable (Fortunati, 1981:40, 81–84). Thus, the separation of the process of production of commodities from that of reproduction, even though the two are indissolubly connected in producing value, is what allows capital to make huge money savings:

> Separated by the line of value, they constitute two distinct moments in the extraction of surplus value. The exchange value and (use) value of the labour-power produced; the first within the process of commodity production and the second within the process of production and reproduction of labour-power functions within the other process as a precondition and condition of its existence. Thus, throughout its entire cycle, capital makes huge money savings for itself and expropriates the maximum, a massive amount of surplus labour. The rift between the two sides of the valorisation process, production and reproduction, requires the product of one to make a 'double somersault' into the other and vice versa ...
>
> (Fortunati, 1981:82)

The theoretical import of this work consisted of showing not only how reproductive labour produced 'externalities', to go back to Hardt and Negri's argument about value becoming immeasurable (1994:154–155), but also why this labour took the form it did in order to reflect on the political consequences deriving from this form (Elson, 1979:123). The point was neither that of measuring these 'externalities' so as to make sure that the (exchange) value of commodities reflected more accurately the (use) value of reproductive labour, for instance, through more accurate accounting processes;[9] nor was it the socialisation of domestic labour through the development of social services and a more equal sharing of its burden as this would not have eliminated exploitation (ie the process through which surplus value is extracted) but would just have redistributed it (Fortunati, 1981:34). Rather the point was to destroy these forms of labour as capitalist labour by creating the possibility for other processes of (non-capitalist) valorisation to emerge. As she puts it:

> Large areas of domestic labor cannot be socialized or eliminated through the development of technology. They can and must be destroyed as capitalist labor and liberated to become a wealth of creativity … The reference here is to immaterial labor (such as affection, love, consolation and above all sex) which among other things constitutes an increasing part of domestic labor.
>
> (Fortunati, 1981:10)

The question of how to instil other processes of valorisation remains open and one to which I will return when thinking about the provocative power of alternative arrangements in Chapters 3 and 4. However, already in the 1970s they had pointed to the fact that (capitalist) value has to do with the historic process through which a particular separation between productive and reproductive activities was institutionalised to enable both its generation and measurement. This separation, their work argued, is what makes this historic process distinctively 'capitalist', in that 'capital must rely on both an immense amount of unpaid domestic labour for the reproduction of the workforce, and the devaluation of these reproductive activities in order to cut the costs of labour power' (Federici, 2012:92). As I will argue in Chapters 2 and 4, the place and articulation of domestic labour in the global economy, particularly in relation to wage labour, is far from being fixed and homogeneous but the argument about the constant creation of divisions and separations that enable the extraction of surplus value remains salient.

This is the first important insight deriving from this work: not that (capitalist) value is irrelevant but that the measuring mechanisms on which it is based, and which make possible its production, need to be confronted so that other production and measuring practices can be instantiated. The other insight, which emerged by looking closer at the multifarious manifestations of immaterial labour, consisted of showing the problematic nature of sorting labour in either material or immaterial terms depending on whether it produced material or immaterial things:

Whilst it may be simple to make a theoretical distinction between immaterial and material labor, it is not so easy in everyday life. In practice, the two are actually closely intertwined. Immaterial labor, as we have seen, often needs supports (tools, technologies) as a vehicle, well-grounded in the material. It needs to be performed in concrete contexts. But, above all, immaterial labor very often sets material labor in motion. Showing one's affection for a person means possibly setting off on a journey, buying a present or preparing a dinner, it means following an immaterial expression with concrete acts.

(Lorente, 2004, in Fortunati, 2007)

The fact that material and immaterial labour are distributed along a continuum of interaction whose boundaries cannot be easily demarcated led these scholars to enquire further into the political work such boundaries were doing. Indeed, rather than aiming at a more clear demarcation between the two spheres, they showed how such distinction naturalised an arbitrary division of labour between what ended up being considered productive (of surplus value) and what did not – and for this reason making an 'invisible', and therefore more easily appropriable, contribution to its generation. Hence, we come to the problematic nature of the current use by post-workerists of the concept of immaterial labour: by arguing that the *old* dichotomy between material and immaterial labour fails to grasp the *new* nature of post-Fordist productive activity, they imply that the distinction existed earlier and the work of feminists who had shown how these categories have always been arbitrary despite being the very ground on which surplus value is extracted, is undermined.

These oppositions are transcended while, at the same time, being reinstated. This is clear in the distinction made by Negri between the primary source of immaterial labour, the intellect, which he says, in 'Kairos, Alma Venus and Multitudo', has acceded to 'the status of sole producer of value' (2000: 227), and, as he and Hardt put it in *Empire*, the other face of immaterial labour which is the 'affective labour of human contact and interaction' (Hardt and Negri, 2001:290–292).[10] Hardt and Negri point to the fact that an understanding of 'affective' labour must begin from women's work. However, as Fortunati has argued, it is not at all clear how they conceptualise 'affects' and in what kind of social relationships they see 'affects' being produced and consumed, with the consequence that women risk being reduced to the body once again (Fortunati, 2007:147). Similarly, Federici argues that the way in which 'affective' labour appears in their work risks stripping the feminist analysis of its demystifying power:

what is 'affective labor?' And why is it included in the theory of immaterial labor? I imagine it is included because – presumably – it does not produce tangible products but 'states of being', that is, it produces feelings ... But the concept of 'affective labor' strips the feminist analysis of housework of all its demystifying power. In fact, it brings reproductive work back into the world of mystification, suggesting that reproducing people is just a matter of making, producing 'emotions,' 'feelings.' It used to be called a 'labor of love;' Negri and Hardt instead have discovered 'affection'. The feminist analysis of the function of the sexual division of labor, the function of gender hierarchies, the analysis of the way capitalism has used the wage to mobilize women's work in the reproduction of the labor force – all of this is lost under the label of 'affective labor'. That this feminist analysis is ignored in the work of Negri and Hardt confirms my suspicions that this theory expresses the interests of a select group of workers, even though it presumes to speak to all workers, all merged in the great caldron of the Multitude.

(Federici, 2008:5)

Indeed, the immaterial worker *par excellence* tends to be the cognitive labourer working in fashion, design, cybernetics, marketing, and research and development, while flight attendants expected to smile at customers are considered emblematic of 'affective' labourers. Aside from the position of the 'affective' worker within the 'cognitive' workforce, their argument about the hegemonic role of the immaterial worker does not take seriously the implications deriving from the contemporaneous existence of 'labour intensive' and 'knowledge intensive sectors', within and across countries (Caffentzis, 1992). Thus, by positing the immaterial worker as paradigmatic of the shift to post-Fordism, the arrangements that constantly impose a separation between material and immaterial production are not called into question. Fortunati (2003) has shown how these arrangements attempt to impose an imperial division of labour between the mind of the service economy, supposed to lead from the North because of its being rich in capital, particularly human capital, technology and know-how, and the body of the manufacturing economy, supposed to develop in the South because of its being 'naturally' endowed with raw materials and labour. The same logic can be seen underlying current European arrangements that aim to separate the mind of finance, which needs to be supported because it is productive and competitive, from the body of a labouring population that can be left to bleed through cuts because it is corrupt and/or unproductive. Of course these attempts cannot be traced along clearly demarcated lines. In *Border as Method* Mezzadra and Neilson (2013a) argue that the terms articulated by any division of labour, whether international or sexual, work through a kind of *differential inclusion* rather than exclusion. Boundaries are continuously drawn across different accumulation regimes that cannot be reduced to the great North/South, Core/Periphery, Developed/Developing, divides. Yet, as argued in Chapter 2, these attempts and their ideological force play a crucial role in the production of these boundaries, even as they defy stable geographical lines.

And this leads to the first point I want to make in concluding my reflections on the immaterial labour debate: by asserting a moment of radical change that has brought about the hegemony of the immaterial worker, these categories are in the end retained; and what feminists started in the 1970s, the process of questioning how and why they are produced and the kind of power effects they generate, gets interrupted. The consequence is that the many complex and ever-changing connections between labour and value that make up our global economy are not attended to and their power effects remain unchallenged. Recognising the importance of these connections does not mean that nothing has changed since the 1970s. Haraway in the 1980s observed the way in which various technologies were allowing forms of domestic labour to permeate society at large (Haraway, 1985:65–108), while Hochschild (1983) used the category of 'emotional labour' to look at the strategic management of emotions for social effect as an increasingly everyday labour practice. However, my point is that tracing these connections and the conditions for their possibility is a much more difficult and laborious process than positing a rupture and the advent of something radically new. Put it differently, and this is the conclusion I draw from the contribution made by 'Wages for/against Housework' scholars, it is more fruitful to ask how these categories are constantly produced, what kind of arrangements sustain them and which ones might help undoing them.

This questioning is, for example, part of the feminist debate on precariety in Italy, which has touched upon, among other things, the phenomenon often described as the feminisation of labour. This is the tendency of 'the current organisational model of work – insecure, adaptable, spasmodic, nomadic' – to model itself on the historical modality of female work (Morini, 2007:48). Now precariousness is seen by some feminists as problematic because it is inflexible, but it is also viewed as the direct result of feminists' demands for freedom from the house, family and work. 'Inflexible flexibility', as Morini puts it, can be seen as the response of capital to the general demands by workers based on the 'refusal to work':

> We are aware of the fact that part of workers' demands in the 1970s, particularly in Italy, were also based on the 'refusal of work', aimed at greater flexibility (which meant winning back time spent on living rather than time spent on machines). Post-Fordist production functioned as social and cultural criticism of the Fordist model of the 1970s ... Today, the reality with which we are faced ... is not configured as a

form of true flexibility but presents itself rather as a form of a growing link between existence and intelligence at work.

(Morini, 2007:48)

While the inflexibility of today's precariousness is condemned, its potential for liberating women from wage labour is celebrated: Morini, for instance, points to the fact that in the few empirical studies that have been conducted, women do not seem to be concerned with the lack of permanent employment or open-ended contracts but mainly with income. The issue for her becomes one of achieving more autonomy with less insecurity (Morini, 2007:52–56). Fantone (2007), however, reflects on the fact that the new subjectivity of the 'precari', which Morini sees as made of 'existence and intelligence at work', is contained within specific historic boundaries that need to be interrogated. For instance, she notes how the movement originated from mainly urban areas in the north of Italy where there is a comparatively low percentage of unemployment and a higher middle-class population. However, as she puts it:

precariety has been a permanent and traditional feature of life in southern Italy for many generations of women, taking the form of submerged labour with no contract, black market and illegal economies (where there is no safety and rights), family self-exploitation, characterised by no clear division between work and house chores, and informal hiring practices through familial connections that have no long term guarantee.

(Fantone, 2007:10)

And one could note here the historical resonance of the 'putting out' system established in England in the sixteenth and seventeenth centuries through which artisans' independence, including women's crafts, was destroyed thanks to the cheap labour which was made available in the rural areas and which relied enormously on the work of rural women and children who worked from 'home' (see Federici, 2004:72, 97, 123). Fantone (2007:10) also notes how the majority of today's domestic workers in Italy are 'poorly paid women coming from previously colonised areas such as the Philippines and Somalia and more recently Poland and Romania'. This, she argues, does not prevent the possibility of a feminist politics in relation to precariety but requires a shift 'to a more complex political analysis that can address gender and reproduction, citizenship and social welfare, immigration and de-industrialisation at the same time' (2007:9–10). Fantone's argument brings us back to the argument made by earlier feminist work, that is, the need to be more attentive to the connections between labour and value, especially when at issue is the kind of arrangements we are advocating: when we talk about precariety, what forms of labour are we valorising and which ones are we devalorising, both within and between countries? What happens when some of the 'freedom' and 'autonomy' that precariety enables comes at the expense of some other women and men's 'freedom' and 'autonomy'? Are we not perhaps contributing to the very production of the (capitalist) value we claim to have now become immeasurable?

These are some of the limits of a feminist politics that does not aim to trace the various connections between labour and value, and such limitation is what the work I have been referring to brings to light. This is also why this work has argued that it makes sense to talk about social reproduction as a terrain of struggle, a struggle over those arrangements that might be able to inject different meanings to our living together. As Picchio (2009:29) puts it, this is not a matter of keeping the economic system, and our conceptions of it, as it is, demanding that it only takes into account social issues, starting with the 'woman issue'. It is rather a question of (re)placing at the heart of political economy the concepts of bodies, minds and desires. Indeed, talking about social reproduction as a terrain of struggle is different from talking about yesterday's 'struggle of the working class against wage labour' (Hardt and Negri, 1994:9) or today's struggle of the cognitive or immaterial worker against an 'entirely parasitic' capital (Hardt and Negri, 2009:137). Both struggles belong to a tradition of thought that, as argued in Chapter 2, privileges certain workers over others, thereby contributing to making invisible the very connections that enable the extraction of surplus value.

This point is linked to the second conclusion I draw from the immaterial labour debate: by implying that labour time was once an accurate measure of value, much of the literature on cognitive labour risks obfuscating the fact that value measurement has always been contested and that institutional arrangements can play a crucial role in processes of contestation. Mirowski, for instance, has argued that value is always 'contingent, hermeneutic, negotiable and non natural' (1990:7) and that measurement is itself a social construct. As such, value cannot have a universal measure. As we shall see in the next chapter, the difficulty of measuring value was acknowledged in the eighteenth and nineteenth centuries as much as it is today, although then the struggle over the kind of institutional arrangements that were to format the value nexus between economy and society was much more visible. The absence of a universal measure of value, Mirowski continues, should enable us to acknowledge that while value and its measurement are neither natural nor inevitable, and there is certainly not 'one "correct" way for a society to measure a commodity … the way its measurement is *instituted* has important consequences' (Mirowski, 1991: 568, emphasis added). The relevance of Mirowski's argument can be seen by turning our attention back to financial derivatives, and the work they do in relation to the value they are supposed to merely reflect, and by asking the question of what it means to acknowledge that value is contingent and therefore contestable while its measure is nonetheless instituted.

Conclusion

Acknowledging the contestability of value is not an easy task. This becomes apparent in the debate about the valuation of financial assets. It is because of its contingency that many economists, for example, prefer to focus on money and prices rather than values. However, as Bryan and Rafferty (2006:36) note, explanations in terms of money end up being unsatisfactory: hence, the need for valuation of something more 'determinant' and 'underlying', such as fundamental value, always reoccurs. In this context derivatives can be seen as providing the crucial link between prices and 'fundamental values' not because the latter are the 'correct' way for a society to measure a commodity (Mirowski, 1991:568), but because 'they represent the way in which the market judges or perceives "fundamental values"' (Bryan and Rafferty, 2006:36). They turn the contestability of fundamental value into a tradable commodity and in so doing they provide 'a market *benchmark* for an unknowable value' (2006:37, emphasis added). Derivatives are therefore significant because they point clearly to the fact that while value is contingent and contestable, its measurement is nonetheless always instituted. My point is that equally acknowledging both aspects requires engaging more critically with the spatio-temporal connections that make the production and measurement of value possible, rather than simply asserting that value is beyond measure. To be clear, 'value' as that which is produced by the specific commodity that is labour power has always been beyond measure and attempts to measure it are always doomed to fail because, as Mezzadra and Neilson (2013a:263) argue, the 'the bearer of labor power can never be fully identified with the commodified form of that same labour power'.[11] Labour power as potentiality precedes all measures (Mezzadra and Neilson, 2013a:204). But, as a form of exploitation pertaining to capitalist production, 'value' presupposes and operates exactly through measurement: indeed, the proliferation of measures is what we see accompanying what Mezzadra and Neilson call the multiplication of labour, the deep heterogeneity characterising the various figures of labour that are both linked and divided by the current spatio-temporal connections (2013a:88, 125).

This takes me to the second important argument made by scholars of post-Fordist capitalism, and that is the fact that financial markets are increasingly becoming the place where value is determined (Fumagalli and Mezzadra, 2009). The precursor of this argument can be found in

Weeks' (1982) account of Marx's 'law of value'. Weeks argues that the gradual monetisation of the inputs into production leads to the minimisation of concrete labour inputs and towards an equalisation of profit rates. Although he leaves out the rise of capital and shares markets, his overall point is that this process confronts producers with more monetary imperatives to meet, pushing them to minimise labour time as they compete with one another. From this perspective, the commensuration of value that derivatives provide through their binding and blending functions seems to be pointing to the strengthening of such a process.[12] This is a process of commensuration that, by means of the monetary or price mechanism, pertains to society as a whole. As De Angelis (2005:82–83) has pointed out:

> Prices, by representing rates of transformation of flows of commodities and money, act as signals to [all] the parts involved in taking decision. The set of prices and the set of signals they send to the different actors of the global economy constitute a sort of map of the nervous system of what we may call the global factory ... [Indeed] price signals capture in a simple quantitative monetary expression a highly variegated range of states and their *differential*. For example price signals can index the cost of effectiveness in which a commodity is produced in relation to the same commodity produced in another place. They can signal the future prospective cost of producing a given commodity. They can register the effect of offloads, strikes, social unrest and political instability, tax policies, advertisement and similar brain washing, 'brand fidelity' and so on. They can, in other words, put order into chaos, but of course, a particular *type* of order, one that is founded on the self-preservation and therefore self-expansion of capital. (original emphasis)

Both Weeks and De Angelis point to the 'law of value' as a specific kind of connectivity, a particular modality of being together in the world, which has to do with the way we produce, measure and distribute 'surplus value'.[13] Now this introduces a powerful qualification to the contingency of value argument: the law of value as a specific kind of connectivity based on competition, and not only for driving costs down or minimising labour time, as Weeks argued (see Terranova, 2000), is an important historical limitation to what value can be.[14] This limitation is neither natural nor irreversible but requires thinking about it as a powerful logic which is merely the result of an historic process that makes it more difficult to enact alternative valorisation processes, whether they actually exist or not. At the same time, it is important to keep in mind that, as with any connectivity understood as a way of assembling or formatting the world, this is neither the only possible nor the most desirable one. Indeed, Weeks was adamant to emphasise the historical specificity of Marx's 'law of value', its being a logic or process specific to capitalism and not a universal law. And as I argue in the next chapter, the fluidity of value and its partial crystallisations is what was at stake in Marx's, and even Smith's, analysis of value, albeit for very different reasons. The dynamic character of the 'law of value' is what is also at stake in De Angelis' argument; relying on Graeber's conceptualisation of value as the importance people attribute to their actions, he suggests that if we understand 'the norms and standards through which people judge this "importance" as emerging from a continuous interacting *process* of social constitution' (De Angelis, 2005:70), the dynamic character of the law of value becomes apparent.[15]

Recognising that the way in which value is currently determined within financial markets is actually a process and not an imperative brings to light our ability to contest such a process, including the institutional arrangements that shape it, which is what I attempt to do in Chapters 3 and 4 when I look at both the arrangements that have strengthened the grips of financial markets over the determination of value as well as those that might be able to format the financial market/value entanglement otherwise.[16] Such contestability entails reflecting on the desirability of the kind of entanglements or connectivity that the law of value articulates. Indeed, one risk that comes with emphasising the contingency of value is that any value making process, including the one currently being carried out within financial markets, may end up being justified. However, recognising the reality produced by derivatives and financial markets more generally does not mean accepting it. As MacKenzie (2008:80) puts it:

> [a]n economic theory or model *posits* a world, so to speak. It is too simple to ask only if that world is realistic ... We must also ask whether the widespread use of the theory or model will make the world it posits more or less real. If either is the case, we need to ask whether that world is to be desired or to be avoided

The interesting questions arising from a perspective that emphasises value's contingency and contestability are not whether the value of the derivative accurately reflects that of the underlying asset, or whether a return to the real economy is possible, but rather whether the reality produced by such technologies is desirable and, if not, what other kinds of economy–society nexus we may deem more desirable.

Notes

1 de Goede (2015:357) has pointed out that recent litigation, unlike the regulatory response I have referred to, has been willing to accept that derivatives' function is to trade on the contestability of value. Although

limited to the US and the first to manifest such an appreciation, the 2013 Tourre trial has signalled the US courts' willingness to abandon the distinction between (illegitimate) gambling and (legitmate) speculation to recognise that what is at stake in derivatives' trading is the commercialisation of contestability. As de Goede argues, the problem for the court was that 'Tourre traded probable default rather than a possibilistic bet on an open, contestable future'. Her argument is that 'Understood as a call to performative ethics, the Tourre judgment enacts financial critique *without* anchoring it in a prior articulation of fundamental value proper social structures. Instead, it produces a legal placeholder as a fictional boundary between legitimate speculation and illegitimate fraud. The boundary can only ever be navigated through an ongoing ethics of practice that renders all financial professionals responsible' (2015:371). Whether this development will lead to a rethinking of the role of regulation, as well as instigating transformation in financial professionals' 'ongoing ethics of practice', remains to be seen.

2 Marx (1863–1883:597), for instance, had already pointed to the role of expectations when analysing the relationship between securities and the capital they are supposed to represent: while 'The shares in railway, mining, shipping companies, etc. represent real capital, i.e. capital invested and functioning in these enterprises, or the sum of money that was advanced by the share-holders to be spent in these enterprises as capital', the capital they refer to does not exist twice as capital value of the share and then again as capital actually invested in the company at issue. For him it exists only in the latter form and 'the share is nothing but an ownership title, *pro rata*, to the surplus-value which this capital is to realise' (1863–1883:597). Thus, expectations of future returns play a role in price formation and this process always involves a speculative element. The point about derivatives is that, by commensurating bits of capital across time and spaces, they affect labour processes around the world.

3 For Marx formal subsumption was characterised by low organic composition of capital (ie labour was the prime input of production), and 'absolute' surplus labour was achieved by lengthening the working day so that the primary determinant of exchange value was 'socially necessary labour time'; real subsumption arose with science and technology allowing for the reduction of the working day, and leading to the production of relative surplus value and the increase of the spectrum of organic composition possibilities. With real subsumption, Caffenzis argues, capitalists 'will demand an equal rate of profit as their brethren (in the long run) even if "their" workers produce next to no surplus value. In other words, these capitalists will demand *the price of production*

(i.e., the sum of their constant capital and their variable capital plus the product of this sum and the rate of profit) in value terms instead of the actual value of their commodities' (Caffentzis, 2005:105).

4 As Caffentizis (2005:102) notes, 'specie-backed monetary systems were always subject to "contingent and purely conventional elements" from debasements to bullion export restrictions', as Foucault (1996) has also shown. Thus 'the determination of the socially necessary labor time required for the production of a commodity inevitably wove together a wide variety of economic, political, social and even personal-cultural considerations in determining its value. The post-1971 monetary environment', he continues, 'might be more subject to political power than the previous periods, but that does not give us any reason to think that Nixon's fiat caused a historical leap from the finite to the infinite in economic value. After all, one can hardly claim that there are no continuities in ratios of economic ratios (e.g., of profitability, exchange rates, and exports) between the pre- and post-1971 periods' (Caffentzis, 2005:102).

5 As Allon argues, one of the most important features of this hybrid system is not the fact that public money exists alongside other financial instruments which have 'moneyness' attributes, but the fact that this system is characterised by debt:'this is more than "debt"' in the simple sense of obligation or liability: the commodification of debt in securitized models of finance enables ever-expanding webs of profitable interconnection between public and private, consumer and corporate indebtedness and financial markets. Asset-backed securities composed of mortgages, student loans, and other forms of consumer debt, for example, are easily convertible into other forms of money in an instant, and so debt itself becomes a highly liquid tradable commodity' (Allon, 2015:297). This, she argues, entails a different relationship between financial capitalism and the state as 'debt represents an accumulation agenda centered not so much on profit through default and repossession but rather on profit through the extension of financial responsibility, ownership, and risk-taking as well as the maintenance of regular, reliable payment streams' (2015:298).

6 Unlike 'formal subsumption' where a surplus in the form of savings, investments, interest payments, etc is extracted 'without transforming the household into "capital"' (Bryan, Rafferty and Jefferis, 2015:317), Bryan et al. believe that the post-2008 process of securitisation of household assets is pointing to the 'real subsumption' of labour to (finance) capital (ie labour becomes productive *within* finance), as 'households are being subject to the same risk/return calculations that apply to capital's evaluation of itself' (2015:321). Their argument is that, whereas conventional financial assets are responsive to the economic cycle, those

linked to households are different and this difference is what makes households central to (finance) capital: 'In conditions of financial crisis, holders of liquid assets will head to cash, causing all asset movements to converge downward; however, households with illiquid assets aspire to stay solvent: to continue living in their house, work, pay the bills, and consume. In this fixity of households lies potential for a new class of financial assets, so long as they are incorporated into their own form of capitalist calculation. If households could be so incorporated, and default risk could be managed, the potential for capital is enormous' (2015:319). This is what they claim has happened through the development of financial assets that give exposure to households and provide for the credible measurement of those risks, particularly with post crisis securitisation which has involved 'the movement of more and more household payments into fixed-period contractual relations, to ensure locked-in future payments on which securities can be built and penalties for non- or even prepayment that disturbs the valuation of securities' (2015:320).

7 By focusing, as I do below, on this particular tradition of Italian feminist thought I do not mean to imply that these scholars were the first to think about immaterial labour or to engage with Marx's theory of value. Also, this work has been the object of subsequent feminist critique, particularly in relation to the reduction of the vast spectrum of human and non-human activities to the category of 'labour'. However, what makes their contribution important is their attempt both to rethink the categories of classical political economy so as to the challenge the unidirectional reading of the relationship between labour and value and to bring to light the spatio-temporal connections that articulate the relationship between production and social reproduction.

8 At issue was Marx's treatment of reproduction, in particular, the fact that reproductive work was reduced to the consumption of commodities that the wage could afford and the work that went into their production so that no distinction was made between commodity production and the production of the labour force (Federici, 2010:1–20). Federici has advanced several reasons why Marx did not investigate further the role of reproductive work in the determination of value. For instance, she points to the fact that until the 1870s, 'consistently with a policy tending to the "unlimited extension of the working day" and the utmost compression of the cost of labor-power production, reproductive work was reduced to a minimum'. Another reason might have been the difficulty that including it in productive labour would have posed to its measurement since it was not subject to monetary valuation (Federici, 2010:3).

9 Other feminist political economists have since shown how accounting for the vast, albeit hidden, wealth produced by reproductive labour is important to show the latter's 'depletion'. For instance, see Rai, Hoskyns and Thomas, 2010.

10 This is something that Virno reaffirms with the primacy of language and the intellect as the generic faculties of the species (Virno, 2004).

11 Indeed, for them 'there is a need to approach labour power as precisely a form of power that exceeds and in a certain sense precedes, processes of discipline and control, dispossession and exploitation' (Mezzadra and Neilson, 2013a:264). This is the important point they raise about the need to pay attention to the production of subjectivity that is intertwined with these processes, a point to which I will return in my Conclusions.

12 I am indebted to Paddy Ireland for the engaging discussions on this point.

13 As De Angelis (2005:73) argues: 'It is by pursuing value within the confinement of market relations that individual "actors" compare values of different products or compare among values of the same products produced with different methods and conditions of production and *act upon* this comparison. The *effect* of this acting enters into feedback relations with millions of others, it contributes to produce new average prices and profit and it produces effects that act as material forces for other actors making similar comparison and acting upon them. The ongoing process of this act of measurement of value and *action* upon it, is what gives rise to what we value socially, and it does so *whatever* is our individual or collective aggregate *ethical* standpoint' (original emphasis).

14 The recent emphasis on 'social value' in the UK, for instance, points to the further strengthening of competition and measurement in 'society' through the creation of a social investment market and the introduction of financial instruments such as the 'social impact bond'. Social value, Dowling and Harvie (2014) argue, provides a new and powerful metric for financialisation whose potential to generate profits is being currently debated within international fora such as the 2013 G8 summit. What is interesting, they point out, is that unlike corporate social responsibility or philanthropy 'where the ethical course is external to the business model... [the social is here] decidedly internal to the ways in which business seeks to create and capture value' (2014:881). And crucially they link such a metric and the attempt to develop a social investment market not only to the crisis of capital accumulation but also to that of social reproduction, particularly since the 'largely invisible reproductive work is no longer being performed – at least, not on a way consistent with capital accumulation', as

evidenced by the increasing panic over youth's unemployability and lack of competitiveness (2014:877). Thus, they conclude,'One way that the social investment model harnesses the social in the pursuit of profit is by accounting for unwaged labour as an activity that produces social value, *not* as an activity that is coded as work' (2014:882).

15 In a different register, this is also part of Mezzadra and Neilson's project to think *Border as Method* (2013a:84) as they try to move away from interpretations of the law of value that privilege capital mobility and the latters' ability to organise labour processes, and focus instead on the complex ways in which 'labour mobilities (and the border struggles and the production of subjectivity that accompany them)' relate to capital mobility in the patterning of the global world.

16 In Chapter 3 I reflect on the potential of two regional arrangements: the potential of the RMA proposed by Ecuador to inject values other than the privatisation of risks and precarisation of life in the current economy-finance hierarchy of values; and that of the ALBA to affect the position that competition has attained in the trade and development hierarchy of values. In Chapter 4 I move the analysis to the realm of wage labour, and ask whether the ELR – a recent proposal articulated by post-Keynesian scholars and feminist economists – has the potential to affect current meanings of work and productive activities. What these experiments have in common, I argue, is the acknowledgement that finance, trade, production and social reproduction are deeply inter-related, rather than being distinct and discrete domains of analysis and action. They also raise the question of what production and work, and not only finance and trade, should be for, which has to do with the kind of economy–society nexus we deem desirable.

Chapter 2

Of value and the contingency of its *law*: the (still) hidden abode of reproduction

To be a productive worker is … not a piece of luck, but a misfortune
(Marx, 1867:644)

Like the land, the body had to be cultivated and first of all broken up, so that it could relinquish his hidden treasures. For while the body is the condition of the existence of labour-power, it is also its limit, as the main element of resistance to its expenditure
(Federici, 2004:140–141)

This chapter continues the exploration of value's contestability by thinking about its fluidity and always partial crystallisations in light of classical political economy, in particular Smith's *Wealth of Nations* and its subsequent critique by Marx in *Capital* Volume I. I engage with Smith and Marx for three reasons: first, because their thinking about value is much more fluid than what is often presented in accounts of so-called intrinsic value. Second, in their work we see an awareness, however problematic, of the crucial importance of social reproduction, an awareness which will gradually disappear from economic analysis. This understanding is what the feminist political economic work referred to in Chapter 1 has relied on, critiqued and expanded, providing a much more provocative approach to value. I return to this approach by reading Federici's *Caliban and the Witch* and its highlighting of the role that the historic separation between productive and socially reproductive activities has played in the generation of (capitalist) value. The third reason has to do with the fact that Smith and Marx's works explicitly acknowledge the importance institutional arrangements have in shaping the nexus between economy and society, including the separation between production and social reproduction, even though the gendered, racial and sexual assumptions on which this separation is based are left unchallenged.

Taken together, these points enable me to articulate more clearly the argument I made in the previous chapter about the limits of arguments that approach the contingency of value as a novel (ie post-Fordist) phenomenon. Value has always been contingent on, among other things, the arrangements that have instituted its measurement, and this, I argue, is what emerges from Smith's and Marx's analyses of the socio-economic system they were intent on investigating and, as I will show, actively contributing to. However, whereas for Smith at issue was the need for statesmen and legislators to depart from the mercantilist credo according to which wealth coincided with the accumulation of money rather than 'stock' (ie capital), Marx's preoccupation was to critique the assumptions on which classical political economy had based its claims about the 'freedom' introduced by the new economic system. One such assumption concerned the theory of value. Since wealth for Smith had to do with the accumulation of the stock needed to satisfy the 'necessaries and conveniences of life', value becomes the compass for making sense of the relationship between the parts and the whole of the socioeconomic system. Rather than in presenting a substance-like approach to value (ie what value is and where it comes from), Smith is therefore interested in seeing how it can function, how it can generate order by relating the parts – what is produced by atomistic individuals – to the whole, that is the national produce. Labour here functions as the measure, rather than the substance, of value. Indeed, as Foucault (1966) has argued, it is only with Ricardo that labour time becomes the source of value.

The most fascinating aspect is that, taken as a whole, Smith's work speaks not of the economic system 'as it really was' but of what it could be if his 'model' were applied: this is a point that Poovey (1998) has also made in relation to Smith's use of numbers. When the first two 'descriptive' chapters are read together with the last three 'historical' ones, *Wealth of Nations* can be seen as attempting to construct a model for the economy–society nexus that diverges from that which Smith thought had prevailed since the fall of the Roman Empire. From this perspective value emerges as a construct made to coincide with labour time so as to envision a whole, a system for the production and distribution of wealth, where parts can be made to relate to one another not in terms of money but of the labour they can buy. Equally significant is the fact that this model is based on a separation between certain activities considered 'productive' of that value and others posited as 'unproductive', despite the latter being, as Federici shows, the very foundation on which the former can exist and produce value.

Marx takes the material effects of such a construct seriously while at the same time challenging the 'naturalness' and desirability of the assumptions on which it is based. The aim is to show that value does not need to take the form it does, that is *labour time* does not need to provide the compass between parts and whole. Marx's approach to value is therefore much more complex than any intrinsic account can give credit for, in that it is far from positing a substance *tout court*. This is even though scores of

Marxist economists continue to quantify the 'substance of value', that is, the ever changing *socially necessary* labour time; and the first three chapters of Volume I, where he introduces key concepts, may be read as pointing in this direction.[1] This is not to say that the law of value no longer exerts any influence: on the contrary, as the discussion of financial derivatives has shown, it is very relevant today. However, the model Marx engages with, which has the commodity as its unit of analysis, is meant to emphasise the political nature of a system which is the result of an historic process and whose workings he believed classical political economy had attempted to naturalise. There is no substance or essence pertaining to value; yet, once *instituted*, socially necessary labour time creates a specific type of relation between the parts and the whole, a particular kind of connectivity or being together as argued in the previous chapter, in which accumulation, centralisation and competition play a crucial role.

What Marx leaves unchallenged, however, are the gendered, sexual and racial assumptions on which the very production of value is made possible. Although he acknowledges that to be a productive worker is 'not a piece of luck, but a misfortune' (1867:644), he does not consider how the 'unproductive' worker in fact provides the very conditions on which this value is extracted: s/he is the subject excluded from analyses of productive processes and political struggles so that the 'productive' subject *himself* can exist. Federici's *Caliban and the Witch* shows how such separations remain crucial to processes of value production today: her work is not the first to point to these very productive exclusions of course. I focus on it, however, because it speaks to a tradition of thought which, as argued in Chapter 1, has challenged and reinvented Marxist categories and practices as well as the possibility for political action; yet, by asserting the analytical and political primacy of particular workers (immaterial/cognitive/ affective), this work risks sustaining those separations on the basis of which (capitalist) value continues to be extracted.

I acknowledge that my strategic reading of Smith's and Marx's texts is selective and partial. However, and besides the point that all readings are, I do think their work can be read as pointing to their being aware of the important intervention they were making, of the value(s) they were setting in motion, and, as we would put it today, of the fact that economic models make the economic reality they claim to simply describe. They both tried to depart from previous orthodoxies and shape in a particular way the imagined whole. If today we recognise that conceiving of systems as a whole, as totalities or unities, is highly problematic, this acknowledgement does not detract from the importance of thinking about the connections that construct the fabric in which we are imbricated and which we constantly make. The question therefore becomes: can the whole be reconceptualised not as a closed system but as the mode of connecting and relating which is always open and in the making and whose tracing, however, always incomplete, is what matters?

This point speaks directly to the question I will address in the next two chapters about the possibility of thinking of more desirable kinds of intervention, interventions which acknowledge the exclusions their partiality and selectivity always entails, while at the same time attempting to bring to light the values that always inform action, whether or not we are explicit about them. As Chapter 3 argues, the privatisation of risks and precarisation of life that are currently being supported by financial markets and instruments such as derivatives are one example of the productive interaction between values and arrangements; and, Ecuador's RMA is one example of possible arrangements aimed at injecting alternative values. Far from being an ideal arrangement, the RMA brings to the fore the issue of intervention, the issue of what to do once we fully acknowledge the blurring of the boundaries between the 'real' and the financial spheres of the economy, as well as that between production and social reproduction. This is why I conclude this chapter by referring to Nietzsche's insights on 'perspectival seeing' which, already in the nineteenth century, had posed the crucial question of intervention, a question which has to do with the 'determination of the *hierarchy of values*' (Nietzsche, 1887:38). Seeing and knowing are always perspectival: as Nietzsche puts it, there is no such thing as a neutral perspective and any 'science', including political economy, needs a 'belief' in order to derive from it 'a direction, a meaning, a limit, a method' (1887:127). As will be argued in the next two chapters, the acceptance of financial markets as the indisputable makers of value is far from being a neutral perspective, one which is the result of inexorable forces; and the precarisation of life that has ensued is only one value in the hierarchy, and one that is highly contestable.

Smith and the economic 'model'

> [P]olitical economy, considered as a branch of the science of a states-
> man or legislator, proposes two distinct objects: first to provide a
> plentiful revenue or subsistence for the people, or, more properly, to
> enable them to provide such a revenue and subsistence for themselves;
> and secondly, to supply the state or commonwealth with a revenue
> sufficient for the public services. It proposes to enrich both the people
> and the sovereign.
>
> (Smith, 1776:417)

We have to wait until book four of *Wealth of Nations* for this statement about the nature and scope of political economy: wealth and its purpose, the means for achieving it and, indirectly, the measure necessary to distribute it to its producers. With this in mind, Smith goes on to examine the two economic systems generated by the 'different progress of opulence in different ages and nations': the system of commerce and that of agriculture (Smith, 1776:417). The analysis of the commercial system is aimed at refuting the prevalent theory of the time, the mercantilist doctrine, which had made European powers overly concerned about increasing their reserves of gold and silver. Wealth is for Smith not money but the annual produce that allows for the satisfaction of 'necessaries, conveniences, and amusements of human life' (Smith, 1776:34). Money is the means through which the produce circulates and, as we shall see, values the precondition for its circulation as it enables its parts to be commensurated. The overarching aim of political economy is that of providing 'plentiful revenue or subsistence for the people' followed by 'revenue sufficient for the public services' or, in other words, that of providing, in one form or another, the means for the reproduction of life (Smith, 1776:34). Social reproduction, here understood primarily as social provisioning, is therefore a central concern in Smith's analysis. The issue of how it is 'organised', in which context value as a measure matters a great deal, is the object of the first two books to which I will return.

In book three, however, it becomes apparent that what Smith considers as 'the Natural Progress of Opulence' (1776:373) has subsistence at its heart: 'As subsistence is, in the nature of things, prior to conveniency and luxury, so the industry which procures the former, must necessarily be prior to that which ministers to the latter'(1776:374). It is interesting that he sees this system made of organic links between country and town as the natural state of affairs, when in preceding sections he has posited commercial society as the most progressive state ever achieved. This is not a contradiction though, as he is merely pointing to the fact that such a society should have developed by relying on a system where country and town are well connected. This is not what had happened to European nations:

> Had human institutions ... never disturbed the natural course of things, the progressive wealth and increase in the towns would, in every political society, be consequential, and in proportion to the improvement and cultivation of the territory of country ... [in Europe instead] the foreign commerce of some of their cities has introduced all their finer manufactures, or such as were for distant sale; and manufactures and foreign commerce together have given birth to the principal improvement in agriculture. The manner and customs which the nature of their original government introduced, and which remained after that government was greatly altered, necessarily forced them into this unnatural and retrograde order.
>
> (Smith, 1776:376–377)

Chiefly responsible for such a state is the transformation of the approach to land which, from being a means to procure subsistence, had become a means to exercise power (Smith, 1776:378–379); thus, whereas the Roman law of succession allowed for the distribution of land among all children, the law of primogeniture that followed ensured that land would be passed to only one of the male descendants. The power that lords acquired over the country as a result led to its lack of cultivation and the fact that some towns, which managed to become relatively independent from the lords by the assent of the monarch, preferred to procure their subsistence through trade from remote parts of the world. This seems to have been the case in Italy with the emergence of the republics where fine manufactured goods were brought and then used to procure subsistence from the lords (1776:397). In England, proprietors and merchants managed to bring about 'a revolution of the greatest importance to the public happiness' as the 'commerce and manufactures of cities ... have been the cause and occasion of the improvement and cultivation of the country' (1776:409). However, an economic system that has relied on trade to develop agriculture, rather than the other way around, is not without its problems as:

> The capital ... that is acquired to any country by commerce and manufactures, is always a very precarious and uncertain possession, till some part of it has been secured and realised in the cultivation and improvement of its lands. A merchant, it has been said very properly, is not necessarily the citizen of any particular country ... [Besides, t]he ordinary revolutions of war and government easily dry up the sources of that wealth which arises from commerce only. That which arises from the more solid improvements of agriculture is much more durable ...
>
> (Smith, 1776:412–413)

What is interesting about this narrative about 'public happiness' is the emergence, despite the unnatural path that England has followed, of a domain of freedom and possibility which is distinguished from that of coercion that had characterised European affairs since the demise of the Roman Empire. Smith is immersed in the theorisation of the shift from coercion to self-rule, a shift which entails a liberal individual who is the object of his analysis in the book that preoccupied him before and after *Wealth of Nations*. In *The Theory of Moral Sentiments* (1759:362–364), but also his *Lectures on Jurisprudence* (1723–1790), he is trying to distance himself from Mandeville and Hobbes, positing sympathy-based benevolence as the virtue *par excellence*. The *impartial spectator*, he who is able to reflect upon himself, separate positive from destructive passions and act accordingly, does not need an omnipresent state. As we shall see, this conceptualisation is part of a tradition of thought which, during the seventeenth and eighteenth centuries had as its object nothing less than the reformation of the person with 'productivity' as its stake.[2]

What is clear is that in his account of the shift from coercion to self rule, commercial society and its institutions come to play a significant role as they enable the flourishing of these 'desirable' qualities, first and foremost productivity. For Smith, the free subject emerges from a coercive state of affairs that had condemned *him* to idleness. Indeed, with the violence that had provided for the 'public happiness' through foreign trade out of sight, idleness itself becomes the source of violence: 'a person who can acquire no property can have no other interest but to eat as much and to labour as little as possible. Whatever work he does beyond what is sufficient to purchase his own maintenance, can be squeezed out of him by violence only, and not by any interest of his own' (Smith, 1776:382). Commercial society, on the other hand, grants unprecedented freedoms as its 'industrious' merchant, who saves and invests part of *his* annual produce in a way that grants more employment to other people, and therefore more prosperity to the nation, comes to replace the idle proprietor of 'ancient' Europe. The latter could not, without commerce or manufacture, employ his revenue in any other way than in maintaining the families directly at his command:

> In the present state of Europe [however], a man of £10000 a year, can spend his whole revenue, and he generally does so, without directly maintaining twenty people ... Indirectly, perhaps, he maintains as great, or even a greater number of people, than he could have done by the ancient method of expense. For though the quantity of precious productions for which he exchanges his whole revenue be very small, the number of workmen employed in collecting and preparing it must necessarily have been very great ... by paying that price, he indirectly contributes to the maintenance of all the workmen and their employers.
>
> (Smith, 1776:406)

The forces that have brought about this shift are 'productivity', inextricably linked with the division of labour, and the introduction of private property, which had set in motion the accumulation of capital and therefore laid the basis for a new political economic system. Marx will later call into question these mythical foundations. What I want to emphasise for the time being is that the way in which this system is supposed to work, that is the way in which it is supposed to ensure that the needs of the whole population are satisfied, is for Smith the desirable outcome of an historical process as much as it is a craft. Indeed, the model he puts forward, and which consists of the division of labour-led productivity and the accumulation of stock – the latter supposed to gradually increase until the annual produce (divided in wages, profit and rent) enables all involved in the process of production to satisfy their needs – is a very artful exercise based on a number of assumptions that are posited as truth claims.[3] Or, put differently, these are statements he sees as able to produce the desired results, an all encompassing and harmonious system of social provisioning, provided they are accepted as true.

The first craft concerns the positing of both the division of labour and the accumulation of capital, as well as their relationship, as natural, achieved and desirable rather than the result of historic, political and institutional processes. As Smith puts it:

> In that rude stage of society, in which exchanges are seldom made, and in which every man provides everything for himself, it is not necessary that any stock should be accumulated, or stored up before hand, in order to carry on the business of the society. Every man endeavours to supply, by his own industry, his own occasional wants, as they occur ... But when the division of labour has once been *thoroughly introduced*, the produce of a man's own labour can supply but a small part of his occasional wants. The far greater part of them are supplied by the produce of other men's labour, which he purchases with the produce, or, what is the same thing, with the price of the produce, of his own.
>
> (Smith, 1776:267, emphasis added)

At this point the 'accumulation of stock' becomes an essential aspect 'of the business of society'. As the workman sells his produce in order to be able to purchase what he needs, it follows that 'a stock of goods of different kinds ... must be stored up *somewhere*, sufficient to maintain him, and to supply him with the materials and tools of his work, till such *time* at least as both these events can be brought together' (Smith 1776:267) (emphasis added). The temporal and spatial mode of society becomes one of accumulation: 'As the accumulation of stock must, in the *nature of things*, be previous to the division of labour, so labour can be more and more subdivided in proportion only as stock is previously more and more accumulated' (1776:267) (emphasis added). There is some circular reasoning at play in the description of the relation between the division of labour and the accumulation of capital: whereas in the first chapter Smith had posited the former as the result of the human propensity to track, barter and exchange, a progressive force that allows us to meet our needs by improving 'dexterity' of labour and saving time (1776:15), in the passage just quoted the division of labour is the result of the accumulation of stock. And although he takes great pain to emphasise how stock accumulates 'naturally', it is apparent that it is the result of a historic process which Smith himself refers to in passing, that is, 'the appropriation of land' (1776:51), a process on whose significance Marx will reflect.

As mentioned earlier, Smith takes this to be a positive development because ownership increases productivity through the care that was absent in 'ancient Europe' and importantly because in the scheme he has in mind, the appropriation-led accumulation *cum* division of labour leads to greater produce (to be distributed among, wage, rent and profit), that is to the satisfaction of more needs. For his all-encompassing scheme to work, a number of assumptions need to hold true, and are indeed presented as truths, starting with the fact that when a man 'possesses stock sufficient to maintain him for months or years, he *naturally* endeavours to derive a revenue from the greater part of it' (1776:270) Why? Because 'A man must be perfectly crazy, who, where there is tolerable security, does not employ all the stock which he commands, whether it be his own, or borrowed of other people' (1776:277). But this is a no more natural or less artful scheme for securing access to subsistence than the one Smith is trying to distance himself from. Unlike the medieval one, which he sees as the realm of unfreedom, poverty and idleness, this is a system providing for the subsistence of all through wage labour. This is why the wage has a central relevance in Smith's analysis (1776:69), a point to which I will return in Chapter 4: it has to provide for the reproduction of the labour force and therefore it is very much the terrain of struggle between 'masters' and 'workmen'.

The second crafting exercise concerns 'value' as the glue that binds the system together, specifically through the establishment of its measure. Smith acknowledges the Aristotelian distinction between 'value in use' and 'value in exchange' and sets out to investigate the principles which regulate the 'exchangeability of commodities', that is 'the *real* measure of this exchangeable value' (1776:32) (emphasis added). What is interesting is his focus on labour not as the source but as the measure of value. As he puts it:

> Every man is rich or poor according to the degree in which he can afford to enjoy the necessaries, conveniences, and amusements of human life. But after the division of labour ... [t]he far greater part of them must derive from the labour of other people, and he must be rich or poor according to the quantity of that labour which he can command, or which he can afford to purchase. The value of any commodity, therefore, to the person who possesses it, and who means ... to exchange it for other commodities, is equal to the quantity of labour which it enables him to purchase or command. Labour, therefore, is the *real measure* of the exchangeable value of commodities ... What is really bought with money, or with goods, is purchased by labour, as

much as what we acquire by the toil of our own body. That money, or
those goods indeed, save us this toil.

(Smith, 1776:34, emphasis added)

According to Smith, value is what allows us to exchange those goods we
need or desire but no longer produce ourselves since we now operate within
a system based on large-scale division of labour. If money is the practical
means of commodity exchange, value is its conceptual tool: it enables us
to make sense of the relations of the parts (commodities) to the whole
(annual produce) in terms of the labour necessary to produce them. This
is obviously the case once we accept that the *labour* for procuring one's
means of existence requires the 'toil' to take the form it does, that is, that
of commodity producer and wage labourer for the accumulation of capital.
However, the question of measure, that is the question of labour time, begs
the question of why labour should take this form. Indeed, Smith recognises
that the craft involved in making it takes such form when he argues:

> [b]ut though labour be the real measure of the exchangeable value
> of all commodities, it is not that by which their value is commonly
> estimated. It is often difficult to ascertain the proportion between two
> different quantities of labour. The *time* spent into two different sorts of
> work will not always alone determine this proportion.
>
> (Smith, 1776:35, emphasis added)

Smith sees the difference as lying in the various degrees of 'hardship
endured', 'ingenuity exercised', the 'constancy or inconstancy of employment' opportunities, 'the small or great trust ... reposed in the workman'
and 'the probability and improbability of success' in these different employ-
ments (1776:110). He acknowledges, for instance, that 'it is not easy to find
any accurate measure either of hardship or ingenuity' (1776:35); what he
does not expressly mention is that ingenuity and hardship are themselves
measures, that is active devices that format the reality they are posited as
to merely describe, ie the exchangeable value of commodities. In other
words, there is an *a priori* decision made about criteria according to which
labour will be known, differentiated and measured. Robinson (1972:9)
made a similar observation when she asked why garbage collectors are paid
less than economics professors: whereas the Smithian justification would
place emphasis on hours spent on education, the possibility of not finding
employment, etc, she saw it as the result of an *a priori* political decision.
The point is that there is nothing natural about these criteria, they are
all *fabricated*, an aspect which, as De Angelis (2005:72) has pointed out,
becomes apparent when we realise that we pay arms dealers more than
nurses for instance.

In Smith's scheme these differences are resolved through the equalising quality of the market: while some 'allowance' for these differences is commonly made through the wage, this allowance 'is adjusted, however, not by any accurate measure, but by the haggling and bargaining of the market, according to that sort of *rough equality* which, though not exact, is sufficient for carrying on the business of common life' (1776:35) (emphasis added). This is what Mann (2010) defines as the logic of equivalence that makes disparate things equivalent and substitutable. Although these 'properties' of the market, first and foremost 'equivalence' and 'substitutability', are what will acquire a self-reproducing quality (at the very least in analyses of neoclassical scholars up to the present point) and will be the object of Marx's critique, it is important to emphasise the perspective from which Smith is writing. He is aiming to *construct* an all-encompassing system: the reading of *Wealth of Nations* as a whole points to at least an ambivalence as to whether he thinks he is describing an already existing system, although I have read it as an effort at actively fabricating one by placing many of the 'observable facts' *qua* 'as ifs'. It is clear that the aim of this system is the reproduction of its members, an aspect which, as will be seen in Chapter 3, has led to the recent revalorisation of Smith's work given its potential to bring social provisioning and institutional arrangements back to the centre of economic analysis (Arrighi, 2009; Offer, 2012).[4]

If in Smith's scheme of things what matters is the gradual increase of the annual produce of the land and labour which in 'every country is no doubt ultimately destined for supplying the consumption of its inhabitants' (1776:327), the issue of the organisation of its production and distribution is crucial. That this is not the result of natural laws as the emergent field of neoclassical economics would soon posit (ie the iron law of wages) but of political and institutional arrangements, Smith is well aware. Indeed, the issue of how to distribute the annual produce between labour and capital is for him of paramount importance, and despite the fact that he ends up siding with the owners of capital – for him the accumulation of capital is what allows the annual produce to increase – he is clear that at least as important is that wages allow for the adequate reproduction of labour.[5]

For the time being, however, I want to reflect further on the *labour* whose reproduction Smith considered crucial to his political economic model. Rather than being a general activity through which the population accesses its subsistence, labour acquires a specific quality, one which is inextricably linked to the production of value. In the same artful way in which he had posited 'hardship and ingenuity' *as if* they were natural qualities according to which it could be evaluated, labour is considered 'productive' of value only if it has the ability to 'fix and realise itself in some particular subject of vendible commodity, which lasts for some time at least after that labour is past' (Smith, 1776:325). Thus, whereas the labour of 'servants' as well as that of 'the most respectable orders in the society ... churchmen, lawyers, physicians, men of letters of all kinds' has its value, in the sense that it deserves its reward as much productive labourers do, it does not produce (exchange) value because 'their service, how honourable, how useful, or how necessary soever, produces nothing for which an equal quantity of service can afterward be procured' (1776:326).

We could say that this is no longer the case, with services having been made exchangeable across borders, thanks, and in no in small part, to international economic agreements such as the WTO's General Agreement on Trade in Services (GATS). But there is a particular aspect of this craft worth noticing: what is at stake in defining labour as un/productive of value is its in/ability to produce equivalence and substitutability in the future. From this angle, we may say that services have been made equivalent and substitutable but this only performs, as in reiterates and extends, rather than departs from, the artifice with which value becomes constructed as equivalence and substitutability and labour as that which produces such 'properties'. This construction results in a particular articulation of the economy–society nexus, whose analytical and political consequences both Marx and Federici emphasise. But it is also the first step towards the formulation of a theory of value that has labour as its source, and whose completion Foucault (1966) considers achieved with Ricardo. Indeed, in *The Order of Things* Foucault sees the field of political economy, in which Smith, Ricardo and Marx are collapsed together, as a pre-critical science because, he argues, labour comes to occupy a metaphysical role, that of a quasi-transcendental. They are all seen as having made it coincide with human essence. This is a claim that Althusser and Balibar (1970) will dispute in relation to Marx, for whom *Capital* departs from metaphysics through a new approach to reading that does not claim a more truthful grounding of economic categories: what is at issue, in other words, is not the description of reality 'as it really is'. The identification of a deeper reality, a cause, an essence, is not what is at stake in Smith's work either, my point being that he acknowledges that the political economic model he puts forward is an 'artifice', not in the sense of being unreal but of being constructed, and in no small measure through conceptual interventions such his own *Wealth of Nations*.

Marx's critical reading strategy

Marx was very well aware that the political economic system that Smith constructed produced very real effects despite being based on a number of problematic assumptions. *Capital* Volume I can be read as an attempt to debunk those assumptions while taking great care to recognise the material effects of the edifice built by the classical school of political economy.

To start with, Marx's view of the objective of political economy is very different from Smith's: rather than considering it the orderly production of the goods which are necessary for the satisfaction of the needs and desires of the entire population, he sees it as naturalising a deeply political, historic and institutional process, a process which has crystallised into a system that views the accumulation of capital as an end in itself. Marx agrees with Smith that a new system has emerged from the dissolution of the feudal order, which was based on the exercise of direct power. He acknowledges that 'to become a free seller of labour power, who carries his commodity wherever he can find a market for it, he must further have escaped from the regime of the guilds, their rules for apprentices and journeymen, and their restrictive labour regulations. Hence, the historical movement which changes the producers into wage-labourers appears, on the one hand, as the emancipation from serfdom and from the fetters of the guilds' (Marx, 1867:875). This, however, is the only aspect of the process that classical political economists take into account. The overall assessment changes when one considers that 'on the other hand, these newly freed men became sellers of themselves only after they had been robbed of all their own means of production, and all the guarantees of existence afforded by the old feudal arrangements. And this history, the history of their expropriation, is written in the annals of mankind in letters of blood and fire' (1867:875).

Unlike Smith, Marx did not consider the shift from feudal to capitalist societies as a movement from coercion to self-rule. Smith (1776:51) had acknowledged that the 'appropriation of land' played a role in the 'accumulation of stock'. However, he did view this process as necessary and desirable. For Marx, instead, it consisted of 'the change in th[e] form of servitude', in which 'conquest, enslavement, robbery, murder, in short, force, played the greatest part' (Marx, 1867:874). In England, for instance, this force included the use of 'bloody legislation against the expropriated since the end of the fifteenth century' and legislation to force down wages (1867:896). If the historic reading of this process is different from that put forward by Smith, so is the analysis of the aims and qualities of the economic arrangements which result from it. While the function of the economic system described by Smith, of which accumulation of stock was a precondition, is the satisfaction of the needs and desires of the population through the annual produce of the nation, the function of the system Marx describes is the endless accumulation of capital, with primitive accumulation and surplus value through commodity production being its fuel.

However, the differences between the two accounts are also of a qualitative order: crucially, Marx argues, the division 'between the product of labour and labour itself ... [not only provides] the real foundation and the starting-point of the process of capitalist production' (1867:716), it also demystifies what is presented as a neutral act of exchange between seller and buyer of labour power on the market, the seller having acquired capital through 'right and labour' according to classical political economists. The separation between labour power and the conditions of labour that follows primitive accumulation is not 'a mere accident' but 'the alternating rhythm' of a process which 'throws the worker back into the market again and again as a seller of his labour power and continually transforms his own product into a means by which another man can purchase him' (1867:723). Once we look deeper at the idea of equivalence which is supposed to characterise the new system we realise that the means with which sellers of labour are bought, that is profits – although this applies equally to rents and interests – arise from the difference between what the workers produce and what they get in exchange for their labour through wages. This difference is nothing other than workers' unpaid labour.[6] Whereas in a feudal society it took the form of physical output, as in the case with 'labour services', feudal rent or the slave owner's livelihood, in capitalist societies it takes the form of surplus value. The assumption about equality in exchange is also complicated by the fact that buyers of labour are not operating under the same compulsion mechanisms as sellers are, since the latter's means of subsistence have been withdrawn from them.

What happens to labour, the form it takes under capitalism, is therefore of paramount importance. The separation of workers from their means of production signals not only the emergence of a new 'kind of servitude', one which is disguised by the notion of equality in exchange. It also inaugurates a society based on a particular modality for producing both goods and social relations. Whereas '[t]he product of labour is an object of utility in all states of society ... *it is only a historic specific epoch of development which presents the labour expended in the production of a useful article as an "objective" property* of that article, *i.e. as its value*. It is only then that the product of labour becomes transformed into a commodity' (Marx, 1867:153–154) (emphasis added). The resulting society of commodity producers is therefore reliant on a logic of abstraction that finds in the law of value its manifestation. To understand how the 'law of value' is qualitatively different from the concept of value employed by Smith, Ricardo and their predecessors, it is important to appreciate the notion of *abstract* labour.

The key issue is for Marx the organisation of labour and production, that is the process through which branches of production develop in a society and labour is consequently allocated among these branches. This is an issue of coordination. Unlike a society where labour is manifestly social and a conscious decision-making mechanism exists between the different segments of production, a society of commodity producers is characterised by the fact that labour is *private*: commodities are here produced by innumerable firms who act independently of one another. This, however, does not mean that a coordinating mechanism is absent. Indeed, such a society too requires a means for making sense of the relations between parts and whole, that is, of the interconnectedness between producers which manifests itself in the exchange of commodity equivalents. Commodity producers are therefore dependent on one another even though they act as (if they were) atomistic entities. Labour is still social, in the sense of being connected, and the modality through which this interconnectedness is realised is (the law of) value:

> [t]he labour of the private individual manifests itself as an element of the total labour of society only through the relations which the act of exchange establishes between the products, and, through their mediation, between the producers ... It is only by being exchanged that the products of labour acquire a socially uniform objectivity as values, which is distinct from their sensuously varied objectivity as articles of utility.
>
> (Marx, 1867:165–166)

For Marx, classical political economy had considered value as the objective embodiment of concrete labour units in a commodity. Now Smith's work, or my reading of it, points in the direction of him being aware of its constructed, socially achieved and, in his view, desirable character. As mentioned earlier, his analysis focuses on labour as a measure rather than the source of value: for him the exchange value of a commodity corresponds to the quantity of labour which the commodity can command. In this context, labour time provides 'the *real* measure of the exchangeable value of commodities'. Marx, however, specifically emphasises the social nature of such a measure, social in the sense of being achieved in the act of exchange but also of occurring at a particular time, and therefore far from being ahistorical and universally valid. Thus, '[t]he division of the product of labour into a useful thing and a thing possessing value appears in practice only when exchange has already acquired a sufficient extension and importance to allow useful things to be produced for the purpose of being exchanged, so that their character as values has already been taken into consideration during production' (Marx, 1867:166). Things therefore become commodities, possessing exchange value, only with widespread commodity production:

> From this moment on, the labour of the individual producer acquires a two-fold social character. On the one hand, it must, as a definite useful kind of labour, satisfy a definite social need, and thus maintain its position as an element of the total labour, as a branch of the social division of labour ... On the other hand, it can satisfy the manifold

needs of the individual producer himself only in so far as every particular kind of useful private labour can be exchanged with, i.e. counts as *equal* of, every other kind of useful private labour.

(Marx, 1867:166, emphasis added)

It is in this context that *socially necessary labour time* asserts itself as the measure of value. But the equivalence, this measure operates on the basis of a powerful abstraction: '[e]quality in the full sense between different kinds of labour can be arrived at only if we abstract from their real inequality, if we reduce them to the characteristic they have in common, that of being the expenditure of human labour-power, of human labour in the abstract' (Marx, 1867:166). Only by abstracting from their uniqueness and specificity, can these different kinds of labour become equivalent values: value, in other words, is the unity to which the heterogeneity of labour is reduced. This does not mean that the results of this process are not material and objective: they indeed are. One effect of such 'construction' is that relations among producers appear to be relations among things, what Marx refers to as the mysterious character of the commodity form: the commodity comes to reflect 'the social characteristics of men's own labour as objective characteristics of the products of labour themselves, as the socio-natural properties of these things. Hence, it also reflects the social relations of the producers to the sum total of labour as a social relation between objects, a relation which exists *apart from and outside the producers*' (1867:164–165) (emphasis added). Marx is not denying the power of these 'things' and their relations, which acquire a life of their own once we consider, for instance, the pressure of competition that the law of value engenders (1867:168); but he is challenging the assumption that these relations exist 'apart from and outside the producers' (1867:165). That they acquire a life of their own, becoming a powerful logic, is evident if we look at the way in which socially necessary labour time crystallises into the measure of value:

The production of commodities must be fully developed before the scientific conviction emerges, from experience itself, that all the different kinds of private labour, which are carried on independently of each other, and yet, as spontaneously developed branches of the social division of labour are in a situation of *all-round dependence on each other*, are continually being reduced to the quantitative proportions in which society requires them. The reason for this reduction is that in the midst of the accidental and ever-fluctuating exchange relations between the products, the labour-time socially necessary to produce them asserts itself *as regulative law of nature* …

(Marx, 1867:165, emphasis added)

This passage can be read as naturalising the law of value. Indeed, one interpretation of the labour theory of value has labour as the real substance of value and socially necessary labour time as its real measure. However, this can be done only if Marx's critical reading strategy, which has as its target the denaturalisation and politicisation of the 'model' Smith attempted to put forward, is put to one side. The point is that, once adopted as the measure of value, and this is the result of an historic process which as Marx suggested was other than natural and inevitable, indeed it was written 'in letters of blood and fire', socially necessary labour time can be understood as instituting and crystallising a powerful dynamic, one that through competition and concentration of capital attempts to realise surplus value, rather than asserting a quantitative order according to which the value of commodities is given by the labour congealed in them.[7] Indeed, although the reference to congealed (past) labour is made several times (1867:129–133), Marx also asserts that 'the value of a commodity is determined not by the quantity of labour actually objectified in it, but by the quantity of *living* labour necessary to produce it' (1867:676–677). We are talking about a different quantity, one that is ever changing but, as argued in the previous chapter, not for this reason immeasurable, and that requires the constant attention of firms that want to remain competitive.[8] Thus, if the law of value works as a powerful coordinating mechanism in society, this is in no way the result of a natural, inevitable and desirable historic process. Indeed, the relation between the parts and the whole that this coordinating mechanism enables acquires here a specific quality of in/dependence in the light of which the ever-changing quantity that is socially necessary labour time can be assessed:

> The quantitative articulation [*Gliederung*] of society's productive organism by which its scattered elements are integrated into the system of the division of labour, is as haphazard and spontaneous as its qualitative articulation. The owners of commodities therefore find out that the same division of labour which turns them into independent private producers also makes the social process of production and the relations of individual producers to each other within that process independent of the producers themselves; they also find out that the independence of the individuals from each other has as its counterpart and supplement a system of all-round material dependence.
>
> (Marx, 1867:202–203)

This system of 'all-round material dependence' finds in value the means through which commodities are made commensurable in the market. This is the continuing significance of the law of value: through various and ever-changing measuring techniques and mechanisms, capital interacts with labour for the purpose of generating surplus value. However, these mechanisms are not part of a universal dynamic but the forms that commensuration takes in capitalist societies. As such they are historically specific and not inevitable. This was one of the major problems with all categories of classical political economy which, Marx emphasised, are 'forms of thought which are socially valid [only] for the relations of production belonging to this historically determined mode of social production, i.e. commodity production' (1867:169). In particular, Marx lamented, political economy focused on value without ever asking the question of why labour took the form it did: 'If [referring to Smith's and Ricardo's analysis of value] ... we make the mistake of treating it as the eternal natural form of social production, we necessarily overlook the specificity of the value-form' (1867:174). And Marx was aware of the fact that other forms had and could indeed exist. As he pointed out, 'the whole mystery of commodities vanishes ... as soon as we come to other forms of production'.[9]

One could certainly argue that other forms of production have always existed and continue to do so. Spillman (2012), for instance, has shown how profit maximisation does not always drive investment decisions and Gibson-Graham (1996) has demonstrated how actually existing economic practices that do not conform with capitalist categories are simply not read by economists (whether of Marxist or other inclination) so that actually or potentially existing alternatives get obliterated. This is a serious concern, and one to which I return in Chapter 4. However, I have suggested that both Smith and Marx can be seen to conceive of value in a much more fluid way than they are often given credit for when they are described as unequivocally supporting a substance-like, intrinsic approach to value. At the same time, recognising such fluidity does not mean ceasing to acknowledge the power of measuring mechanisms, particularly considering the influence that competition, or global competitiveness in today's parlance, continues to exert.[10] The difficult task is thinking about alternatives, actually existing or not, together with the ways in which the law of value continues to be re-enacted and this entails seeing the relationship between the two as not necessarily one of exclusion but of complex, if fraught, co-constitution. For Marx, the continuous re-enactment of the law of value had to do with the reproduction of social relations alongside the production of commodities, and in particular with the *separation* between labour-power and the conditions of labour. Thus 'seen as a total, connected process, i.e. a process of reproduction, [the capitalist process of production] produces not only commodities, not only surplus value, but it also produces and reproduces the capitalist relation itself; on the one hand the capitalist, on the other the wage labourer' (1867:723–724).

Although the focus on the reproduction of social relations is crucial for understanding how the law of value continues to get re-enacted, whilst coexisting with alternative forms of production, I want to pause on the significance of Marx's positioning of the separation between wage labourers and capitalists as constitutive of this complex dynamic. To be clear, the question for me is not whether Marx's reliance on wage labour and commodity production, the latter mainly associated with 'material' production, make his insights into value extraction and measurement problematic given their presumed decline in post-Fordism.[11] Indeed, Marx's analysis extended beyond the world of material commodities.[12] The relation between value and immaterial labour and production is already present in his work, as is the acknowledgement of the coproduction between different spheres of the economy (production, consumption, exchange and circulation), an idea he develops further in *Grundrisse* (1857–1858). The boundaries of these spheres cannot be easily demarcated, not even when attempting to retrieve the proper place of the production of value: it is impossible, he says, that:

> outside the sphere of circulation, a producer of commodities can, without coming into contact with other commodity-owners, valorize value, and consequently transform money or commodities into capital. Capital cannot therefore arise from circulation, and it is equally impossible for it to arise apart from circulation. It must have its origin both in circulation and not in circulation
>
> (Marx, 1857–1858:268)

Value is therefore produced at the intersection between these spheres: this much Marx acknowledges, his point being that the law of value functions as a powerful logic of commensuration that enables endless accumulation.

What I think is important to emphasise is that Marx's privileging of a particular relationship, that between the capitalist and the wage labourer, gives a partial account of the complex ways in which the law of value gets constantly re-enacted. It has, for instance, ended up obscuring the important ways in which the production of value is premised on the enormous pool of unwaged labour, starting with reproductive labour. It is not only that the exploitation of unwaged labour provides the very conditions of existence for the exploitation of wage labour (Mies, 1986) but that this is a system that relies on the constant creation of separations and divisions for the extraction of surplus value. This is, as alluded to in the previous chapter, one of the most important theoretical insights that has emerged from the work of 'Wages for/against Housework' scholars, for whom reproductive labour is a constitutive element of (capitalist) value and one that is gendered, sexed and racialised, as well as classed from the very beginning. Federici's study of the historic position of (mainly European) women in the so-called transition to capitalism has been invaluable in tracing one important way in which these separations are essential to the reproduction of capitalist relations and therefore to the re-enactment of the law of value.[13]

Caliban, the witch and the 'misfortune' of reproduction

Marx had been very careful to show how Smith's 'mythical' moment of accumulation was based on the historic expropriation of land from the European peasantry as well as on the exploitation of the colonies. However, there is hardly any mention in his oeuvre 'of the profound transformations that capitalism introduced in the reproduction of labour power and the social position of women ... [starting with] the "Great Witch-Hunt" of the 16th and 17th centuries, although this state-sponsored terror campaign was central to the defeat of the European peasantry' (Federici, 2004:63). Federici's study of the historic position of women in Europe from the fourth century to the nineteenth century sheds a different light on the so-called transition to capitalism as it shows the crucial role that separations and divisions, starting with that between production and reproduction, play in the generation of (capitalist) value. It also points to the fact that these separations continue to be sustained through extra-economic force and the power of narratives that make such divisions invisible, including those that too easily celebrate their overcoming (eg Hardt and Negri, 2009).

The first contribution of *Caliban and the Witch* is therefore historical. Primitive accumulation required not only the expropriation of European workers and the enslavement of Native Americans and Africans but also 'the transformation of the body into a work-machine'; bodies had to be made 'productive' and crucial to this enterprise, which was fully achieved in the nineteenth century, was the control over women's reproductive powers (Federici, 2004:).[14] There is indeed for Federici a specific historic context within 'which the history of women and reproduction in the transition from feudalism to capitalism must be placed' (2004:66): not the end of the famine in the eighteenth century, as Foucault had argued, but 'the population crisis of the 16th and 17th centuries ... turned reproduction and population growth into state matters as well as primary objects of intellectual discourse' (2004:86). Several factors contributed to this crisis: from the 'refusal to work' struggles, such as those of the Heretics across Europe, to the Black Death, which decimated more than one third of the European population between 1347 and 1352, with the consequent demand for labour and high wages across Europe, and people's regained access to the means of subsistence. These events threatened the reproduction of the feudal system as well as the possibility of a capitalist society to 'evolve' from it (2004:32, 40, 62).[15]

The emergence of classical political economy with its emphasis on population, productivity and growth can be seen from this perspective, one in which concerns over the reproduction of the labour force are inextricably linked with women's control over their reproductive powers.[16] Indeed, Federici argues, land privatisations, which inaugurate the sale of labour power in the market, and the Price Revolution, with which prices were inflated to reduce self-sufficiency, were not on their own sufficient to produce a self-sustaining process of proletarianisation: the need for new sources of labour that would drive accumulation required new forms of 'regimentation and division of the workforce' (2004:68). For life to be made 'productive' of (capitalist) value a special attention to women and their reproductive powers was necessary (2004:68). This attention finds its most evident manifestation in the Witch-Hunt, which exterminated hundreds of thousands of women throughout Europe (2004:180–186). However, far from being an abomination, the remnants of an obscurantist past the Enlightenment did away with, it was part of a concerted strategy consisting of women's social degradation, legal infantilisation and economic devaluation (2004:95–100) for which the state took control, and which went in tandem with the reformulation of racial and sexual hierarchies in the colonies (2004:229–236).

The main outcome of this concerted strategy was the loss of control women had over their bodies as well as the loss of their status as workers. This is not to say that unequal power relations did not exist in feudal societies, but to be specific about the new forms of power this strategy brought about, the disappearance of the different contraception practices (and associated knowledges) women had been responsible for during the Middle Ages and the introduction of reproductive crimes are only two ways in which intervention took over 'life'. The relegation of their labour to the 'unproductive' sphere was the other: a gendered division of labour certainly existed in pre-capitalist Europe but the separation of production from reproduction rendered reproductive activities 'the carriers of different social relations' (Federici, 2004:74).[17] The nuclear family and the housewife emerge as 'natural' states of affairs only in the nineteenth century, by which time women had effectively become a natural resource, a 'commons', from which value could be extracted (2004:97).[18] Reproductive labour was parcelled out, regulated and put directly at the service of accumulation while its crucial role in the extraction of value was rendered invisible. What, therefore, seems like an exclusion of women and their reproductive labour from the public sphere, was at the same time a very productive inclusion.

To be sure, as Marx pointed out, 'to be a productive worker is not … a piece of luck, but a misfortune' (1867:644); however, neglecting the crucial importance of reproductive activities misses the very conditions on which the production of value, such as 'misfortune', is made possible. If labour power is not like any other commodity (Picchio, 1992) the powers necessary for its reproduction are not like any other labouring activity, and that is why reproductive powers required specific forms of intervention to be made productive of (capitalist) value. That this crucial aspect is absent in Marx's analysis is evidenced by the fact that accumulation for him proceeds regardless of population numbers: as the 'productivity' of labour increases, the labour needed diminishes compared to the capital invested in machinery and other assets and this process results in what Marx calls 'surplus population'. The description of this dynamic, however, would hold:

> [i]f procreation were a purely biological process, or an activity respond-
> ing automatically to economic change, and if capital and the state did
> not need to worry about 'women going on strike against childmaking'.
> This is, in fact, what Marx assumed ... In reality, so far are procreation
> and population changes from being automatic or 'natural' that, in all
> states of capitalist development, the state has had to resort to regula-
> tion and coercion to expand or reduce the work-force ... Marx never
> acknowledged that procreation could become a terrain of exploitation
> and by the same token a terrain of resistance. He never imagined that
> women could refuse to reproduce.
>
> (Federici, 2004:91)

In other words, what Marx refers to as the separation between labour power and the conditions of labour is a deeply gendered, sexed and, as argued below, racialised process. This, I think, is the second important contribution Federici's work makes, one which is both analytical and political: whether 'women' remain a legitimate category of analysis today is an open question which requires careful attention to be paid to the way in which reproductive labour is currently organised.[19] However, the crucial impor-tance of *Caliban and the Witch* rests on having shown how the myth of primitive accumulation Marx was trying to denaturalise 'was not simply an accumulation and concentration of exploitable workers and capital. It was also an *accumulation of differences and divisions*' (Federici, 2004:63, original emphasis) which operate as both exclusions (from sight) and inclusions (in value making processes). This is still the case today with the continuous, if ever-changing, making of these separations, a process which, as Federici has also poignantly illustrated, relies on powerful narratives as well as the use of (extra-economic) force.

We can, for instance, see how the narrative of the 'productive' worker – which permeates Keynesian as well as neoliberal approaches to work but also, albeit in a different register, accounts about the primacy of the immaterial or cognitive worker – is linked to the specific construction of the individual which has accompanied the transition to capitalism. Smith's mythical narrative of an individual who overcomes his idle nature by realising the virtues of accumulation is built on a particular idea of the person, the *Impartial Spectator*, he who, through Reason, can stand outside of himself reflecting on and judging his different and often conflicting interests and passions. This idea is part of a long philosophical discussion that, Federici argues, saw a battle unfolding in the seventeenth century for the 'reformation' of the person. This reformation resulted in the person's 'dissociation' from *his* own body, a body 'attacked as the sources of all evils and yet ... studied with the same passion that, in the same years, animated the investigation of celestial motion' (2004:137). And although, Federici acknowledges, it would be simplistic to attribute economic motives or interests to these investigations, we can see the contribution the various approaches to human nature made to the science of work that was emerging around the same time: '[t]o pose the body as a mechanical matter, void of ... the "occult virtues" attributed to it by both Natural Magic and the popular superstition of the time – was to make intelligible the possibility of subordinating it to a work process that increasingly relied on uniform and predictable forms of behaviour' (2004:139).[20]

The question was how to achieve this and it is in this context that Federici places the philosophical investigations of Descartes and Hobbes who, despite their differences, contributed to the articulation of those distinctions and separations that were to become so crucial to the production of value. For Descartes the body cannot define the person because what makes the latter human are its pure immaterial faculties, chiefly the presence of thought (Federici, 2004:148). Like the role of Smith's *Impartial Spectator*, that of Reason, the counterpart of the mechanisation of the body, is that of 'judge, inquisitor, manager, administrator'. Here we find the origins of 'subjectivity as self-management [and] self-ownership', and this is why Descartes' theoretical impact was to be more long lasting than Hobbes' for whom the absence of a body-free Reason, which can manage passions and appetites, requires externalising the function of command to the state (Federici, 2004:150).[21] The conflict between these two approaches is in the end resolved in their respective assimilation as one cannot exist without the other: Descartes' model makes the individual more 'productive' through self-management although the state is to intervene when self-management goes too far.[22]

The crucial point is that 'productivity' is achieved through the split of the Self/Reason from its body: what is interesting, Federici argues, is that if the 'soul' is displaced from the cosmos and corporeality, where it was for Natural Magic, it is, however, not done away with. Rather, it returns at the centre of philosophy 'endowed with infinite power under the guise of individual reason and will' (2004:148). But there is something important that happens with this move and that is the fact that the self loses 'its solidarity with its corporeal reality and with nature' while becoming obsessed with dominating both (2004:148). Two points are worth noting with regard to this move. The first concerns the various forms of abstractions that emerge from the development of individual identity understood as 'otherness' from the body:

> The emergence of this *alter ego*, and the determination of a historic conflict between mind and body, represents the birth of the individual in capitalist society. It would become a typical characteristic of the individual molded by the capitalist work-discipline to confront one's body as an alien reality to be assessed, developed and kept at bay, in order to obtain from it the desired results.
>
> (Federici, 2004:152)

This double movement between an *alter ego* which is inalienable and a corporeal or external reality that becomes alienable is what Bhandar also argues, expanding on Balibar's reading of Locke, is at the basis of modern subjectivity and property formation. Propriety and property are brought together in Locke's theorisation of individual subjectivity so that 'the proper subject is not only he who actually owns property, or is able to "freely" alienate his labour, but is, fundamentally, he who has the capacity to engage in the conscious reflection that marks out or defines the internal stage, "an indefinitely open field in which [self-consciousness] is both actor and spectator"' (Bhandar, 2015:12). This moment, she argues, is denied to the black slave, the native and the non-European through what Ferreira da Silva refers to as the 'analytic of raciality', the dynamic through which racial subjects are continuously placed within 'an exterior realm of Nature by scientific and philosophical discourses that give primacy to the subject of interiority' (2015:12).

From the eighteenth century onward, the logic of abstraction inherent in this interiority/exteriority play is what comes to constitute the realm of the racial as 'the effect of the interior tools of pure reason' (Ferreira da Silva, 2007:60–61) as well as that of property. We cannot, for instance, understand how individual subjects became objects of ownership through slavery, Bhandar writes, without appreciating 'the ways in which transformations in conceptualisations of ownership (from Locke's use to Bentham's expectations of use) shaped emergent racial abstractions in the figures of the savage and slave, the very figures that were required to effectively dehumanise slaves as chattel property (and financial instruments) and to render indigenous communities immaterial to land appropriation' (Bhandar, 2014:218). Not that this logic has resulted in the disappearance of possession altogether: if the latter is no longer used as a legal justification, it continues to inhabit the life of property as 'the possession of particular qualities and attributes that give rise to a sense of entitlement and security ... Notions of privilege and entitlement shape the contours of one's consciousness, based on the possession of particular qualities and characteristics that constituted the pre-requisites of one's ability to own property' (2014:218). We can see this logic operating through the laws that construct 'Indian status' in Canada (Bhandar, 2015:3–8), for instance, as well as in 'the wasteland rationale [still] used to appropriate the lands of others ... reflecting the persistence of the notion of a proper subject of ownership who is quite thoroughly saturated with raciality' (Bhandar, 2012:121). Like Federici's category of the 'woman', the analytic of raciality is not as an adjunct to an analysis of modern subject formation and capital accumulation but is constitutive of both, as capital cannot accumulate and the unitary, self-governing subject cannot emerge without 'differentially including' bodies and natures, those of the slaves, the natives and the non-Europeans. These separations or 'differential inclusions' (Mezzadra and Neilson, 2013a:159), which different forms of abstraction make possible, are therefore the very premise on which the re-enactment of the law of value takes place.

And this takes me to the second point about the move to Reason and self-government, that is the role that extra-economic force continues to play in aiding these separations – a force which continues to manifest itself in the era of financial capitalism with the paradigmatic figure of the cognitive worker as much as it did when the *free* seller of labour power became the paradigmatic figure of industrial capitalism. As Rosenberg (2014:8) has argued, 'financial forms of profit-rendering are part of a larger system of ... accumulation – one that ... is not only the means by which capitalism begins, but also the means by which it continually reconstitutes itself'.[23] The point she makes is that, alongside the important attempts currently made to understand 'the "leap" of capital into finance', we need to understand the relation the latter holds with the intensification of forms of imperial violence. And that is why she insists on the concept of *primitive* accumulation, 'not only to describe the ongoing violent character of capital's self-perpetuation, but the kinds of transitions internal to the capitalist mode of production (in this case from an industrial capitalist system to one in which finance is predominant), and the narrative forms that accompany those transitions as well' (2014:10). This is true of the land grabbing going on around the world, as well as of the way in which in Europe we are witnessing a massive squeeze on living conditions at the same time as huge financial profits are being made. Tracing the links between financialisation and settler colonialism, Rosenberg argues, is one way to make visible the simultaneous presence of accumulation and immiseration on a global scale (2014:13). Another one, as argued in Chapter 1, would be to trace the connections between the price signals sent by financial derivatives – through the commensuration of bits of capital across time and space that they enable – and the decisions made by companies with regard to their production processes and labour forces on the basis of these signals as well as on the political struggles ensuing from such decisions. But making these connections visible also means seeing how certain narratives end up invisibilising the separations on which the extraction of value takes place, including those which posit the immaterial, cognitive worker as paradigmatic of the new, post-Fordist, mode of production where measures have disappeared and valuation happens in a domain of sheer contingency.

This is why I retain the term 'capitalist' to describe past and current processes that shape the economy–society nexus despite important warnings about the fact that the more we zoom into any practice, logic, dynamic or 'law' for that matter, the more we realise there is no essence that pertains to them (see eg Gibson-Graham, 1996). Indeed, the denaturalisation and politicisation of the concepts described by classical political economy are exactly what is at stake in Marx's critical reading strategy: while no essence can be ascribed to concepts, practices and processes, such strategy shows how abstractions become a real force in the world. I also see, and in this respect Federici's work has been crucial, the constantly shifting demarcation of the boundaries between production and reproduction as one important way through which this force is renewed, and this is because reproductive labour is the ground constantly relied upon for the extraction of surplus value. This labour, which is deeply gendered, sexed and racialised, gets different kinds of 'remuneration', giving rise to different distributions of the value it produces, depending on whether it is marketised, socialised by the state (with the important role played by immigration policies) or, as is increasingly the case, sustained through debt.

This point about the constantly shifting demarcation of the boundaries between production and social reproduction adds another dimension to the analysis of financial derivatives carried out in the previous chapter. I think we miss something important if we limit our analysis of financial innovations, and more generally of the processes that have led to the financialisation of the economy, to 'the increasing role of financial motives, financial markets, financial actors and financial institutions' (Epstein, 2005:3). What is also needed is an appreciation of the restructuring of the production–reproduction nexus that sees credit, rather than commodities, as the starting point for the reproduction of labour power and general economic calculus and enterprise as the organising principles of household 'management' (Williams, 2007, 2013; Bryan, Martin and Rafferty, 2009; Allon, 2011, 2015). Indeed, it may well be that, as Bryan, Rafferty and Jefferis (2015:318–321) have argued, what is at stake in the present reconfiguration of this nexus, at least as far as financialised economies are concerned, is the 'real subsumption' of labour to finance, a process which sees labour becoming productive *within* finance as 'households are being subject to the same risk/return calculations that apply to capital's evaluation of itself' (2015:321). This is a process which the authors claim had started before the crisis but has become evident through the post-crisis securitisation of household assets which has involved 'the movement of more and more household payments into fixed-period contractual relations, to ensure locked-in future payments on which securities can be built, and penalties for non- or even prepayment that disturbs the valuation of securities' (2015:320). The central role the household plays in what the authors see as a novel process of value production in finance does not detract from, but only confirms, the point that reproductive labour, despite not being coterminous with the household, remains a crucial site for the extraction of surplus value.

Finally, and relatedly, I continue to talk about capitalist processes and practices because, as the analysis of financial derivatives in Chapter 1 has shown, the 'law' of value continues to exert an enormous influence, despite no essence pertaining to it, thanks to the equivalence and competition the logic of abstraction makes possible. What a critical reading strategy of these historical processes enables us to see is that neither equivalence, nor the abstraction on which it is based, sprang up naturally. The history of their instantiation was written in 'letters of blood and fire', and in the writing off of the woman, the Black, the native and the non-European from the Self that was to dominate. Acknowledging both seems to me necessary to enable different practices, actually existing or not, to emerge and other processes of valorisation to be instantiated.[24] As Bedford and Rai (2010:4) have put it, this task can be accomplished only if we address 'both the structural and the agential elements of social relations in ways that include an interlinked analysis of the capitalist processes of production, social reproduction, and exchange as well as resistance to and within the system'.

Conclusion

In a different context, that of the critique of Christian and liberal humanist values, the violence that equivalence disguises was central to the work of another nineteenth-century thinker. If for Marx and Federici the *transition* to capitalism entailed something other than the shift from coercion to self-rule, for Nietzsche (1877) the values of equality, justice and compassion are not eternal universals, and the institutions of justice, religion and the state which support them are not based on consensual agreement. Rather, they are the product of economically sanctioned violence: '[w]here has this ancient, deeply rooted, and by now perhaps ineradicable idea, this idea of the equivalence' (asks Nietzsche's *On the Genealogy of Morals*) 'drawn its strength from? ... from the contractual relationship between *creditor* and *debtor*, which is old as the concept of "legal subjects" itself and which points back in turn to the fundamental forms of buying, selling, exchange, wheeling and dealing' (Nietzsche, 1887:45) (original emphasis).

The point, as Douglas Smith has put it, is not the historic accuracy of the claim – indeed one doubts the existence of such a contract in the first place – but its use as a device to challenge the Enlightenment fiction of the free and equal citizen. Rather than deriving from the consensual agreement between parties, institutions are imposed from above and without, and the values they promote are the result of an intense and long struggle between competing systems of values – the aristocratic morality and the slave morality – with the concept of 'equivalence', which has come to characterise social relations, disguising exactly such struggle (Smith, 1966, in Nietzsche, 1887:xv, 46). Despite seeing the former as active and characterised by an ethics of 'ruthless self affirmation', and the latter as a reactive response motivated by *ressentiment*, Nietzsche's account of morals is not one of origins: it does not provide any foundation for a true or untainted, and therefore freer, system of values. If at various points his focus is on cruelty, rather than benevolence or compassion as in Adam Smith's case, what is interesting is that his methodology undoes any such claim to 'truth'. What is at stake in *Genealogy* is not 'truth' but interpretation, that is, the power of making and remaking the world, a power which is renounced exactly through our appeals to truth.[25]

There are two interconnected points about the power of interpretation worth noticing here, and which concern the relationship interpretation holds with both objectivity and intervention. Nietzsche is clear that interpretation is not a task to be accomplished from a neutral perspective: any science needs a 'belief' in order to derive from it 'a direction, a meaning, a limit, a method' (1887:127), which does not mean to say doing away with objectivity if objectivity is:

> understood not as 'disinterested contemplation' (which is a non-concept and a nonsense) but as the capacity to have all the arguments for and against *at one's disposal* and to suspend and implement them at will: so that one can exploit that very diversity of perspectives and affective interpretations in the interest of knowledge. From now on ... let us beware of the dangerous old conceptual fable which posited a pure, will-less, painless, timeless knowing subject, let us beware of the tentacles of such contradictory concepts as 'pure reason'... [and] 'knowledge in itself' ... Perspectival seeing is the *only* kind of seeing there is, perspectival 'knowing' the *only* kind of 'knowing'; and the

more feelings about a matter which we allow to come to expression, the *more* eyes, different eyes through which we are able to view this same matter, the more complete our 'conception' of it, our 'objectivity', will be.

(Nietzsche, 1887:98, original emphasis)

This is an argument that resonates with many constructivist approaches to science and certainly pertains to political economy: that the economy is not a neutral terrain to be studied by a 'timeless knowing subject', that both the economy and the subject are constantly made and remade through an incessant process of interaction, and that objectivity has less to do with 'knowledge in itself' than with its perspectival construction would certainly not escape the attention of the performativity of economics scholars with whom I engage in the next chapter. And perspectival seeing, this being the second point about interpretation, is also connected to intervention: if, as Douglas Smith (1966:xiii) points out, *Genealogy* is understood as 'the historical study of the multiple intersecting forces which produce [thereby crystallising] the meaning of a given phenomenon or practice' this intersection is also 'an *ongoing* struggle whose outcome is yet to be determined, and so allows for the possibility of intervention'. Indeed, Nietzsche writes, 'only that which is without history can be defined' (1887:60). Everything else is intervention: 'everything which happens in the ... world is part of a process of ... reinterpretation, a manipulation, in the course of which the previous 'meaning' and 'aim' must necessarily be obscured or completely effaced' (1887:57–58). This does not mean that meanings and aims do not stabilise: my reading of Smith and Marx's work was motivated exactly by what I see as their potential to point to how processes take on a certain form, as well as to the possibility of affecting them.

The importance of perspectives, values and beliefs in this process of reordering and rearranging is what Nietzsche's *Genealogy* brings to the fore: if perspectival seeing is the *only* kind of seeing there is, and perspectival 'knowing' is the *only* kind of 'knowing', we need to be much more explicit about the values or beliefs with which we are making our intervention, the traditions such values embody, and the exclusions they carry, aware of the fact that the reality produced by such intervention will be very different from that envisaged in the first place. Again Nietzsche (1887:58) was prescient about this:

The 'development' of a thing ... does not in the least resemble a *progressus* towards a goal, and even less the logical and shortest *progressus*, the most economical in terms of expenditure of force and cost. Rather, this development assumes the form of the succession of the more or less far reaching, more or less independent processes of overpowering which affect it – including also in each case the resistance marshalled against these processes, the changes of form attempted with a view to defense and reaction, and the results of these successful counteractions. *The form is fluid but the meaning even more so*. (emphasis added)

It is in this sense that I envisage the provocations that follow in the next chapters as conscious interventions–conscious not as in coming from a 'timeless knowing subject' but as explicit about the *perspectival seeing* from which they are made, aware of the violence and exclusions this *seeing* entails and also of those which it opposes. But there is one more aspect of Nietzsche's *Genealogy* that I consider important in thinking about the sort of provocations that might be able to shift current value making processes in the context of the real economy versus financial sphere debate examined in the previous chapter. The irretrievability of 'origin' and 'truth' about values and the acknowledgement of the presence of both *ressentiment* and *perspectival knowledge* say something important about our fixation with intrinsic, fundamental values. From this angle, calls for the need to anchor valuations to fundamental values can be interpreted as the reactive movement to the actively shaping forces of finance, which we attempt to exorcise by discarding them as unreal. However, *ressentiment* is not the only lens through which to approach such evaluations: as an active intervention rather than reactive movement, we can accept that what is at stake when we invoke real or fundamental values is the struggle over competing perspectives and arrangements. Nietzsche (1887:38) concludes his first essay by posing exactly this question, the question:

> of the *value* of previous evaluations ... The question: what is the value of this or that table of commandments and 'morality'? should be examined from the most varied perspectives; in particular, the question of its value *to what end*? cannot be examined too closely ... From now on, *all* disciplines have to prepare the future task of the philosopher: this task being understood as the solution of the *problem of value*, the determination of the *hierarchy of values*. (original emphasis)

We have not yet engaged with such a task because, in Nietzsche's view, our 'democratic prejudice against everything which dominates and wishes to dominate ... has already succeeded ... by conjuring away one of its basic concepts, that of essential *activity*'. What has come to dominate instead is the passive concept of 'adaptation' to 'external circumstances' (1887:59). As a mode of existence, this approach has much to say about the passivity or *ressentiment* with which we look at markets as the indisputable makers of value, accepting this situation as a *fait accompli* and sometimes lamenting our incapacity to act. But if we are not to renounce that 'essential activity'

Nietzsche calls 'form giving capacity', how are we to think of value(s) and intervention today?

Graeber (2005:18–23) has invited us to think of value as the importance people attribute to their action. What, he asks, if we start from the assumption that what has been evaluated is actually not a thing but an action? Thinking about action and process has been difficult, he writes, because Western philosophy has opted for Parmenides', rather than Heractlitus' approach to reality: recognising the state of constant flux would have created problems of boundary settings and measurement. But in fact reality has always been messy and crystallisations have nonetheless taken place exactly through measurement. Seeing value as the importance we attribute to our action has to do with meaning making, with interpretation, to stay a little longer with Nietzsche. For all classical tradition meaning making has been a matter of comparison, of relating parts to a whole. We have seen this in Smith but also in Marx's analysis. Thus:

> parts take on meaning in relation to each other, and ... process always involves reference to some sort of whole: whether it be a matter of words in a language, episodes in a story, or 'goods and services' on the market. So too for value. The realisation of value is always, necessarily, a process of comparison; for this reason it always, necessarily, implies an at least imagined audience
>
> (Graeber, 2005:57)

This is the case despite the fact that 'any closed system is just a construct, and not necessarily a very useful one; nothing in real life is really so cut and dried. Social processes are complex and overlapping in an endless variety of ways' (ibid). Indeed, arranging and formatting takes place all the time. Yet, Graeber argues, this is possible because of the possibility of relating parts to an imagined whole. Now, we know how problematic totalities and unities are, how violent 'form giving capacity' can be. The question is: would our approach to intervention be any different if the whole we refer the parts to were reconceptualised as the open-ended tracing and remaking of the dis/continuities that make up our global economy?[26] What if we were explicit about our perspectival seeing, and about the fact that our tracing can only ever be a partial and incomplete process? And that our action will always involve exclusions while producing outcomes that are different from those we envisage? It is with this understanding that I approach the issue of arrangements as provocations in the next two chapters, while I return to the specific way in which I think of tracing and intervention in conclusions.

Notes

1 Indeed, scholars have tried to calculate socially necessary labour time to ascertain the value of commodities. It might even be arrived at, as Mandel, for instance, argues, although this would require firms to 'open up their books' (see 'Introduction' to Marx, *Capital*, Volume I, 1867:45). See also Mohun (2004). Those who have challenged Marx's law of value have instead focused on the impossibility of such a task, emphasising that although costs of production, labour included, play a role in deciding whether a product is going to be produced in the first instance, this in no way gives an indication of the value of the product, which requires that we look at valuation as a complex process.

2 Productivity was indeed crucial to the battle for the 'reformation of the person', which Federici traces back to the philosophical interventions of Descartes and Hobbes, as well as to a concerted strategy by church and state which resulted in the person's dissociation of *his* body, and the latter becoming the object of the emergent 'science of work' (Federici, 2004:139).

3 For Smith (1776:75–76) this system would eventually reach a stationary state where the accumulation of capital would be brought to an end. Presumably this would happen provided all labour were employed by capital savings, thus generating the amount of annual produce necessary to satisfy the needs of the entire population.

4 As Chapter 3 shows, this revalorisation is also based on Smith's multi-dimensional approach to human interaction which, scholars such as Arrighi, Offer and Hirschman claim, has been reduced by subsequent economic analysis to the pursuit of self-interest. The field of Smith's enquiry, they argue, was much broader and complex and cannot be reduced to this simplistic assumption about human nature. Although this is an important argument, Federici's work points to the need to pay careful attention to the transformation this field of social inquiry underwent in the seventeenth and eighteenth centuries, and which had at its core the 'reformation of the person'. This reconceptualisation of the person entailed, among other things, the dissociation of the mind/will/reason from the body, which was to be made increasingly productive of (capitalist) value. This movement, Federici argues, provides the conceptual resources for the enactment of old and new separations on the basis of which value is extracted: it is by focusing on these separations that we can see how certain 'bodies' and activities are devalued, even as they are celebrated, while value is extracted from them. Smith's *Impartial Spectator* has been an important conceptual intervention in this respect and, as Chapter 3 argues, any attempt to revalorise his contribution needs to take into account its significance and effects.

5 At various points Smith refers to the careful studies that had been made on the maintenance of a labourer's family (1776:81–82). Noticing that the 'real recompense of labour, the real quantity of the necessaries and conveniences of life' (1776:82) had increased in the century in which he was writing, he argued that 'what improves the circumstances of the greater part, can never be regarded as an inconveniency to the whole. No society can surely be flourishing and happy', he adds, 'of which the far greater part of the members are poor and miserable' (1776:83).

6 The difference with Smith is that 'capital ... is not only the command over labour, as [he] thought. It is essentially the command over unpaid labour ... The secret of self-valorisation of capital resolves itself into the fact that it has at its disposal a definite quantity of the unpaid labour of other people' (Marx, 1867:672).

7 In Marx's scheme, surplus value is achieved first by lengthening the working day (absolute surplus value) and later by making labour more productive within a given time (relative surplus value). Although these strategies exist in varying degrees at the same time, there is a point where the extension and intensification of labour become mutually exclusive so that lengthening the working day is possible only with a lower degree of intensity and vice versa. This point, Marx claims, is given by the corporeality of the workers. This is the limit that Mezzadra and Neilson (2013a:89) see as having become unbalanced since 'at stake [today] is less a lengthening of the working day [or the intensification of labour which for Marx followed its shortening] than the tendency for work to occupy more life'. While I do not dispute the tendency for work to occupy life, and think their careful study of the multiplication of labour through the proliferation of borders is one of the most compelling in post-Fordist analyses, I wonder to what extent this is qualitatively a new phenomenon: we can say that more life is invested with work today only if the boundaries between labour and leisure time are considered to have been clearly delineated before. However, even in Fordist economies (they do indeed see the multi-plication of labour as having always been a post-colonial 'reality') this was never completely the case, a point which Federici's *Caliban and the Witch* crucially makes.

8 This 'quantity' is also, importantly, the result of political struggles (see De Angelis, 2005:76–79).

9 From medieval Europe 'where personal dependence characterizes the social relations of material production [and the products of labour take the shape of] services in kind and payments in kind' to patriarchal rural industry of a peasant family where the labour of the individual members is 'regulated by the difference of sex and age as well as by seasonal variations in the natural conditions of labour'; the form

that labour takes has important political consequences for each society (Marx, 1867:169–171).

10 Bryan and Rafferty's argument about derivatives' role as that of commensurating bits of capital across space and time is one example (2006).

11 The argument is that services, considered as immaterial, have come to represent the largest share of the Gross Domestic Product of many countries (Rifkin, 2000:115). More significant, Vercellone argues, is the qualitative, rather than quantitative, shift to an economic system that is based on the production of wealth through knowledge itself, that is, through the preponderant use of labour's cognitive qualities (Vercellone, 2006:221). Now whether, and where, knowledge-related industries and activities have become the distinctive feature of a new economic system is disputable. One could argue that the complexity in distinguishing between material and immaterial labour, as well as accounting for material and immaterial production, is becoming more evident in recent debates. This was demonstrated by the debate economists had during the negotiations leading to the adoption of the General Agreement on Trade in Services (GATS) of the WTO over the definition of, and distinction between, goods and services (see Trebilcock and Howse, 2005: Ch 12).

12 As Marx acknowledged: 'a Schoolmaster is a productive worker when, in addition to belabouring the heads of his pupils, he works himself to the ground to enrich the owner of the school. That the latter has laid down his capital in a teaching factory, instead of a sausage factory, makes no difference to the relation ... *to be a productive worker is therefore not a piece of luck, but a misfortune*' (Marx, 1867:644) (emphasis added).

13 Federici and Fortunati's initial work, *Il Grande Calibano* (1984), focused on the history of women during the period that can only euphemistically be described as 'transition to capitalism', as their perspective is one that focuses on the centuries-long social struggles of which women were an integral part, thereby problematising any linear and progressive reading of such a shift. This is the premise with which Federici's *Caliban and the Witch* starts: '[c]apitalism was the response of the feudal lords, the patrician merchants, the bishops and popes, to a centuries-long social conflict, that in the end shook their power ... This much must be stressed, for the belief that capitalism "evolved" from feudalism and represents a higher form of social life has not yet been dispelled' (2004:21–22).

14 Indeed, what Foucault has referred to in terms of the 'disciplining of the body' is for Federici a process where the 'attempt by state and church to transform the individual's powers into labour powers' figures prominently (2004:133).

15 '[W]e deduce its dimension from some basic estimates indicating that between 1350 and 1500 a major shift occurred in the power-relation between workers and masters. The real wage increased by 100%, prices declined by 33%, rents also declined, the length of the working day decreased, and a tendency appeared towards self-sufficiency. Evidence of a chronic disaccumulation trend in this period is also found in the pessimism of the contemporary merchants and landowners, and the measures which the European states adopted to protect markets, suppress competition and force people to work at the conditions imposed. As the entries in the registers of the feudal manors recorded "the work [was] not worth the breakfast … " It was in response to this crisis that the European ruling class launched the global offensive that in the course of at least three centuries was to change the history of the planet' (Federici, 2004:62).

16 And the same point can be made of the Mercantilist doctrine that that preceded Classical Political Economy.

17 As Federici points out, 'In the feudal village no social separation existed between the production of goods and the reproduction of the workforce; all work contributed to the family sustenance. Women worked in the fields, in addition to raising children, cooking, washing, spinning and keeping an herb garden; their activities were not devalued and did not involve different social relations from those of men, as they would later, in a money-economy, when household would cease to be viewed as real work' (2004:25).

18 In contrast, Federici argues, medieval towns had seen women working as 'smiths, butchers, bakers, candlestick makers, hat makers, ale brewers, wool-carders, and retailers … In England seventy-two out of eighty-five guilds included women among their members. Some guilds, including silk-making, were dominated by them; in others, female employment was as high as that of men. By the 14th century, women were also becoming schoolteachers as well as doctors and surgeons' (2004:31).

19 Federici asks: '[I]f "femininity" has been constituted in a capitalist society as a work-function masking the production of the work force under the cover of a biological destiny, then … the question that has to be asked is whether the sexual division of labour that has produced that particular concept has been transcended. If the answer is a negative one (as it must be when we consider the present organisation of reproductive labour), then "women" is a legitimate category of analysis, and the activities associated with "reproduction" remain a crucial ground of struggle' (2004:14).

20 As Federici's opening quote indicates, the body required intervention in order to be made productive. But, she adds, for 'knowledge'

to become 'power' its prescriptions needed to be enforced, and this is where the intervention of state and church to discipline the body can be seen most evidently: 'the mechanical body could not have become a model of social behaviour without the destruction by the state of a vast range of pre-capitalist beliefs, practices and social subjects whose existence contradicted the regularisation of corporeal behaviour promised by Mechanical Philosophy' (2004:141). That is why the system of sympathetic relations Foucault describes in *The Order of Things* (where matter and cosmos are a *living organism*) had to be broken (Federici, 2004:142) and that of representation emerged.

21 It is here, Federici observes, that we can also find the origin of the proliferation of micro powers that Foucault has described. Thus 'the mechanisation of the body did not only involve the repression of desires, emotions, or forms of behaviour that were to be eradicated. It also involved the development of new faculties in the individual that would appear as *other* with respect to the body itself, and become agents of its transformation' (2004:151).

22 As Federici argues: 'The centralisation of the mechanisms of command, through their location in the individual, was finally obtained only to the extent that a centralisation occurred in the power of the state ... the democratisation of command would rest on the shoulders of a state always ready, like the Newtonian God, to reimpose order on the souls who proceeded too far in the ways of self-determination' (2004:151).

23 Whereas the role of the 'free' labourer and the colonial system is well recognised in Marx's analysis of primitive accumulation, '[f]ewer of us', Rosenberg argues, 'know well Marx's claims about the relationship of finance and public debt to primitive accumulation'. Marx had presciently noticed how 'The public debt becomes one of the most powerful levers of primitive accumulation. As with the stroke of an enchanter's wand, it endows barren money with the power of breeding and thus turns it into capital, without the necessity of its exposing itself to the troubles and risks inseparable from its employment in industry or even in usury ... [T]he national debt has given rise to joint-stock companies, to dealings in negotiable effects of all kinds, and to agiotage, in a word to stock-exchange gambling and the modern bankocracy' (Marx, in Rosenberg, 2014:8).

24 This is what is also at stake in engaging with the institutional arrangements I examine in Chapters 3 and 4. ALBA, it will be argued, acknowledges the hold that competition has at the level of free trade history, practices and institutions; and yet, by promoting complementarity, solidarity, cooperation and reciprocity, it does not accept competition as the only practice informing trade relations. Similarly, the RMA proposed by Ecuador recognises that markets play a role in

the determination of exchange rates but, instead of accepting them as the sole makers of value, it invokes inter-governmental activity and cooperation between states and markets, and in a way that explicitly links together finance, production and social reproduction. Here the dichotomy between the real and the financial spheres of the economy is done away with and exchange rates' determination is considered together with investment in areas ranging from food, health and education to energy and technology. Finally, the Employer of Last Resort recognises the hold that the wage and the work ideology have over social relations. However, by engaging with both the state and wage labour, it attempts to transform the meaning of work and productive activities by changing the system of (capitalist) valuation that characterises most economic activities.

25 What this renunciation expresses, Nietzsche (1887:127) argues, is 'the belief in a *metaphysical* value, the value of *truth in itself*, as it alone is guaranteed and attested in each ideal (it stands or falls with each ideal)' (original emphasis).

26 Mezzadra and Neilson (2013a:129) have brilliantly illustrated how, for this tracing to be a meaningful analytical and political project, we must account 'for the proliferation of borders and reorganisation of space that radically questions the inevitability of networks of social relations converging on a "coherent whole", particularly when the whole is associated with the bounded space of the modern state'. And, as they also point out, we must keep in mind that capital itself reduces living and concrete labour to unity by means of the various mechanisms through which its commensuration is accomplished.

Chapter 3

Value making in financial and trading arrangements: of provocations and *perspectival seeing*

Strictly speaking, there is absolutely no science 'without presuppositions', the very idea is inconceivable, paralogical: a philosophy, a 'belief' must always exist first in order for science to derive from it a direction, a meaning, a limit, a method, a *right* of existence'

(Nietzsche, 1887:127, original emphasis)

We see a strange phenomenon occurring: what we practice is often not what we value and what we value is often not what we practice (and in saying this let us not forget that 'practice' means many diverse things: work, shopping, eating, filling forms, writing, taking the train, watching the telly, harvesting a crop, reading, struggling, changing nappies … and each and one of these involve direct or indirect relations to the 'other'). Yet, anthropologists tell us, value is what guides our practices and the latter are in turn constituted by values. Could it be then that struggles are clashes among values and correspondent practices (value practices) and that what constitutes our daily existence is the front line, the battlefield?

(De Angelis, 2005:1)

As seen in Chapter 1, financial derivatives complicate the argument according to which it is possible to return to a real economy made of assets whose 'fundamental values' can be accounted for and distinguished from financial ones. My argument there was that recognising the contingency of value does not mean accepting that any value making process goes; but, on the contrary, that it requires engaging more fully with such a process, the values that accompany its trajectory, and the institutional arrangements that have supported it. It is by reflecting on the desirability of the reality produced by current arrangements, rather than the real or fictitious nature of the value they generate, that other forms of action can be thought of. Desirability is of course a matter of 'perspectival seeing' where at stake is the 'determination of the *hierarchy of values*' (Nietzsche, 1887:38). In this chapter I engage with the question of the hierarchy of values that inform, while also being shaped by, current institutional arrangements. I understand the relationship between the two as one of a constant feedback loop: arrangements are informed by, and inform, such hierarchy. Thus, whereas the privatisation of risks and uncertainty and the precarisation of life are only two of the most important values informing, and being provoked by, arrangements such as financial markets, competition is high up the hierarchy of values shaping and is, in turn, being affected by trading arrangements.

The first section of this chapter therefore starts where Chapter 1 left off and asks what kind of institutional arrangements might be able to shift current value making processes, not because these processes are unreal but because they are undesirable. I invoke the technology of financial derivatives once again to consider the potential of one particular arrangement, the Ecuadorian proposal for a RMA, to affect such processes. Before doing so, however, I delve deeper into the relationship between values and institutional arrangements by reflecting on the contribution that STS-inflected SSF, particularly by performativity scholars, have made to our understanding of markets as made by and through economic models. As I have argued, such an awareness was already present in both Smith's and Marx's work, although performativity scholars have opened up to scrutiny the role that 'intentionality' plays in such 'form giving activity' and shown that closer attention should be paid to the shaping force of material and technical devices. My aim is to reflect on what I see as an important limitation of their work while also showing the complementarity between their endeavours and that of the critical and feminist political work I have been referring to so far. The potential for collaboration rests on the fact that they all share a commitment to complexity, contingency and contestability, a commitment which makes it possible to ask the question of the 'perspectival seeing' or values that, implicitly or explicitly, inform action.

The second section transports this discussion to an altogether different area, that of the trade and development debate within the multilateral trade arena. This is a debate that has challenged the values informing one of the most prominent institutional arrangements in multilateral trade, that is the World Trade Organisation (WTO). Trade and development scholars have argued for more flexibility from its legal strictures, particularly from those provisions which have extended the logic of equivalence-based exchange to areas previously exempted from trade regulation. At a time when the one-size-fits-all orthodoxy of the 1990s seems to have been called into question and flexibility to have been gradually accepted, I aim to show how competition, through a renewed emphasis on global competitiveness, continues to inform trade and development debates; and why the reality that is shaped by, while also constituting, global competitiveness is undesirable. I conclude by reflecting briefly on the potential of one regional arrangement, the Bolivarian ALBA, to affect the position that competition has attained in the trade and development hierarchy of values.

This chapter therefore aims to think of alternative values, actually existing or not, while at the same time retaining a focus on, so as to show the pervasiveness of, those which dominate the current hierarchy, that is the privatisation of risks and uncertainty in financial markets, and competition in the multilateral trade arena. My intention, however, is not that of producing a concrete agenda or blueprint for action. Rather, I conceive of these two international economic arrangements as provocations, and am proposing to think of institutional arrangements more generally as provocations, in three interrelated respects: first, as attempts to think of desirable forms of intervention in the economy–society nexus capable of engendering alternative valorisation processes; second, to acknowledge that non-humans (such as technical and material devices) as well as humans participate in such processes and that the reality provoked by these interventions might be very different from that envisaged by humans; third, to bear in mind that whatever the goals we aim to achieve through interventions, the act of formatting markets will always permit, as well as oppose, particular exclusions. What provocations make clear, however, is the particular, partial and perspectival quality of their intervention.

Financial derivatives, the privatisation of risks and the precarisation of life

In Chapter 1, I explored the modality through which derivatives participate in value making processes, that is, the processes through which economic value is produced in today's financialised economies. I have shown how, rather than simply deriving their value from those of the underlying assets, derivatives participate in their actual construction; and how this process points to the extreme difficulty of disentangling 'real' and 'financial' values. The question I ended up with was whether acknowledging such uncertainty means we should give up on 'fundamental values' or any anchor between production and finance and take the market as the sole arbiter and maker of values. The argument I intend to make here is that acknowledging contingency in value making processes implies neither ignoring the constraints within which such processes take place nor doing away with judgments about their desirability. To articulate this point, I draw on the contribution that STS-inflected SSF have made to our understanding of how economic models, technologies and innovations do not simply mirror or represent an underlying economic reality but actively make it. While recognising this important contribution, I also point to what I see as a limitation, that is the fact that STS-inflected SSF have up until now refrained from putting forward their *perspectival seeing* so as to format markets in a different way. My argument is that thinking about contingency in value making processes characterised by financial uncertainty is a necessary, albeit not sufficient, condition for conceiving of desirable forms of intervention. I conclude by referring to an instance of such (always imperfect) intervention in the context of currency futures. The point I make is that it is on the desirability of current value making processes, the values they rely on and engender, that struggles over different kind of arrangements should be conducted, not on their fictitious or real nature.

On performativity

STS-inflected SSF emerged in the 1990s, motivated by the desire to distance themselves from the emphasis that classical economic sociology placed on human action as embedded in institutions, norms, relationships and structures to explain economic activities. Turning their attention to the way in which such action takes place through hybrids made of humans as well as technical and material devices, this body of work has particularly focused on economics, arguing that economic models and theories actively shape and format the economy, rather than simply describing it. As Callon (1998:2) put it in *The Laws of the Markets*:

> Saying that economics has failed by neglecting to develop a theory of real markets and their multiple modes of functioning, amounts to admitting that there does exist a thing – the economy – which a science – economics – has taken as its object of analysis. The point of view that I have adopted in this introduction, and which the book strives to defend, is radically different. It consists in maintaining that economics, in the broad sense of the term, performs, shapes and formats the economy, rather than observing how it functions.

This understanding of the economy as the real 'thing' that constitutes the object of economic analysis cannot be said to characterise all classical economic sociology, and my reading of Smith's and Marx's work was meant to trouble such an assumption. It is, however, the case that the belief in an economic order governed by natural laws has come to gradually dominate economic analysis. The *performativity* thesis has challenged such belief by highlighting the multifarious ways in which economic theories and models become a material force embodied in market practices, arrangements and infrastructures. For instance in *An Engine, Not a Camera: How Financial Models Shape Markets*, MacKenzie (2008) gives substance to the argument that economics and the economy coproduce one another by focusing on one such instance of coproduction. He carefully traces the process through which the adoption of the modern financial theory of option pricing, among other theories, has managed to transform financial market practices since the 1970s. The story he tells is that of the Black-Scholes-Merton model which offered a formula for pricing options: he shows how, although the prices the formula produced did not resemble the actual prices in the market when it was first adopted, the match improved with its wide-spread use. The fact that economic theory is able to influence, in the sense of affecting, the direction of financial markets is today widely accepted. MacKenzie, however, sees the Black-Scholes-Merton model as something other than mere 'influence'. He considers it as an instance of 'Barnesian' performativity, that is of a theory that gradually constructed the reality it claimed to be representing, mirroring or discovering, in this case, the 'right' prices of options, at least until the crash of 1987 (MacKenzie, 2008:119–210). Barnesian performativity, he points out, differs from both 'generic' performativity, which takes place when a theory or model is used as a tool in an economic process, and 'effective' performativity, which implies that the model or theory is used so as to generate change. What characterises this specific type of performativity is the fact that the theory or model actively formats the reality it claims to be merely representing.

Performativity therefore differs from the concept of self-fulfilling proph-ecy developed by Merton in 1948. The latter notion implies a relationship between beliefs and behaviour such that the prediction will turn out to be true; in Merton's words, '[t]he self-fulfilling prophecy is, in the beginning, a *false* definition of the situation evoking a new behaviour which makes the original false conception come "true"' (1968:477). The difference is not only that, contrary to self-fulfilling prophecy, performativity does not imply falsehood in the belief that comes to be performed. The most impor-tant aspect of performativity is that it is concerned 'with the incorporation of economics in the infrastructures of markets' so that it exceeds beliefs and mindsets, however important these are. As MacKenzie (2008:19) puts it:

> an aspect of economics that is incorporated only into beliefs 'in the heads of economic actors' may have a precarious status. A form of incor-poration that is in some sense deeper is incorporation into algorithms, procedures, routines, and material devices. An economic model that is incorporated into these can have effects even if those who use them are skeptical of the model's virtues, unaware of its details, or even of its very existence.

Two aspects of the performativity argument are worth reflecting on to illustrate the contribution that STS-inflected SSF have made to our understanding of the co-constitutive relationship between theory and practice, economics and the economy, and I would say the financial and the real spheres of the economy. The first is that performativity exceeds the sphere of human beliefs as the mere psychological realm. 'Incorporation' highlights the role of material devices with which the theory or model interacts. At the same time, and this is the second important aspect, it brings to light the constraints within which the model operates. Thus, to say that the Black-Scholes-Merton formula was performative 'is not to make the crude claim that any arbitrary formula for option prices, if proposed by sufficiently authoritative people, could have "made itself true" by being adopted. Most such formulas could not do so, at least other than temporarily' (MacKenzie, 2008:20). As he points out, even if initially adopted widely, the formula would soon have been abandoned had it led agents consistently to lose money or conduct arbitrage so as to gain from systematic price discrepancies.

The issue becomes one of understanding why certain formulas have durable consequences and this requires expanding as far as possible the radar of research so as to delve into the reality in which formula, models and devices have become immersed. The concept of *agencement* is important in this respect as it sheds light on how markets take different forms in different places: '*Agencements* denote sociotechnical arrangements when they are considered from the point [of] view of their capacity to act and to give meaning to action' (Callon and Caliskan, 2005: 24–25; quoted in MacKenzie, 2009:20–21). What *agencement* does is to place the emphasis on the *tools* that enable performativity. MacKenzie, for instance, argues that the performativity of financial theory has become incorporated in financial markets in three specific ways. From a technical perspective, the growth of financial markets would have been impossible without the development of infrastructures, with financial theory built into software so as to enable risk calculation and semi-automatic fast trading. From a linguistic perspective, financial theory provided words and concepts with which to manage and reduce the complexity inherent in market transactions. In this respect, 'implied volatility' is an engineered concept that has reduced the complexity inherent in, and has therefore made possible, the pricing of options. Finally, from a regulatory or legitimising perspective, financial markets would not have developed without the active intervention of economists and regulators who 'purified' previously contentious practices and instruments from their association with gambling by making them efficient and rational realms of transactions (Latour, 1993; de Goede, 2005).

In the specific case of the Black-Scholes-Merton formula, the journey from the theoretical model to trading practice included all these aspects: many members of the University of Chicago were involved in the process of legitimising derivatives' trading and contributed to setting up the Chicago

Board Options Exchange; Black himself sold sheets with option prices to traders; and although it is not clear to what extent the authority these financial economists enjoyed played a role in spreading the formula, the latter had the advantage of 'cognitive simplicity', with the sheets themselves being extremely easy to read and handle when compared to others in circulation (MacKenzie, 2008:78). The entanglement of human and non-human agents which emerged as a result produced a situation where the practice started to resemble the theory more and more: without these forms of technical, linguistic and legitimising and regulatory intervention, however, the Black-Scholes-Merton formula would not have created its reality. Thus, by opening up to scrutiny the complex web of socio-material practices constituting markets, work on the performativity of economics points to contingency within constraints, material and technical as well as human.

This work, however, has not gone uncontested: if performativity scholars have made clear that engaging socio-material practices always necessarily entails a partial account, however serious the attempt is to widen out the reality being accounted for, concerns have been expressed in relation to the kind of entanglements that have ended up being privileged in their analyses. Mirowski and Nik-Khah in particular have lamented the fact that in their attempt to do away with structures, forces and intentionality, performativity scholars and STS-inflected SSF more generally have ended up concentrating on machine metaphors, theories and models in a way that has consistently diverted attention from other important processes. In *Do Economists Make Markets?*, a collection edited by MacKenzie, Muniesa and Siu (2008), Mirowski and Nik-Khah take issue with the account of the Federal Communication Commission (FCC) spectrum auctions which Callon, Muniesa and Guala provide as a clear instance of successful performativity, successful in the sense that economists' game theoretical accounts of auctions shaped the format of the auctions adopted. Mirowski and Nik-Khah argue that concentrating on economists' theories has led these authors to ignore both the role of the government and that of telecommunication companies 'in orchestrating the outcome' of the auctions. As they put it: '[it is] only when you leave out the government and the telecoms on the one hand, and that notorious shape-shifter the computer on the other, that you can conceive of the auctions as the result of the free play and creative tinkering on the part of the economists' (2007:216–217).

As Mirowski and Nik-Khah admit, this 'partial' account might have depended on the fact that performativity scholars relied on economists' own accounts of the event (2007:202) rather than on a careful description of the phenomena. The latter would have required them to follow all actors, and not only the economists and their account of the 'successful' auction. Indeed, placing the emphasis on *agencement* would have required opening up to scrutiny the 'sociotechnical arrangement', ie the FCC actions in its various articulations; and, I would argue, nothing prevents the observer from recognising how the articulations which are more 'connected, related, associated' are also those which exert most power in the arrangement (Latour, 2005:177). In other words, there is nothing in the performativity thesis which prevents one from talking about powerful actors as long as that power is carefully traced in action. Similarly, there is nothing in the performativity thesis that prevents us from seeing that certain theories and models cannot be made to work. Mirowski and Nik-Khah's specific reference is to the neo-classical story which they see as 'so persistently flawed that it cannot be made to "work" for much longer than it takes to come up with another (possibly contradictory) story to take its place'. Indeed, they add, 'over the course of the twentieth-century alone, the neo-classical orthodoxy with regard to its core price theory has "flipped" at least three times (Marshallian supply/demand/Walrasian general equilibrium/Nash non-cooperative equilibrium)' (2007:216). This is a point MacKenzie has acknowledged in relation to the Black-Scholes-Merton model as he recognises that not all formulas for pricing options could have worked.

Mirowski and Nik-Khah's critique, however, speaks to a more general concern I have about the performativity school: this has to do with the fact that recognising contingency within constraints, however important, is not sufficient to start thinking about, and devising, ways to organise markets differently. Entering the debate about their desirability is therefore crucial and this means confronting economists on the reality they attempt to construct through their theories and models. What is significant in this respect is that, recently, neoclassical economists have abandoned their comparison of the price system to a natural mechanism and revealed their ambition is to '*fabricate* markets, and not simply treat them as States of Nature' (Mirowski and Nik-Khah, 2007:215–216). In other words they have admitted that markets are achieved and normative rather than neutral and natural, making more explicit the fact that, as argued with respect to classical political economy, the struggle has always been one over the reality which different actors attempt to construct. This is a point which Callon acknowledges in the concluding chapter of the edited collection where he proposes to explore different market formations as 'struggles of performation … between competing programs which make the disassembling and reassembling process possible, necessitating investments that measure up to those by which actual markets were formatted' (Callon, 2008:349).

Yet, I would argue, work on the performativity of economics has up until now fallen short of making substantial 'investments' that measure up to those which have formatted financial markets so far, and which have furthered a vision and provoked a reality from a specific 'perspectival' seeing, one based on the privatisation of risks and uncertainty and the precarisation of life. This is the challenge the performativity of economics confronts, I believe, if it is not to become redundant: not to provide a blueprint for action, but to think of partial, limited and always precarious attempts to reassemble markets differently. This point is emerging more generally within STS. As the 'inherently contextual nature of not only the application of scientific knowledge but also its means of production' (Pickersgill, 2012: 599) is re-emphasised, questions about ethics and technology announce a possible 'turn to politics and the normative' (Bijker, Hughes and Pinch, 2012: xxvi; Johnson and Wetmore, 2009; Collins and Evans, 2002; Jasanoff, 2003; Wynne, 2003). Such a turn, however, requires reflecting on the values that have accompanied the growth of financial derivatives as well as those that have emerged as a result, while also asking the question about their desirability.

Performation and perspectival seeing

How does this all relate to the discussion of financial derivatives? STS-inflected SSF have been mainly concerned with the second order economy, that is, with circulating 'goods' such as contracts (securities, currencies, bonds, derivatives), rather than with the production side of the economy. As Marx had presciently noticed in his analysis of value, however, much is to be gained by concentrating on both sides. Indeed, financial derivatives show how the two are deeply entangled: their trading clearly impacts on production as decisions on investments in the so-called real economy are made based on valuation processes taking place in financial markets. Acknowledging that value is produced at the intersection between the real and the financial sphere of the economy, with the two spheres coproducing one another, presents a dual task: it requires us to take into account the contingency, within constraints, of such a process and, at the same time, to pose the question of its desirability. If performativity scholars have significantly contributed to this task by opening many 'black boxes' of financial practices and showing their productive, as opposed to merely parasitical, role, they have so far refrained from making substantial 'investments' in reformatting the economy and articulating the *perspectival seeing* from which such investments are made.

Yet, as the discussion in the last two chapters has indicated, this dual task is not new: if neoclassical economists have only recently acknowledged, at least explicitly, that markets are fabricated, Smith and Marx understood this to be precisely the case. For them economic models and theories did not simply mirror or represent an underlying economic reality but actively made it; and this included Marx's 'law of value' despite subsequent interpretations tending to dehistoricise and naturalise it.[1] This more nuanced, although not conventional, reading of their work is what has allowed scholars like Dalla Costa and James (1972), Dalla Costa and Fortunati (1977) and Federici (1980) to reject both objective and subjective theories of value and to put forward an understanding of value making as a process rather than an imperative, which is what led them to explore alternative valorisation practices. An instance of these was the 'Wages for/against Housework' initiative which required the state to recognise domestic labour as 'productive' of value. As argued in the next chapter, this campaign was not without its problems as it risked extending the power of the measurement processes they were critiquing. However, understood as a provocative demand, this form of intervention was deployed because of its potential to shift exactly those value making processes.

The more general point I am making is that this body of critical and feminist political economic work can provide crucial resources for interrogating and intervening in today's value making processes. This is because it enables us to see that regarding value as always 'contingent, hermeneutic, negotiable and non natural' and its measurement as a social construct (Mirowski, 1990:706) does not imply that measuring mechanisms are inexistent or without power. Rather, it makes us appreciate that while there is no, one 'correct way for a society to measure a commodity ... the way its measurement is *instituted* has important consequences' (1990:568) (emphasis added). In the context of financial derivatives, for instance, this argument demands that we pay attention to the ways in which their power has come to materialise. For instance, it enables us to see how, in addition to the technical, linguistic and legitimatory mechanisms MacKenzie has identified in relation to the performativity of financial theories, institutional arrangements have played a crucial role in supporting derivatives' growth. It was with the demise of Bretton Woods that old risks previously managed by the state were revealed while new ones started to proliferate; and firms' and governments' increasing need to protect themselves against price volatility was met by the proliferation of financial instruments such as derivatives. Indeed, as the state withdrew and old and new risks were not only revealed but also made private, firms and governments started to take into account, and calculate, the risk of variability of interest and exchange rates, the socio-political risks of unstable countries where they might be operating and the risk of weather variability, etc (Pryke, 2006). Indeed, anything that in the production cycle was prone to change and could be traded became the possible underlying asset of a derivative. Private risk was to be found everywhere and the market was the place to calculate any sort of risk. Risk, as Arnoldi has argued, seems to have become the asset to invest in (2004:39).

Certainly the belief in the calculation of risks did not spring up naturally but was made possible through financial innovations such as the

Black-Scholes-Merton model of option pricing that promised to deliver a risk-free portfolio, in addition to the theories that provided modern finance with its conceptual unity, a unity that would result in the primacy of shareholder value.[2] At the same time, and this is a point Mirowski and Nik-Khah make in relation to neoclassical theory more generally, we know that the risk calculation hypothesis at the core of modern finance and financial innovations has 'flipped' several times.[3] Thus, to understand why it continues to maintain 'the appearance of monolithic continuity and placid confidence' (Mirowski and Nik-Khah, 2008:216), we need to look at the factors that have contributed to risk becoming the principal rationale for thinking about investments, at the level of the company as well as that of the individual. This is certainly not the only factor but I do believe that both the proliferation of risks connected to global investing and the obsession with, and dependence on, shareholders' value cannot be thought of in isolation from the 'profit squeeze' of Fordist capitalism that resulted in the move towards stock managerial capitalism (Harvey, 2010:65–66). As Marazzi puts it (2010: 31–32):

> at the height of its development, in a determinate organic composition of capital (i.e. the relationship between constant and variable capital), Fordist capitalism was no longer able to 'suck' surplus-value from living working labour ... We know how it went: reduction in the cost of labour, attacks on syndicates [i.e. unions], automatization and robotization of entire labour processes, delocalisation in countries with low wages, precarization of work and diversification of consumption models. And precisely financialization, i.e. increase in profits not as an excess of cost proceeds (that is not in accordance with manufacturing-Fordist logic) but as an excess of value in the Stock Exchange.

The 'profit squeeze' did not last long: as Seguino has pointed out, while increasing productivity has been recorded in many countries in the last three decades, the share of national income going to workers has decreased 'in the USA, Europe, sub-Saharan Africa, the Middle East, Latin America and the Caribbean' (2010:180). Thus, profits have increased as a result of the responses to the 'profit squeeze' described by Marazzi and the maximisation of market value has, since the 1980s, become the principal concern and objective of the company, regardless of its capital structure or the way in which it finances its activities. And the significance of this process is not limited to the private realm of the firm. Financial deregulation and liberalisation, coupled with the reduction of public spending and the privatisation of social security, have resulted in what Paulré defines as the 'new asset economy' where individuals' welfare, and ultimately life, is made dependent on the value of assets invested in financial markets (Paulré,

2009:169). Thus, as flexibility in the labour market increases and more public and common resources central to the needs of daily social reproduction (such as water, electricity, health and education) are privatised, financial markets have come to replace the state as the 'social insurer' (Fumagalli and Mezzadra, 2009:210). In this respect, they argue, financial markets signal the privatisation of the productive and reproductive spheres of life at the same time as life is put to work for the extraction of more value. New attachments are produced through private indebtedness and the investment in private pensions, private insurance and the eventual channelling of part of the salary to the financial market, which sees people worrying constantly about the value of their financial assets and their present and future solvency. Life is made ever more precarious and investment in the future becomes a totally individualised and privatised enterprise (Dowling and Harvie, 2014). This is a very partial and therefore limited account of the financialisation story but one that I consider important and indeed shapes my own perspectival seeing, the one from which I evaluate the desirability of current arrangements as well as the potential of alternative ones.[4]

I also acknowledge that an analysis that focuses on how different phenomena grouped together under the financialisation umbrella have impacted on everyday life, unidirectionally producing attachments (to financial markets for instance), misses the manifold ways in which financial logics have tapped into, and were provoked by, individuals and households' desires. Allon (2011), for instance, has shown how the complex dynamics between the two has led to the reconfiguration of the household as an asset to be invested in, with household members seeing themselves more and more as investors rather than citizens. The significance of this dynamics and its implications for the kind of 'investments' we wish to make when it comes to rearranging the economy–society nexus cannot be underestimated. However, I do believe that recognising these attachments as real and productive does not mean doing away with judgments about their desirability. In the context of the discussion about financial derivatives, for instance, the role they have played in the crisis has shown important aspects about what we might refer to as the risk mentality as well as its relationship to financial markets and instruments, aspects whose desirability we can certainly judge. First, derivatives have shown that risks, as well as values, are constantly made and that financial markets are not simply technical realms where risks are calculated: markets are performed and the act of participating in a market itself changes the market, as well as the risks that it is supposed to merely calculate. Second, and importantly, the uncertainty characterising financial markets and exemplified by the difficulty of retrieving 'fundamental' values does not mean that any value making process goes. From my 'perspectival seeing' if derivatives have demonstrated something concrete about the 'values' that have accompanied their growth, this is the undesirability of a social vision predicated on the privatisation of risks and uncertainty, with the resulting precarisation of life. The point is that if a world in which financial markets are the arbiters of value 'is to be avoided' (not because they are unreal but because the reality they produce is undesirable), then thinking of how to deal with such uncertainty differently – and be 'invested' otherwise in the economy – provides a fruitful perspective from which to start shifting the terms of the debate with the aim of articulating an alternative vision of the *real* (in our) economy. And this may include thinking of alternative institutional arrangements capable of affecting such value making processes.

The Ecuadorian proposal for a New Regional Financial Architecture and the Plan *Para el BuenVivir*

I turn briefly to one such example to illustrate the possibility of dealing differently with financial uncertainty and the contestability of value revealed by financial derivatives. I do not take this example as a blueprint for macroeconomic action but I see it as a provocative attempt to rearrange the prevalent finance–production nexus by setting in motion values other than the privatisation of risks and uncertainty and the precarisation of life. In 2010 I conducted research on the RMA, a proposal for dealing with exchange rates tabled by the Republic of Ecuador at the UN as part of a broader initiative for the establishment of a New Regional Financial Architecture.[5] Although the proposal has since been abandoned, I refer to it since it represents an attempt to take financial uncertainty seriously by recognising, while participating in, the coproduction of the financial and real spheres of the economy (Ecuador, Permanent Mission to the United Nations, 2008). Exchange rates are indeed quite significant from a perspective that focuses on the contingency of value as they are supposed to represent the worth of one currency, and therefore the state of one economy, in terms of another. But how does one think about this relation of equivalence? How does one measure it? According to neoclassical theory, and in particular its Purchasing Power Parity variant, exchange rates (as the relation of equivalence between two countries' average prices of goods and services) are determined on the basis of trade flows: the theory holds that what explains their movement over time is the trade balance so that an increase in exports of one economy's goods and services leads to an appreciation of its currency. Capital flows play no role in the Purchasing Power Parity world (Harvey, 2005:4).

However, in financial markets, actual exchange rates are determined on the basis of the supply and demand of the currencies and it is here that expectations play an important role. Although these expectations are supposed to be based on so-called real variables such as price index, interest rates, macroeconomic stability and inflation rates, and aside from the question of how real an account of the state of the economy these variables can ever give, the point is that in today's financial markets 'forecasts and asset prices (including exchange rates) are not independent of one another; far from it – aggregate expectations *determine* prices' (Harvey, 2005:5–6) (emphasis added). What Harvey argues is that expectations about the future impact of such variables, including anticipations of others' expectations, are always already affecting today's value. Indeed, such expectations are behind portfolio capital flows which, he argues, are what really explains the movement of exchange rates in the long term. In addition to this first layer of interaction between expectations and prices, studies are now pointing to the fact that exchange rates' derivatives, forward exchange rates in particular, are driving spot exchange rates (Maldonado and Saunders, 1983; Jabbour, 1994; Chatrath, Ramchander and Song, 1996). This is the double circularity I have described in Chapter 1 in relation to financial derivatives more generally. Hence, the question of how to determine what one currency is worth in terms of another remains unanswered.

And this uncertainty shows exactly the limits of the regulatory approach to derivatives: measures, such as the prohibition of short-selling, the introduction of the Tobin tax and the separation between commercial and investment banking, can be introduced to limit speculative attacks against currencies and generally to limit the volume of derivatives' trading.[6] However, the uncertainty that derivatives point to is deeper in two respects. First, as long as derivatives provide crucial hedging functions there will be a need for them and as long as there is such a need, speculation cannot be effectively controlled. Second, even if the impact of derivatives on prices were reduced, the value that exchange rates are supposed to express (the average prices of goods and services) would remain contestable. Indeed, how is the 'real' value of goods and services, whose relation of equivalence exchange rates are supposed to express, to be measured in the first place?

These are the two aspects the proposed RMA aimed to address. First, by proposing to deal with exchange rates in a cooperative manner, through mutually agreed bands based on the sharing of information about macroeconomic policies (Ecuador, Permanent Mission to the United Nations, 2008:2–3), it aimed to remove a critical source of uncertainty from the realm of private dealings.[7] In this respect, it offered an alternative to current regulatory approaches by targeting the source of uncertainty directly, thereby reducing the need for hedging in the first place. Second, by acknowledging, while trying to shape, expectations, and agreeing on optimal exchange rates within bands, policymakers would have immersed themselves in the construction of exchange rates, thereby removing this process from the exclusive realm of financial markets. The proposal saw three different options reflecting different degrees of cooperative arrangements among countries, ranging from the monitoring and exchange of information to the setting-up of soft bands for exchange rates, up to the most committed level consisting of a fixed, but adjustable, exchange rate regime with compulsory bands.

The underlying rationale was that by exchanging *ex ante* information about national policies, and agreeing on bands within which 'optimal exchange rates' would be decided and communicated to markets (Ecuador, Permanent Mission to the United Nations, 2008:4), agents would have had access to important information on which to model and shape their expectations. At the same time these bands would serve another purpose, that of alerting policymakers to information coming from outside that would lead to 'specific consultations ... when indicative band limits of the soft target zones are approached or breached' at the market level. As the proposal stated: 'Such consultations would serve to spur policy adjustments or otherwise to adjust the target zones conformant with some new regional reality' (2008:4). To put it schematically, the proposal envisaged interaction between governments and market agents in the following way: governments would give an indication of exchange rate through bands; the rates would, however, be left free to fluctuate within these bands until governments' projections were called into question by market agents. Then a reassessment would take place and a decision by governments made again.

The proposal therefore envisaged a different kind of arrangement between states and markets, recognising the participation of both in the determination of exchange rates' value. What is worth noting is that, although the proposal talked about anchoring expectations, its actual aim was not that of making exchange rates reflect equilibrium prices (ie the average price of goods and services). When I asked to what 'real' variables exchange rates' expectations would be linked, Pedro Paez, the then President of the Ecuadorian Technical Commission, pointed out that 'equilibrium prices' have not existed for a long time, and in Latin America this becomes apparent if one looks at the 'historic matrix of dependence' that has its roots in the colonial period: hence the difficulty in setting any (exchange rate) parity at the beginning of the institutional arrangement.[8] This, however, did not mean abandoning the attempt to connect exchange rates with the economy (in this case average prices); nor did it mean influencing exchange rates for trade competitiveness and growth reasons as is often done through competitive devaluation and overvaluation. On the contrary, it meant participating more actively in the making of the economy. This is why the proposal made clear that the financial architecture could not be thought of in isolation from the changes that needed to occur 'at the level of the relationship between states, firms and the heterogeneous spectrum of popular economies' (2008:6). And this is why, as Paez pointed out, the proposal must be read in conjunction with the Ecuadorian *Plan Nacional*

Para el BuenVivir 2009–2013 (National Plan) which aimed to promote a new 'productive matrix' that places the production and re-production of life as the central concern and principal end of the economy (Republica del Ecuador, 2009:296).

Negotiated by a broad alliance of social forces against the neoliberal policies of the last three decades, the 2008 Ecuadorian Constitution contains a reference to the *BuenVivir* (the good living) as a post-development project that merges aspects of the cosmovision of indigenous people (*Sumak Kawsay* or *la vida plena*) with those deriving from feminist economics and environmental politics (see Leon, 2008). The conceptual shift this vision implies is more explicitly articulated under the National Plan, where it is recognised that 'underlying the idea of development, progress and modernisation is the conceptualisation of a linear time in which history has only one meaning and direction: developed countries are ahead, positing the model for all societies to follow' (Republica del Ecuador, 2009:31). This is a world mentality which, as Escobar has poignantly argued, has produced prominent ontological assumptions such as the separation of humans from non-humans, and of certain humans from others, and the separation of 'the economy' from other realms of life (2010:9). These are also the assumptions the Plan targets by declaring them at odds with the 'full life' or *vida plena* to which *Sumak Kawsay* refers and according to which 'the world above, the world below, the world outside and this world are connected to each other and are part of a whole within a spiral, and not a linear perspective of time' (Republica del Ecuador, 2009:32), a perspective that emphasises 'relationality and reciprocity; the continuity between the natural, the human and the supernatural ... and the embeddedness of the economy in social life' (Escobar, 2010:9). Moving away from the ideological orbit of 'development', therefore, means thinking of other ways of producing and consuming as well as organising and sharing *life* (Leon, 2009:17). In this respect, the Plan aims to promote the transition from an extractivist model of colonial origins to a 'bio pluralist' economy that recognises and valorises different forms of life, different forms of economy, and different property relations (Republica del Ecuador, 2009:43). This, the Plan continues, requires an active investment in the production and, importantly, the reproduction of life, with investments in areas ranging from food, housing, health and education, to energy, technology, environmental and bio-services as well as wide-ranging agrarian reforms (Republica del Ecuador, 2009:296–362).

It is not my intention to idealise such arrangements. Indeed, writing before the 2009–2013 National Plan was released, and referring to the social policies promoted by progressive regimes in South America, Gudynas et al. (2008) have pointed to the lack of coherence between statements and actual practice.[9] Others have argued that the moment of openness and possibility brought about by the alliance of social forces coincided with the constituent process but ended with the adoption of the Constitution. However, reflecting on the potential of the RMA and the Plan is important for two reasons: first, because the immediate contribution they make to the current debate about the regulation of finance is to show the inadequacy of responses that focus on the separation between the real and the financial spheres of the economy, such as those aiming to curb the speculatory excesses of derivatives. More important, however, is the emphasis they place on the economy conceived of not in isolation from the other realms of life but as the (very contested) terrain on which the production and reproduction of life takes places. Crucially, they show how seeing value as contingent does not mean accepting any value making process; on the contrary, this requires engaging more fully in its construction, rather than letting the market be the maker and arbiter of value. From this perspective 'fundamental' value appears as that which does not need to be abandoned but rather reconceptualised; no longer seen as that which is pure and untainted by financial activity – and therefore outside financial markets which attempt to capture its substance – but rather as that which is constantly made. What emerges is the real economy as that which needs to be constantly constructed, a construction which can take place from a 'perspectival seeing' that struggles for an altogether different kind of *investment in life* than that promoted by financial markets so far.

This is the provocation the RMA and the Plan are potentially capable of, injecting 'values' or 'beliefs' other than the privatisation of uncertainty and the precarisation of life in the current international financial hierarchy. This question pertains to another arrangement of which Ecuador is part and upon whose potential to shift current value making processes I want to reflect. As a regional trade agreement, ALBA may be considered as an attempt to inject values which are very different from those currently dominating the multilateral trade arena, first and foremost that of global competitiveness. Before considering such potential, I turn to the debate about flexibility that has attained centre stage within critical trade and development literature, highlighting the role that competition continues to play in these debates.

The WTO and the flexibility debate: from competition to global competitiveness

Established in the 1990s, the WTO embodied the belief in the universal beneficial role of trade liberalisation. Ostensibly motivated by the acceptance of the logic of comparative advantage according to which all countries can benefit from trading with one another, it reduced the scope of so-called special and differential provisions on which countries could rely on 'development' grounds and introduced more equally binding rules than those imposed by its predecessor, the General Agreement on Tariffs and Trade (GATT), while at the same time extending the reach of the latter to areas previously exempted from trade regulation.[10] The logic of equivalence, which Marx saw as deriving from a violent process of abstraction that intensifies exchange and accumulation, was made to apply to areas as disparate as services, investment and intellectual property rights (IPRs) through legal provisions such as National Treatment and Most Favoured Nation.[11] These are the principal rules through which multilateral liberalisation has taken place, particularly in the first decade of WTO life.

The extent to which WTO rules have in actual fact reduced members' policy space has been the object of more recent enquiry, with some trade and development scholars pointing to the creative interpretation WTO rules are capable of and to the dangers of monolithic interpretations of such law (Santos, 2012). For instance, scholars within the Law and New Developmental State (LANDS) approach do not dispute the restriction of policy autonomy that WTO law has introduced. However, they argue that 'mainstream' critical trade and development literature does not always acknowledge the active role that states are reasserting in the pursuit of development. This new role, which Trubek and Santos (2006) see materialising in several South American countries, is based on the acknowledgement that past policies, both developmentalist and neoliberal, have failed to deliver prosperity for all (see also Bresser-Pereira, 2006; Trubek et al., 2014). As Trubek (2007:4) puts it:

> The past looks like a battle field on which all sides lie defeated. We have lost faith in big ideas and universal solutions. Neither markets nor states seem like the panaceas they once were thought to be. We have confronted the complexity and embeddedness of legal systems, cultures and traditions and learned that one size does not fit all. We have seen that the developmental state can be a tyrant as well as an emancipator, the market a source of oppression as well as of energy and innovation, external assistance a tool of hegemony as well as a gesture of goodwill.

The New Political Economy of Development that has emerged as a result is premised on the rejection of the one-size-fits-all model that has prevailed in the last three decades and the reformulation of 'development' as learning and experimentation: since '[t]here is no sure fire formula for development – the best that can be done is to proceed from a contextual and detailed analysis [and to] experiment' (Hauserman, 2007:547). Thus reformulated, 'development' requires much more policy autonomy to experiment with different strategies, including at the WTO level. Although LANDS scholars are carefully monitoring these experiments and paying attention to the shifting role of domestic law, which they see oriented towards more hybrid forms (Trubek, 2008), they argue that the move towards greater flexibility is already observable in relation to WTO law. Their argument is therefore that, as the neoliberal economic orthodoxy is coming under increasing scrutiny, WTO law is much more indeterminate and less inflexible than many critical trade and development scholars recognise, and that states with a clear development strategy are able to influence its development. Santos (2012), for instance, has demonstrated how countries with 'developmental legal capacity' have been able to intervene at the level of litigation, thereby affecting the interpretation of WTO law (see also Ratton and Badin, 2011). This position highlights the limitations of an exclusive emphasis on the legislative moment for struggles over the meaning of WTO law, pointing to the myriad of other sites, such as litigation and trade expertise, that participate in meaning making processes (Lang, 2009).

The objection LANDS scholars have raised to what they call 'mainstream' trade and development theory is crucial in two respects: it invites us to look at the way in which states interact differently with WTO law so as not to make broad sweeping generalisations about its effects; and it also requires that we carefully examine the processes of knowledge production that have allowed previously unregulated practices to come to light and be constructed as trade-related so as to appreciate how they become the object of multilateral trade regulation (Lang, 2011). The call to be attentive to the processes through which meaning, including that of trade law, is created, stabilised and also continuously challenged is particularly important in demystifying the power of WTO law. At the same time, it is equally important to recognise that once practices have been made trade-related, they produce powerful and at times long-lasting effects on member states: indeed, the way we come to know and define practices as trade related affects our understanding of 'autonomy' in the policy realm, however relative such autonomy always is. Thus, while acknowledging the flexibility of WTO law as LANDS scholars invite us to do, the question about the significance of the extension of the trade rationale into more domains of life, and the way this constrains the possibilities that might be enabled by more creative interpretations of WTO law, remains important, although not one I am going to address here.

What I want to focus on is another aspect of this debate: when examining the conditions that have made the extension of the WTO remit possible, critical trade and development scholars point to the problematic acceptance of the universal beneficial role of trade liberalisation: despite their differences as to the actual stringency of WTO rules, they share a commitment to troubling the logic of comparative advantage on which the case for uniform liberalisation rests. However, the point I want to make through the short digression into trade theory that follows, is that what seems to be taking the place of the troubled comparative advantage logic is the acceptance of a discourse about the inevitability of global competitiveness. This acceptance poses serious questions about the way in which multilateral trade relations are conceptualised and conducted; and, consequently, about the extent to which states can experiment with 'development' strategies. At stake, once again, is the hierarchy of values that informs action, this time in the multilateral trade arena.

Of comparative and competitive advantage

The standard theory of free trade, the so-called Hecksher-Ohlin-Samuelson theory, posits that countries benefit from trading with one another by specialising in the production of the goods in which they have a comparative advantage.[12] These are the goods produced by utilising the most abundant, and therefore cheaper, factors of production; the implication is that countries endowed with abundant capital/labour will gain from producing capital/labour intensive goods and services. As a result, a certain international division of labour emerges which is deemed to benefit all trading partners since trade is supposed eventually to equalise real wages and profits across countries (ie it will make countries all equally competitive). Such theoretical construction has informed much post-war multilateral trade activity. As Shaikh (2007:53) has pointed out, however, for this theoretical apparatus to work three assumptions need to hold true, namely that 'the terms of trade fall when a nation runs a trade deficit; the trade balance improves when the terms of trade fall; and finally there is no overall job loss generated by any of these adjustments'. These assumptions have not only been challenged theoretically but also empirically: reality has neither conformed to the model of balanced trade nor known of any tendency towards full employment.

There have been standard responses to these findings: for instance, neoclassical economists have argued that assumptions about exchange rates' movements are valid only in the long term (Rogoff, 1996); and the New Trade Theory has focused on imperfect competition and increasing returns to scale to argue that liberalisation is not always beneficial and states should at times intervene so as to support strategic sectors (Krugman, 1981, 1983). A more radical challenge has come from economists who have critiqued the theory of comparative advantage on its own terms. Authors such as Shaikh and Millberg have argued that what is at issue is competitive (absolute) cost and advantage, not comparative advantage (Shaikh, 2007; Millberg, 1994). The point of departure for these analyses is the classical theory of competition, which is different from the neoclassical theory of 'perfect competition', and which points to the fact that companies operating transnationally, similarly to those which operate at the domestic level, 'utilize strategies and tactics to gain and hold market share, and price cutting and cost reductions are major features in this constant struggle' (Shaikh, 2007:57). Moreover, Shaikh continues, 'because a nation's international terms of trade are merely international common currency relative prices, they will be regulated in the same manner as any relative price: by real costs. However the terms of trade will then not be free to automatically adjust to eliminate trade imbalances unless real costs themselves did so' (2007:57).

This means that free trade will always benefit countries which are stronger in terms of absolute costs; hence, contrary to what both classical and neoclassical theories assume, free trade never works in the interest of all countries (Shaikh, 1980, 1996). This, Shaikh argues, is confirmed by the international trade practices not only of Britain and the US but also of Japan, South Korea and the Asian Tigers. From this perspective the postwar life of the multilateral trade regime can be read as a history of selective trade liberalisation to promote particular trade interests. However, as LANDS scholars have pointed out, these interests are being challenged by the ascendancy of emerging economies in Asia and South America, not only through their faster growth but also by means of litigation through which they dispute orthodox interpretations of WTO law.

Hence, by rejecting the comparative advantage axiom, the competitive advantage approach provides for a greater degree of state intervention, bringing to the centre of debate industrial policy and managed trade so that governments can 'consider trade liberalisation in a selective manner, [and] as individual countries become sufficiently competitive in the world market' they can move up the development ladder (Shaikh, 2007:64). The role of competition therefore underpins flexibility arguments as the need to enhance one's competitiveness becomes ever more crucial: countries should compete in the international arena when they are ready and in order to be ready they need actively to intervene in the economy. A cursory look at the countries identified as adopting an interventionist approach clearly points to the central role, at least at the level of political economic discourse, that global competitiveness plays in the pursuit of such a strategy.[13] What seems to be happening is therefore that competitive advantage is taking the place of comparative advantage and that global competitiveness is increasingly providing the framework within which policy autonomy and development strategies need to be pursued: this is the 'need to prosper in conditions of global competition' (Trubek, 2014:19).

The question is: what does it mean to say that this process *needs* to take place in conditions of global competition? Or, put differently, do these conditions end up constraining the extent to which states can experiment with well-being and development? In their comprehensive survey of the global competitiveness literature, Green, Mostafa and Preston point to the fact that although competitiveness has achieved the status of global discourse, and definitions by national and international institutions proliferate,[14] it in fact remains quite a loose term. What they see emerging from historical debates is the acknowledgement that economic competitiveness applies not only to the level of the firm but also to that of national economies, and that these two levels are deeply interrelated. However, they point out that although national economic competitiveness is 'defined variously in terms of labour productivity, total value creation, economic growth and living standards ... no single measure can capture all that is important in policy terms about economic competitiveness' (Green, Mostafa and Preston, 2010:5). More importantly, even if one takes into account the final measure of competitiveness strategies, that is the extent to which, in the long term, they promote sustainable improvements in living standards, current indicators such as Gross Domestic Product (GDP) per capita tell us nothing about 'how purchasing power is distributed' (2010:5). In other words, economic competitiveness tells us very little about living standards and well being. If this is the case, what is one to make of the current emphasis on global competition?

There are two lines of enquiry that can be pursued. One would take the 'need to prosper in conditions of global competition' at its face value, that is, it would accept the constraints seemingly dictated by the international economic system, and ask for what purpose competitiveness is being pursued 'on the ground'. What we see in the countries surveyed by the LANDS literature so far is that redistribution and social policies are being devised and implemented albeit in contradictory and piecemeal fashion (Trubek, 2012; Alviar Garcia, 2014). From this angle we might conclude that the answer depends on what will be done with the GDP generated by competitive exports. This perspective highlights the importance of continuing with case studies, as LANDS scholars are currently doing, so as to assess the kind of reality generated by different policies in different countries.

However, a complementary line of enquiry, and one I am more interested in pursuing, asks what the acceptance of the competitive advantage logic underlying the global competitiveness argument does in both normative and positive terms. I believe that this is an important question to address if we want to keep two crucial levels of analysis open, namely, that of carefully tracing the material reality produced on the ground so as to avoid the risk of overgeneralisations; and that of attending to the need to always ask what is lost in thinking within the confines of the prevailing conceptual framework, in this case competition or global competitiveness. This is, in other words, a question about the current hierarchy of values in multilateral trade relations and its desirability.

Of competition and complementarity

The argument that states should be able to promote innovation and avail themselves of industrial policy before they are able to compete and liberalise trade is, while important, also one that accepts the inevitability of competition as the foundational modality of trade relations. The rejection of the one-size-fits-all model of liberalisation promoted by the WTO thus far is certainly the point of departure for experimenting with new trade practices that do away with the acceptance of the logic of comparative advantage. However, the question is whether competition is the only framework for conceptualising multilateral trade relations. It is clear that the intellectual and analytical apparatus upon which this framework relies for explaining international economic relations is premised on a zero sum, competitive model that cannot deliver well-being for all. In order to develop one has to climb a ladder; to trade one has to become competitive; and to grow one has to constantly accumulate. However, not all countries can specialise in high value-added goods and services: the current international division of labour presupposes that there will always be countries producing low(er) value-added products.

To be sure, the competitive advantage theory put forward by Shaikh acknowledges that international trade cannot benefit all countries: this is indeed the consequence of taking competition as a driving force of capitalist relations seriously (Shaikh, 2007). Accepting competition as the only possible trade strategy, however, does little to challenge the current international division of labour. Put crudely, it means accepting as inevitable that while states might change their position on the development ladder, the ladder itself will remain in place. Now, thinking of challenging a principle that is so integral to capitalist relations might be seen as utopian, the likely objection being that unless such relations are radically transformed, competition will continue to inform multilateral trade practices. However, problematising the primacy of competition is important from a normative as well as a positive angle: that is, because accepting it means also accepting that there will always been countries left at the bottom of the development ladder; and, equally important, because competition is not the only value actually and potentially underpinning trade relations. To illustrate both points, I will go back to Smith's *Wealth of Nations* as his reflections on the relationship between competition, trade and development, together with those on human and social interaction that he articulated in *The Theory of Moral Sentiments*, provide a fruitful terrain for interrogating the inevitability and desirability of competition in trading arrangements and economic relations more generally.

As Arrighi (2009:43) has pointed out, although Smith conceived of competitiveness mainly in terms of price competition between firms, his position on economic development and the role of the state is much more complex and nuanced than one would get from his often cited argument that the state should intervene in the economy by removing barriers to domestic competition. Arrighi writes (2009:43):

> [f]ar from theorizing a self-regulating market that would work best with a minimalist state or with no state at all, *The Wealth of Nations*, no less than the *Theory of Moral Sentiments* and the unpublished *Lectures on Jurisprudence*, presupposed the existence of a strong state that would create and reproduce the conditions for the existence of the market; that would use the market as an effective instrument of government; that would regulate its operation; and that would actively intervene to correct or counter its socially or politically undesirable outcomes.

Indeed, as seen in Chapter 2, *Wealth of Nations* can be read as presenting policymakers and legislators with a model for actively shaping the economic system it appeared simply to describe. Arrighi's focus, however, is on the significance of the argument Smith makes about the 'unnatural' path that European powers had followed in developing principally through the means of foreign trade. The 'natural' path for Smith consisted instead of organic linkages between agriculture and industry, links that had to be actively cultivated, with trade entering the picture and increasing the size of the market only once these linkages had been consolidated so as to provide subsistence for the entire population.[15] The interesting point for Arrighi is Smith's idea that, regardless of the path followed, there would be a point for all states when the intensification of competition would lead to the reduction of the rate of profits and therefore to the achievement of a 'stationary state'. This is, for instance, what Smith thought had occurred to late imperial China (Arrighi, 2009:69). Although it is not clear to what extent he believed that states' intervention could help overcome this barrier, the speculation was that endless growth and capital accumulation would sooner or later be called into question. In different registers this point is also raised by Marx and Keynes: Marx (1973:334) by arguing that competition on a global scale would eventually challenge the ability of capital to overcome barriers to its accumulation; and Keynes by prefiguring 'a world in which, when investment had been kept at the full employment level for thirty years or so, all needs for capital installations would have been met, property income would have been abolished, poverty would have disappeared and civilised life could begin' (Robinson, 1972).

Smith's reflections on the 'stationary state' are for Arrighi one of the most promising aspects of *Wealth of Nations* for they present current policymakers with the possibility of rethinking the model of 'growth, development and trade' pursued so far (2009:386). While I share Arrighi's view about the undesirability of such a 'model', I am less persuaded that its unsustainability can be based on the realisation that sooner or later competition will reach its limits and growth and accumulation will consequently be overcome. This is the critique that Federici (2004) has levelled on Marx in *Caliban and the Witch*, by showing how capital, in its pursuit of self-valorisation, relies on the constant remaking of separations that both divide and unite in order to extract value. The 'stationary state', in this sense, is no more a reality than the state of equilibrium or the balance of trade, while competition, as we can see in the discourse about global competitiveness, is very much alive. This is the case even as we recognise how problematic the international division of labour which is supposed to undergird competition is, particularly once we start questioning 'the capacity of borders to circumscribe homogeneous economic spaces'.[16]

On what other basis can the hold of competition be challenged then? Smith's work is also relevant for interrogating competition from a positive angle, that is, from a perspective that questions its role as the only, or even most desirable, lens for looking at social and economic relations. Indeed, scholars have increasingly made the case that Smith's thinking about the multi-dimensional character of human interaction, which emerges from his oeuvre, has been subject to economic reductionism particularly by those who have sought to rely on his work to either confirm or deny intellectual validity to free trade theory.[17] These more recent interpretations of Smith's work have drawn our attention to the complex relationship between *The Theory of Moral Sentiments* and *Wealth of Nations* with respect to Smith's account of the many 'passions and interests' populating social relations. They have, for instance, pointed to the fact that his notion of 'sympathy', that is the ability to place ourselves in the situation of other people which he considered the source of all sentiments informing human activity, cannot be easily reconciled with accounts about the primacy of self-interest.[18] The problem, Hirschman (1997:112) has argued, is that scholarly and policy debates after Smith have reduced his complex thinking to the proposition that 'the general (material) welfare is best served by letting each member of society pursue his own (material) self-interest'. We can certainly appreciate how this move has enabled competition to acquire primacy as the norm guaranteeing an efficient market: at both the domestic and international level the destructive force of competition could be moved out of sight, but in actual fact accepted, because of a belief in an 'invisible hand' able to bring harmony to chaos.[19] The question as to what the consequences of competition would be in the absence of such a 'benevolent' force could thus be ignored. And yet, as Shaikh's argument about competitive advantage points out, the absence of equilibrating mechanisms is what trade reality constantly shows, for instance, through the trade imbalances that states continuously experience contrary to what standard free trade theory posits.

But there is something else to ponder on if we are to understand how competition continues to exert its force, besides dispelling the myth of natural or equilibrating mechanisms on which subsequent economic analyses have relied to justify and entrench particular economic relations, and however reductive the reliance on Smith's work has been for establishing the central relevance of these mechanisms. For Hirschman the problem is that after Smith 'the field of inquiry over which social thought had ranged freely up to then' (1997:112), and which had looked at the complex interplay between the various sentiments animating social interaction, has been considerably narrowed. Now, while it is important to show that the richness of Smith's thought has been reduced to a limited set of propositions by subsequent economic analyses, it is also crucial to acknowledge that the 'social field of enquiry' to which Smith contributed was, as Federici has argued, also the terrain on which a battle for the 'reformation of the body' took place between the sixteenth and seventeenth centuries. This was a battle in which the body was conceived of and made 'productive' in specific ways, with important consequences for how we have come to think of and practice social and economic relations in the world, and in which competition, starting with that between mind and body, figures prominently. Thus, at the same time as we come to appreciate how in Smith's thinking 'self-interest' finds its basis on sympathy-based benevolence, making it just one of the many sentiments informing social and economic interaction, it is important that we recognise how his *Impartial Spectator*, he who is able to separate out, judge and act upon all sentiments, remains a crucial mechanism through which separations are constantly enacted in order to extract value.[20]

Paying attention to the constant remaking of these separations and the redrawing of their boundaries may give us a better appreciation of how competition draws renewed strength while also enabling us to remain attentive to all the other 'sentiments' and practices that animate social and economic interaction and that get obfuscated through an exclusive emphasis on competition. Focusing on the two simultaneously, as I argued in Chapter 2, remains the crucial challenge. Again, this is not to detract from the important consequences of the economic reductionism after Smith that scholars like Hirschman, Arrighi and Offer point to. We can see, for instance, how, thanks to the 'splendid generalisation' Hirschman talks about, the market has gradually come to be presented as an institution founded on impersonal relations of exchange based on equivalence and characterised exclusively by self-interested behaviour. Thus, during the 1976 Mont Pelerin Society's celebration of the bicentenary of *Wealth of Nations*, Coase (1976:544) could argue that:

> The great advantage of the market is that it is able to use the strength of self-interest to offset the weakness and partiality of benevolence ... [which] should not lead us to ignore the part which benevolence and moral sentiments do play in making possible a market system. Consider, for example, the care and training of the young, largely carried out within the family and sustained by parental devotion. If love were absent and the task of training the young was therefore placed on other institutions, run presumably by people following own self-interest, it seems likely that this task, on which the successful working of human societies depends, would be worse performed.

However, economic reductionism alone cannot explain how and why such a separation gets created, naturalising a split between a non-market economy characterised by 'moral sentiments' and personal relationships, on the one hand, and a market economy characterised by self-interest and impersonal relations, on the other. The fact that the realm of non-market, private relations coincides with that of reproduction, which for the most part remains unpaid despite providing the very conditions for production, is not a coincidence. It is only by focusing on the work that this separation does that we can see how certain activities (and bodies) get 'devalued' at exactly the same time as they are celebrated, all the while enabling the production of more value. Acknowledging how these separations and divisions continue to be produced is the precondition for challenging them, and indeed much work has already been done in troubling their boundaries.

Feminist economists, for instance, have rejected the presumption that mainstream economics makes about beings who come onstage fully formed before the social relations that constitute them, and have shown how these relations have very few neutral, impersonal and law-like characteristics. Some have argued for the need to adopt a 'social provisioning approach' to the study of economics as an alternative methodology that looks at production and reproduction together (Power, 2004; Picchio, 1992; Beneria, 2007; Folbre and Nelson, 2000). From this perspective, economic analysis encompasses both the paid and unpaid economy and brings to light the fact that the question of the economy is always already a question of how we organise social provisioning, our living together, and that this is informed by a myriad of values, beliefs and practices that exceed those recognised by mainstream economics (ie self-interest, competition, profit maximisation). Similarly, relational economic sociologists have shown how economics has neglected the social context within which economic transactions take place. Granovetter (1990:100), for instance, has insisted on the fact that 'the economic action of individuals as well as larger economic patterns, like the determination of prices and economic institutions, are very importantly affected by networks of social relationships' (see also

Granovetter, 1999). Pushing the boundaries between the social and the economic further, Zelizer (2011:5) has argued that once we accept that all economic transactions are social interactions, 'the search is on for a better theory of social process to account for economic activity' to show how 'in all areas of economic life people are creating, maintaining, symbolizing, and transforming meaningful social relations' (see also Zelizer, 1994, 2005, 2010).

We can see how, by tracing and unpacking the complexity of social relations, such approaches bring to light the numerous exceptions to the competition rule. Beneria (2007:20), for instance, has explored the various 'passions and interests' that motivate people to engage in creative and/or in poorly remunerated work: 'Volunteer work, such as that carried out at the community level, might be motivated by a sense of collective well-being, empathy for others, or political commitment; and artistic work is often associated with the pursuit of beauty and creativity, irrespective of its market value'. Levin (1995) has argued that investment decisions are always socially and emotionally constituted and, in her extensive work on American Trade Associations, Spillman (2012) has shown how reasons other than profit maximisation play a role in strategic decisions. The objection that can be made is that, whereas it is easier to appreciate the importance of such work in the realm of interpersonal transactions, it is much more difficult to discern its relevance in the case of impersonal markets characterised by standardised production such as those with which multilateral trade is concerned. However, as Offer (2012:5) remarks:

> Even within [impersonal] markets, a good deal of exchange involves interpersonal interaction, e.g. in marketing, hospitality, and personal services. The share of services has come to dominate output in western developed societies, and services typically require interpersonal interactions and trust. Teachers, doctors, lawyers, waiters, hairdressers, salespeople and financial managers too, all owe the client a duty of care.

But in fact even the privileging of the services sphere as the domain 'proper' of personal relations in the context of standardised production needs unpacking, as mass manufacturing can only be constructed as the domain of impersonal relations once we abstract from the social relations that enable its production.

What does this all mean in the context of the discussion on multilateral trade carried out so far? First, that it is through the rearrangement of boundaries, whether drawn conceptually or through the use of force, that competition fuelled growth and accumulation gains continuous strength. However, recognising the hold that competition has at the level of free trade history, practices and institutions, does not mean that it is the sole belief and practice informing trade relations. The point is that of allowing other values and practices, actually existing or not, to inform trade practices at the same time as we trouble the ways in which boundaries are drawn for the extraction of more value. More generally, however, what this all points to is the fact that trade is only one part of a larger question about how to format the economy–society nexus, and this implies considering it together with the issue of production starting with the question of what to produce and how, which is inextricably connected with the question of the organisation of labour and finance. These questions involve a rethinking of the model of 'growth, development and trade' pursued so far and this rethinking is crucial if the policy autonomy that countries claim to be struggling for, within and beyond the WTO, is to translate into a project that, as Arrighi (2009:386) writes, rejects the 'Western success along the extroverted, Industrial Revolution path [which] was based upon the exclusion of the vast majority of the world's population from access to the natural and human resources needed to benefit rather than bear the costs of global industrialisation'. This is not an easy task, and certainly the line of enquiry suggested here is not meant to provide a concrete agenda. However, I conclude by reflecting on the potential of another experiment going on in South America aimed at affecting the 'productive matrix' of the region.

Conclusion

ALBA is a trade agreement launched in 2004, currently comprising of 11 members and built on the normative principles of complementarity, solidarity, cooperation, reciprocity and sustainability. Complementarity is loosely defined as 'the commitment to identify and develop joint projects that permit the integration and/or synergies of the capacities in accordance with their potentialities and interests'. This is the 'recognition of the fact that each member ... has its own unique economic, social, and cultural strengths' (Muhr, 2010:20) on which to build common projects (see also Burges, 2007; Costoya, 2011). Therefore, ALBA provides a framework for governments to negotiate exchanges of goods and services in ways that reflect their respective strengths. For instance, Venezuela and Cuba exchange oil for doctors and teachers; have several projects concerning the production of soy beans, rice, poultry and dairy products as well as steel and nickel; and are supporting Bolivia in its attempt to expand its natural gas industry in exchange for natural gas, mining, agriculture, agroindustrial and industrial products and indigenous knowledge and medicine.

Exchange is still crucial here: however, at issue is the potential of thinking of something other than the equivalence-based exchange that abstracts from the concrete and unique quality of goods, services, relations and aspirations of states. ALBA is committed to a strategy that is designed to enhance the ability of participating governments to improve the well-being of the majority of the population, with this being the ultimate aim of the alliance (see Hart-Landsberg, 2009). This is in contrast, for instance, to the East Asian strategy which is structured by 'profit-making transnational corporations that have competitively linked economic activity across nations to form a regional production system aimed at exporting goods outside the region' (Hart-Landsberg, 2009:5). And it certainly departs from the WTO privileging of 'non-discrimination' and 'equal treatment' in trade relations.

As with the RMA and Ecuador's Plan, there are numerous limitations to ALBA that I do not go into here, including the fact that it continues to rely on extractive industries to fund its activities, with the increasingly problematic relationship with indigenous communities and organisations; and the fact that the whole strategy is very much based on state-centred collaboration with small input from the Council for Social Movements, despite the latter's formal inclusion in ALBA's governance structure.[21] Moreover, if we take seriously Mezzadra and Neilson's argument about the complex articulation of capital frontiers and territorial borders (2013a:241–242), ALBA may appear as an anachronistic arrangement in that it holds on to an idea of the state as the primary actor of economic activity. Yet, I think it is problematic to reduce it to an attempt to 'invert' current trends so to 'shift back' to a system of command and control of the economy where the state knows it all. On the contrary, ALBA can be understood as an experiment that aims to intervene in, rather than reverse, current trends. In the last three decades in particular, regional and multilateral trade and investment frameworks have put forward a specific understanding of the role of states in trade and investment activity that has become almost unchallengeable. As Backer and Molina (2009–2010:747) point out, states' participation in market activities is accepted as legitimate only when they conceive of themselves, and act, as 'idealised private investors'; and, when they come to the market through publicly owned enterprises, they are supposed to insulate the management of the company from their political control while at the same time 'private actors are supposed to exercise no significant political power'. ALBA, on the other hand, presents a different model, one 'grounded in the political use of economic power. More specifically, it represents an attempt to conflate the economic and political at the state level' thereby challenging the current model of private markets-based globalisation (2009–2010:748).

What this challenge, assuming it materialises, can result into is an open question and one that, as Backer and Molina write, is inextricably linked to the issue of the borders within which complementarity and cooperation are supposed to apply. It is not so much, as they put it in relation to the trade with non-members, that 'borders, even the borders of trade and investment arrangements, include those within ... and exclude those outside' (2009–2010: 750). Borders are constitutive of the very internal 'reality' they seem to both circumscribe and insulate from. Rather than whom and what ALBA's borders are excluding, the more interesting question concerns the reality they are constituting: in Mezzadra and Neilson's words, it is 'the quality of the social relations that are constituted and reproduced by and through borders that matters' (2013a:279).

In this respect, ALBA has arguably opened up a conceptual space for thinking of and practising economic relations differently, and not only at the intergovernmental level. Like the RMA examined in the previous section, it has raised the question of what production – and not only trade and investment, or finance for that matter – should be for, which has to do with the kind of economy–society nexus to be formatted. As an experiment, its potential rests on the fact that, while acknowledging the power that competition exerts on economic relations, it questions it from both a positive and a normative angle, thereby seeking directly to affect the hierarchy of values that informs such relations. What quality of social relations this conceptual space can and will enable remains to be seen, but this concern is different from that about ALBA's marginal role and unrealistic contribution. It speaks of the need to interrogate the *differential inclusion* that any arrangement and formatting necessarily entails, that is of the 'varying degrees of subordination, rule, discrimination, and segmentation' to which inclusion in any realm, including trade, can be subject (Mezzadra and Neilson, 2013a:159); as well as the *perspectival seeing* from which differential inclusions are enacted and to which it contributes. At the same time, this is the potential of any institutional arrangement that, conceived of as a provocation, seeks to format the economy–society nexus differently, aware of the fact that the reality produced will be very different from that envisaged through the intervention.

Notes

1 Latour and Lepinay (2009) have argued that the problem with current understandings of political economy is the fact that the nexus between economy and society has been obfuscated because of a belief in an economic order governed by natural laws that exist 'out there' and that society is supposed to discover and implement. While this 'belief' characterises most neoclassical approaches to the economy, I have argued that it is reductive to attribute it to Marx's thinking on value, and even to Smith's.

2 MacKenzie shows how, despite being developed separately, the four

tenets of modern finance (the efficient market hypothesis, the relationship between risk and return based on the Capital Asset Pricing Model,
the Modigliani-Miller theorems positing the irrelevance of capital
structure and the Black-Scholes-Merton approach to option pricing)
achieve their conceptual unity around the end of the 1970s and the
beginning of the 1980s (2008:38–67).

3 In 1994 Orange County went bankrupt when US$1.6 billion was
lost due to investments in derivatives by one man; the same account
was given with regard to the 1995 failure of the 233-year-old Baring
Banks, when US$27 billion was lost in derivative bets on the Japanese
Nikkei by one 'rogue trader', Nick Leeson; again, the miscalculation of
risks emerged during the Asian Financial crisis of 1997; in 1999 with
the collapse of Long Term Capital Management; and in 2008 when
Bear Stearns went bankrupt.

4 As mentioned in Chapter 2, financialisation cannot be understood
simply as the 'the increasing role of financial motives, financial markets, financial actors and financial institutions' (Epstein, 2005:3)
but needs to be appreciated in light of the restructuring of the
production–reproduction nexus that it entails and that sees credit as
the starting point for the reproduction of labour power and general economic calculus and enterprise as the organising principles of household
'management' (Bryan, Martin and Rafferty, 2009; Allon, 2011, 2015).

5 This research was supported by funding from the British Academy
(grant number SG090138) and conducted in Quito, Ecuador in 2010. I
wish to thank Pedro Paez (former President of the Ecuadorian Technical
Commission for a New Regional Financial Architecture) and Maria
Elsa Viteri (former Finance Minister), for being extremely generous
with their time and expertise.

6 This was, for instance, the thrust of the US financial bill passed on 15
July 2010 which includes the establishment of a Consumer Financial
Protection Agency, the obligation for most OTC derivatives to be
traded on exchanges and the obligation for deposit-taking banks not
to buy or sell financial products for their 'trading accounts' (Dodd-
Frank Wall Street Reform and Consumer Protection Act 2010). This
is also at the basis of proposals by the European Commission requir-
ing more transparency on short-selling and restrictions on so-called
'naked shorting' – the practice of buying or selling derivatives without
owning the underlying asset (Moya, 2010).

7 Ecuador adopted the US dollar in 2000. The RMA, however, was one
of the three components of the proposal for a Crisis Response Agenda
from the South. The others are the Bank of the South and the new
intra-regional currency, the Unified System for Regional Compensation
(SUCRE), which will replace the dollar for intra-regional trade.

8 Pedro Paez, conversation with author, Quito, 23 March 2010.

9 An instance of this tension can be seen at the intersection between the passage of the 2009 Organic Law on Food Sovereignty (Asamblea Nacional, 2009) meant to create access to land and means of production as well as prioritise financing mechanisms for small and medium producers; the extension of social security to all persons meant to give effect to the recognition that all beings are productive; and, as put to me by Finance Minister Viteri, the *need* to still rely on the extractivist sector, albeit in a more sustainable way, so as to accomplish these objectives and facilitate the transition towards an economy less reliant on petroleum (Maria Elsa Viteri, conversation with the author, Quito, 29 March 2010).

10 I am not going to dwell on how contested the concept and meaning of 'development' is. I have elsewhere focused on the way in which development has operated like a scientific discourse within the multilateral trading system since decolonisation (Alessandrini, 2010; see also Escobar, 1995). I consider development to be a very fraught concept meaning different things to different people in different parts of the world: see Chimni (2006). I use 'development' here to refer to the struggles over 'well-being' broadly conceived, including the attempts states make to improve that of their populations.

11 National Treatment and Most Favoured Nation are the legal provisions through which 'non-discrimination' and 'equal treatment' have been applied to multilateral trade relations since the post-war period, although in different forms they could be found in bilateral trade treaties well before the entry into force of the GATT. They require states not to discriminate against and between foreign 'like' products, services, services providers and IPRs.

12 For an overview of the classical and neo-classical theories of free trade, see Trebilcock, Howse and Eliason (2012:1–16).

13 This is particularly the case of Brazil. For a list of studies conducted to date by LANDS scholars, see Trubek et al. (2014).

14 For instance, the World Economic Forum defines it 'as the set of institutions, policies, and factors that determine the level of productivity of a country. The level of productivity, in turn, sets the sustainable level of prosperity that can be earned by an economy. In other words, more competitive economies tend to be able to produce higher levels of income for their citizens. The productivity level also determines the rates of return obtained by investments in an economy. Because the rates of return are the fundamental drivers of the growth rates of the economy, a more competitive economy is one that is likely to grow faster over the medium to long run.' While for the Institute of Management Development 'Competitiveness of Nations is a field of

economic theory which analyses the facts and policies that shape the ability of a nation to create and maintain an environment that sustains more value creation for its enterprises and more prosperity for its people' (Green, Mostafa and Preston, 2010:4).

15 Indeed, the purpose of Smith's political economy was as much 'to supply the state ... with a revenue sufficient for the public services', as it was 'to provide a plentiful ... subsistence for the people, or more properly to enable them to provide such a ... subsistence for themselves' (Smith, 1776:43).

16 In one of the most compelling critiques of the new international division of labour, Mezzadra and Neilson (2013a:84) have argued that its major shortcoming is that it remains 'primarily a theory of capital mobility, rather that a theory of how labour divisions, process, mobilities and struggles relate to the transitions of capitalism under pervasive financialisation and the accompanying deep heterogenization of global space'. The heterogenisation of labour and proliferation of boundaries they meticulously map 'cut across the map of the world', destabilising the very possibility of thinking alongside North/South, developed/developing, core/periphery divides. By making this point they do not claim that the concept has become redundant but that it 'is no longer able to organise a stable fabric of the world or possesses an ontological consistency and force sufficient to undergird an act of *fabrica mundi*'. While I am not convinced it was ever able to do so, I appreciate that their effort is to emphasise the more fragmented character of the dis/connections between capital and states: 'Obviously', they write, 'we do not live in a smooth world where geography no longer matters and the gap between capital's command (and frontiers) and political sovereignty (and borders) is vanishing. This gap continues to exist but is articulated within shifting assemblages of territory and power, which operate according to a logic that is much more fragmented and elusive than it was in a classic age of the nation state' (2013a: 85).

17 Polanyi, for instance, has argued that because Smith posited 'human propensity to barter, track and exchange one thing for another' as the fundamental norm among others, for instance, reciprocity and redistribution, competition has acquired primacy in political economic analyses. See Beneria (2007:14).

18 'What are the advantages which we propose by that great purpose of human life which we call bettering our condition? To be observed, to be attended to, to be taken notice of with sympathy, complacency, and approbation, *are all* the advantages which we can propose to derive from it' (Smith, 1759, in Offer, 2012:3).

19 Even though, as Offer has argued, Smith only mentions the 'invisible hand' once.

20 In a different register from that of the *Impartial Spectator*, we can also
see how, by taking the willful wage labourer as the representative or
standard worker in capitalism, the multiplicity of labour figures with
which *he* was connected could be displaced from sight (Mezzadra and
Neilson, 2013a:85).

21 Indeed, in 2008, social movements which had become dissatisfied with
the Council started another process, the Social Movement Articulation
towards ALBA, which runs parallel to the Council. While supporting
the latter, the articulation aims to 'build a wider space of integration
of hemispherical popular sectors', and a space that is meant to be
'coordinated in a more autonomous way'. See Bacallao-Pino (2014:93).

Chapter 4

Re/production as the nexus: of (non)wage labour and alternative valorisations

[W]hile the future is unmade, it is *being* made. Various plans and projects, many of them conflicting, shape material life over time. Institutions change, and can be changed because those institutions are being remade by people's participation in them and use of them. This does not mean that the future is entirely open or random: at this moment many, many people are busily working to shape it. But neither is it determined or closed; if that were the case, it would not require such effort to construct.

(Danby, 2004:60)

... when we struggle for a wage we do not struggle to enter capitalist relations, because we have never been out of them. We struggle to break capital's plan for women, which is an essential moment of that division of labour and social power ... to demand wages for housework does not mean to say that if we are paid we will continue to do this work. It means precisely the opposite. To say that we want wages for housework is the first step towards refusing to do it, because the demand for a wage makes our work visible, which is the most indispensable condition to begin to struggle against it, both in its immediate aspect as housework and its more insidious character as femininity.

(Federici, 2012:15–19)

The arrangement I consider in this chapter is perhaps the most controversial. Although I have hinted at the fact that I look at institutional arrangements as provocations rather than blueprints for action, I have not explained why I have only considered institutional and not also other kinds of arrangements. This chapter gives me the opportunity to clarify how I see the relation between the two by going back to the work of 'Wages for/against Housework' scholars. This is the tradition that, as mentioned in Chapters 1 and 2, has critically interrogated Marx's labour theory of value by paying specific attention to the role of social reproduction. I draw on this scholarship again for two reasons: first, because it offers important resources for thinking about the links between gender, labour and value in today's post-Fordist economies, exactly at a time when these links appear to have become more tenuous; and, second, because it provides the opportunity to interrogate the sort of arrangements that might be able to affect these links, thereby shifting current value making processes, in the contested realm of wage labour.

The context of this exploration is provided by the recent engagement of some feminist economists with a proposal put forward by post-Keynesian scholars. This proposal demands that the government acts at once as the ELR and a social provider, particularly of care. I ask why and how such a proposal appeals to feminist economists who have long argued for the inclusion of social reproduction within the general analytical framework of political economy; and explore what I think is a crucial concern, that is, that by participating in institutional programmes such as this one we might end up sustaining, rather than undoing, the very relations we seek to challenge. It is with this concern in mind that I go back to the work of 'Wages for/against Housework' scholars who have argued not only against the wage society but also the welfare state; my focus is on how to make sense of an institutional arrangement such as the ELR in light of this tradition of feminist work which has instead highlighted the importance of self-valorisation processes. Rather than setting these two different moments of feminist struggle in opposition to one another, however, I intend to reflect on what is at stake for both, and this, I would argue, is the promotion of arrangements able to 'provoke' alternative valorisation processes, whether institutional or otherwise.

Social provisioning and the employer of last resort

The collaboration between post-Keynesian and feminist economists is a recent phenomenon. Although potential links between the two schools have been identified and discussed since the early 1990s, collaborative projects have largely remained negligible (Danby, 2004:55). As a symposium on post-Keynesian and feminist economics has highlighted (van Stavaren and Danby, 2010), this is due, among other things, to the tendency by post-Keynesian scholars to exclude from the terrain of economic enquiry non-monetised activities and production. This has meant that the separation between the productive and reproductive spheres feminists have long problematised has remained unchallenged. However, a post-Keynesian proposal for the state to become a permanent guarantor of jobs has more recently attracted the attention of feminist economists. Before exploring the reasons for its appeal, I describe briefly the proposal and its main tenets.

Although the idea goes back to the seventeenth century, its revival and further elaboration within the framework advocated by Keynes for the socialisation of investment can be attributed to Minsky, who started working on it in the 1960s. In *Stabilizing an Unstable Economy* (1986) he put forward its main proposition, that is, that the ELR would create 'an infinitely elastic demand for labour at a floor or minimum wage that does not depend upon long- and short-run profit expectations of business. Since only government can divorce the offering of employment from the profitability of hiring workers, the infinitely elastic demand for labour must be created by government' (1986:308). Several other economists have since contributed to its refinement (Vickrey, 1993; Mitchell and Watts, 1997; Wray, 1998; Forstater, 1999; Majewski, 2004).

The central tenet of the programme is that the government becomes a *permanent* guarantor of jobs for anyone able and willing to work for a socially established wage. Although permanent in time, the programme is meant to change in size so that it expands in periods of recession to absorb workers who have been made redundant and contracts as the economy recovers and the private sector is able to hire more workers. Thus, the first feature of the programme is that it operates as a buffer stock employment mechanism (Minsky, 1986; Wray, 1998). Post-Keynesian economists point to the fact that, when jobs are guaranteed, uncertainty and precariousness are reduced for people while firms' expectations of effective demand become more stable. Second, it sets the 'floor' price of labour and thus ensures price stability since private sectors jobs are provided at a mark-up over the ELR fixed wage (Kaboub, 2007:11). Third, by providing continuous training to displaced workers, the programme is expected to contribute to the appreciation of skills that unemployment drastically interrupts and furnishes the private sector with a constant pool of skilled workers. In order to provide job training in the most effective way, ELR promoters argue that there should be planning in cooperation with union leaders and business so as to identify structural changes in the economy and provide a 'systematic preventive program to minimise the damage caused by [structural and technological change] STC' (Kaboub, 2007:13–14). Thus, leading to the fourth feature, the relationship with the private sector is one of cooperation rather than competition. As Wray (1998) points out, the programme is supposed to focus on activities that are either undersupplied or not supplied at all by the private sector, usually because they are not profitable when pecuniary considerations are the major determining factor.

Overall, by having in place a system that guarantees an infinitely elastic demand for labour at a socially determined wage that does not depend on profit expectations (Minsky, 1986:343), and therefore on the pecuniary valuation of investment, the programme comes very close to the socialisation of investment as advocated by Keynes since full employment is guaranteed irrespective of the level of demand. However, post-Keynesian scholars emphasise that the proposal departs from post-war Keynesian policies, which aimed to guarantee full employment at times of crisis by promoting government spending in *some* activities. As Wray (2007:17) points out, these policies often resulted in '"hiring off the top", largely stimulating spending on output from the more advanced sectors – taking the most technically proficient workers away from other work, and hoping that some jobs might trickle down to the least skilled workers'. This interpretation of Keynes' theory was, as Joan Robinson has trenchantly argued, highly problematic.

As Robinson highlights, the pressing issue for Keynes was to demonstrate that it is 'the process of investment, not its fruits, that matters' (Robinson, 1960:90–91). Keynes' point about investment was that it generates effective demand and therefore employment. In a capitalist system where employment is the means through which workers secure access to income and therefore subsistence, a premise which he never challenged, Keynes believed that it is the responsibility of the government to ensure full employment conditions; but he never wanted employment to be reduced to the act of digging and filling holes (Robinson, 1972:6). Starting from the same premise, Robinson's argument was that, once the idea that it is the responsibility of governments to create conditions of full employment became the new orthodoxy, the focus should have shifted from the level to the content of employment (1972:6) and the question should have become: what is employment for? As she puts it: 'the fruit of investment becomes more important than the process of investment and "digging holes" or building battleships is seen in its true light as an onerous burden in the community, not as a source of wealth. If resources were not used for these dismal purposes, they could be used for something useful or pleasant' (Robinson, 1960:91).

The problem is that the focus post-Keynes never changed and Keynesian orthodoxy became a case for government spending 'on something or other – no matter what' (Robinson, 1972:6). In this way the military industrial complex took off and became the favourite beneficiary of successive budget deficits. While countries, especially those which did not waste resources on arms but 'put all their investment into productive forms', experienced a great increase in economic wealth, she warned against the faith in growth as such, pointing to the fact that 'not only subjective poverty is never overcome by growth but [also that] absolute poverty is increased by it' (1972:7). She was therefore critical of an economic system that promotes accumulation of wealth per se regardless of the social and environmental costs associated with it, save 'a few minor points discussed under the heading of "externalities" that could easily be put right' (1972:7).

The ELR purports to be a different programme in that it focuses on those sectors left out because pecuniary considerations are the determining factor in investment decisions – one needs only to think about low income households.[1] It intervenes when private demand is insufficient to employ all resources and is supposed to do so by hiring workers 'at the bottom'. Their spending is in turn supposed to stimulate demand, production and therefore private employment, with some of the jobs filled by drawing on the ELR workers' pool. The programme would therefore stop increasing aggregate demand as soon as full employment was achieved. This aspect has allowed post-Keynesian economists to respond to arguments about the rise of inflation the programme might cause, as well as its costs and therefore sustainability. In relation to the threat of inflation, for instance, the concern is that by 'enforcing' a living wage there will be a push-up for all wages. However, Kaboub has argued that this is likely to result in a one-off (and desirable) wage increase followed by a one-off profit reduction rather than generating an inflationary spiral (Kaboub, 2007:14). Referring to available estimates he argues that the costs of financing such a programme relative to GDP size are too small to generate inflation (Kaboub, 2007:14) and this directly relates to the issue of sustainability of such a programme. Several studies have shown that its contribution to budget deficits and national debt is not going to be an obstacle to its implementation: for instance, in the US, UK and Australia, costs for financing ELR would range between less than 1% to 3.5% of GDP (Mitchell and Watts, 1997; Gordon, 1997; Majeswski, 2004). Thus the programme would certainly add to the annual deficit and national debt but, as Todorova argues, these levels 'are accounting indications of the private sector's desire to net save and do not represent financial burden on the government' (Todorova, 2009:6). Relying on the principle of functional finance developed by Lerner, ELR promoters argue that it is the function of the deficit or national debt rather than its size that matters and the reason is that:

> the logic of government finance is totally different from that of the households or firms ... tax payments do not and cannot finance government spending; for, at the aggregate level, only the government can be the 'net' supplier of fiat money. As a result, the starting point is government expenditure. Once government spends (creates or supplies) fiat money to purchase goods and services, it provides the private sectors with the necessary amount of money to meet tax liabilities, save, and maintain transaction balances. The government can safely run a deficit up to the point where it has provided the quantity of non-interest-earning fiat money and interest-earning bonds desired by the public.
>
> (Kaboub, 2007:12)

This does not mean that governments do not face financial constraints: as ELR supporters point out, when full employment is achieved, further deficit leads to what Keynes termed 'pure inflation', with higher aggregate demand increasing prices rather than employment or output. Thus, deficits become 'excessive' when aggregate demand is increased beyond the full employment level. However, the design of the ELR programme is such that spending will be counter-cyclical:

> so that if implementation of ELR does boost aggregate demand and cause the economy to grow quickly, ELR spending will automatically fall sharply (even as government tax revenue grows). The 'open-ended promise' to employ those willing to work at the ELR wage *cannot* cause government spending to grow without limit for the simple reason that ELR *cannot* grow without limit; indeed it will *fall* as the economy gathers steam and pulls workers out of ELR.
>
> (Wray, 2007:16, original emphasis)

According to post-Keynesian scholars, therefore, the programme is not only capable of eliminating unemployment, generating decent living-wage jobs across the board and possibly in a socially and environmentally sustainable manner, but it is also 'financially' sustainable. It is a matter of shifting register from the 'sound finance' to the 'functional finance' approach that moves beyond notions of scarcity, implicit in the often heard claims about the 'imperative' of deficit reduction, and inevitability of trade-offs, such as that between employment and inflation.

However, rather than enquiring further into post-Keynesians' claims about the sustainability of the programme, my interest lies in exploring the question of why and how it appeals to feminist economists. One obvious reason is that it moves the debate about how to organise social provisioning away from attempts to allocate unemployed workers among scarcely available jobs and also welfare programmes based on the punitive means-tested approach to securing income (Todorova, 2009:13), hence providing an opportunity to start thinking about Robinson's question of what kind of employment and investment we should be promoting. In this respect the programme comes close to the so-called social provisioning approach to the study of economics which has been the methodological starting point of feminist economists.

Although there are a variety of traditions that inform feminist economics (Tong, 1998), a point of agreement is the understanding of economic activities as interdependent social processes. As Power (2004:7) puts it: 'to define economics as the study of social provisioning is to emphasize that at its root, economic activity involves the ways people organize themselves collectively to get a living' and manifestations of such an approach have included analyses of unpaid and caring labour. However, social provisioning does not only concern 'unpaid' and 'caring labour'; nor is it a distinctive 'woman's issue'. At a methodological level, Power continues, 'starting economic analysis from this standpoint illuminates the ways a society organizes itself to produce and reproduce material life ... and the outcome of such a process is social production and reproduction' (2004:7). Thus, the specificity of the social provisioning approach is that it is not an adjunct to economic analysis but its very starting point. It is an approach that emphasises the interconnectedness and mutual constitution of the productive and reproductive spheres contra economic understandings that foster an ever-growing disconnect between the two. From this standpoint, then, we can understand the fascination of feminist economists with the ELR programme because it has the potential for putting at the centre of economic activity the 'planning and implementation of life-supporting and life-enhancing projects' (Todorova, 2009: 9).

How so? By intervening in the job 'design' of the programme. The assumption is that applying such an approach, the ELR could potentially contribute to making a whole range of valuable non-performed, under-performed or unremunerated activities emerge as remunerated 'jobs'. And this process would not only mean incorporating caring labour within the creation of new jobs, however important this aspect is for challenging the distinction between productive (paid) and unproductive (unpaid) care labour.[2] It would also mean including the whole spectrum of activities encompassing the broad terrain on which the reproduction of life is made possible, from child care to health care, from care for the elderly to environmental care, from restoration to engineering, from transport to housing, from manufacture to finance. In other words, applying the social provisioning approach would allow the myriad of activities that sustain our life process to come to light and be 'valued': this is clearly the potential that engaging with such a project offers. However, here also lies the problem: making a whole range of 'hidden vacancies' become visible seems akin to preparing them for marketisation. Indeed, as Antonopoulos argues, the fact that the whole programme remains an institution of wage labour requires us to consider the consequences of supporting such a comprehensive macroeconomic policy (Antonopoulos, 2007:19):

> while the problem of economic instability and depressed effective demand is central across regions subject to capitalist production, we need a consideration of the consequence of adopting any blanket macroeconomic policy that assumes a desire to preserve (or enhance) these very capitalist relations. To the extent that local communities may already engage in other ways of organising their social provisioning (not necessarily based at all on wage work), it is legitimate to ask would ELR be in conflict with these values.

This is a crucial point and one which resonates with the argument 'Wages for/against Housework' scholars made in the 1970s, not only against the wage society, which has made people dependent on wages for their survival while simultaneously denying access to work, but also against the welfare state, which they saw as the protector and guarantor of a social division of labour that promotes cooperation at the point of production and atomisation and separation at the point of reproduction (see Dalla Costa, 1972, 2002; Dalla Costa and James, 1972; Fortunati, 1981; Federici, 2004, 2008). For these reasons, rather than taking up wage labour, they thought it important to think of arrangements able to promote alternative (ie non-capitalist) processes of valorisation. In this respect, the premise from which they were working is very different from Keynes and Robinson's. This, however, did not amount to an outright refusal to engage with both the state and wage labour but, I want to suggest, a very particular way of doing so. Thus, while they insisted on the collectivisation of social reproduction through the creation of self-managed and alternative social services, for instance, in the areas of health, birth control, abortion and the prevention of domestic violence, they also strategically supported the 'Wages for/against Housework' initiative. It is to this particular modality of engagement, this for and against movement and its potential to generate social transformation – a potential which Kathi Weeks captures by referring to the campaign as a *provocation* (Weeks, 2011:131–132) – that I now turn.

Dis/continuities in labour, value and social reproduction

As seen in Chapter 3, this praxis derived from a profound reconceptualisation of political economy which these scholars saw as the nexus between economy and society, two realms which have long been kept separate by a belief in an economic order governed by natural laws that exist 'out there' and that society has to discover and implement, for instance, the law of demand and offer, the law of equilibrium, that of 'sound finance', and even certain interpretations of the law of value.[3] Through their work on reproductive labour in particular, these scholars showed how value is actively made and measured, rather than being objectively determined, under capitalism. Recognising that the way in which capitalist value is produced and determined is a process rather than an imperative meant confronting its contingency and contestability, which in turn opened up the possibility of exploring alternative processes of valorisation. These insights led them to rework the important category of self-valorisation: whereas for Marx it had denoted all that which is involved in the expanded reproduction of capital, they used it to indicate those labour activities which do not simply react to capital but are able to exceed it through creativity and invention (Dalla Costa, 1972). For instance, they engaged with Gabriel Tarde (1902) whose work on value had argued that classical political economy 'was at fault for the omission of affections, and especially of desire, in analyses of valorization' (Fortunati, 2007:142).

Picchio's work in this respect has been crucial. She has shown how, after Smith and Ricardo, the vast spectrum of 'passions and interests' that were the subject of classical political economy has been gradually reduced to one, that is the maximisation of material wealth through exchange and competition. Once these had been posited as the principal means and objective of our economic system, a specific division of labour between production and reproduction was established that serves this purpose (Picchio, 1992, 2009). It is worth reflecting a little longer on how such division of labour takes places, excluding from social analysis other modes of existence and introducing the wage as a central mechanism for regulating social interaction. Picchio's interest in classical political economy derives from her meticulous study of the transformations which by the eighteenth century had radically reshaped the economy–society nexus in England. One such transformation concerns the place and function of reproduction: whereas previously the household produced for the reproduction of its members, the new system used 'the reproduction of the labouring population for the accumulation of capital'. Smith and Ricardo, however, understood capital not only 'physically, as tools or goods, but as a specific historical relationship between the labouring population and its means of reproduction' (Picchio, 1992: 8).[4] They took for granted that this relationship was regulated by certain constraints, such as the imperative for capital to make savings and expand,[5] and acknowledged that this process happened chiefly by reducing the costs of reproduction. However, Picchio argues, they saw these constraints, as well as the consequences deriving from them, as historic and institutional. Thus, the tendency to reduce the costs of reproduction made this relationship a conflictual one and that is why the wage was so central to Smith's and Ricardo's analyses. For both it was 'the outcome of a complex series of social and political forces, embodied in a variety of institutions and expressed through a variety of social norms'; thus, although wages had to be kept 'within the bounds necessary for a viable relationship between social production and accumulation', it was clear to them that they were contingent and the product of struggle (Picchio, 1992:29).

Crucially, Picchio argues, this notion of the wage as the cost of social reproduction is what gets displaced through the work of subsequent thinkers such as Mill, Torrens and McCulloch, who introduce the concept of the 'Wage Fund', that is the idea that wages are determined in the market by the supply and demand of labour. This conception creates an inversion of analytical focus: wages are no longer 'taken as a reflection of the exogenous modes of reproduction, but reproduction – in quantity and standards – [is]

seen as depending on wages determined by the allocation of quantities of capital and population' (1992:56). This inversion provides the foundation of the modern approach to economics and we see it at work when notions of scarcity and economic imperatives or laws are used to justify unemployment and the need to freeze or cut wages. This loss of analytical focus has also had political consequences as the conflict is no longer between wage and profit within the total value produced but between sections of the labouring population within a given fund. In this context, competition emerges as the chief mechanism regulating social interaction, the latter reconceptualised as exchange, while other actually existing desires, passions and interests are removed from the terrain of legitimate economic enquiry. As Picchio (1992:53) points out:

> while the concept of social reproduction and subsistence could easily embody an idea of equality, solidarity and collective cooperation for survival ... competition of large numbers of workers for access to a limited wage fund implies destructive struggles within the labouring population ... This new analytical method expressed a new view of the world. A broad historical and social analysis was replaced by a simplistic mechanical framework in which specific historical processes were homogenised by universal laws, and social conflicts were mystified by theories of technical and natural constraints.

By making the historical relationship between production and reproduction explicit, Picchio's work has aimed to show how the functional link between waged work and housework becomes a general concern rather than being a woman's issue. She acknowledges that women 'are deeply divided by differences of class, nationality, and race as well as by their own individual histories' (1992:114); and these divisions, as the engagement with Federici's work in Chapter 2 has shown, are productive of (capitalist) value. This is a point that scholars who have looked at race as a constitutive aspect of gender analysis have further elaborated, emphasising the radically different experiences of Black women with both paid and unpaid labour (see Hill Collins, 2000). As Bhandar has argued (2013:4), too often:

> The word 'woman' is used as though it applies to all women when it actually represents and signifies the experiences and histories of white women. This means that the experiences of Black women, Asian women (and, in other contexts, indigenous women) are erased or suppressed by the theories and politics of left feminisms. It means that the analyses of political problems that are being presented are partial and incorrect – because (as we know), capitalism has been forged through colonial dispossession, the Atlantic slave-trade, and now, a globalised

form of capitalism that depends on third world labour whose value remains fixed – to some degree – by racism and a persistent belief in white superiority.

The persistence of white superiority is not simply a matter of racism but of a mixture of attributes that are at the same time 'metaphysical, embodied, and affective [and that] shape the very constitution of modern legal-political subjectivities' (Bhandar, 2014:218). Indeed, the concept of the 'human' that emerges from Smith's analysis is a very specific one: as seen in Chapter 2, *he* is the one who is endowed with the ability to barter, track and exchange in order to accumulate; and also able to reflect upon himself, separating good from destructive appetites and passions, in order to act both rationally and sympathetically as the *Impartial Spectator*. This interplay of interiority and exteriority which has been at the heart of Western legal subjectivity since the nineteenth century is also at the basis of what Ferreira da Silva calls the analytics of raciality which allows us 'to see how since the last third of the nineteenth century at least, modern political economic architectures – in Europe and its colonies – have been accompanied by a moral text, in which the principles of universality and historicity also sustain the writing of the "others of Europe" (both a colonial and racial other) as entities facing certain and necessary (self-inflicted) obliteration' (Chakravartty and Ferreira da Silva, 2012:370–371).

That this logic continues to reverberate in current constructions of the proper economic agent is apparent if one looks at the figure of the irresponsible borrower in the US, mostly Black and Latino/a: it is not purely by chance that the US Community Reinvestment Act came to be seen as an important trigger of the 'subprime' mortgage crisis. This is not just a matter of blaming the usual suspects. At stake, Chakravartty and Ferreira da Silva have argued, is the very production of specific persons and places as 'unsuitable economic subjects' (2012:365) in order to create opportunities for value creation and accumulation. 'How could anyone expect to profit from unpayable loans', they ask, 'without debtors who were already marked by their racial/cultural difference ensuring that at least some among them would not be able to pay? This is precisely what makes "high risk securities" profitable.' This is why they argue that what is missing in many progressive accounts of the subprime crisis is the 'consideration of how these "new territories" of consumption and investment have been mapped onto previous racial and colonial (imperial) discourse and practices' (2012:368). The rich special issue they coordinate sees 'the subprime crisis as a "relative" of crises that transformed the political economic horizons of Africa, Asia and Latin America in the 1990s'; and reflects on the 'resonances approximating national and global responses to neoliberalism to profit from calculating "mistakes" (like lending money to persons and nations precisely because they would not be able to pay it back)' (2012:364). Tracing these connections is an important task and one which requires that we pay attention to these dis/continuities, to the modalities, past and present, old and new, that resolve 'moments of economic expropriation into *natural* attributes of the "others" of Europe (2012:364) (emphasis added). In the context of the present day, irresponsible borrowers, for instance, adopting the analytic of raciality on a par with gender and class enables us to see how specific persons can be marked as 'intellectually (illiterate) and morally (greedy) unfit', precisely because they are being measured against the 'descriptors of the modern economic subject: the (liberal) rational self-interested, the (historical-materialist) productive-creative labourer, the (neo-liberal) obligation-bound debtor-creditor' (2012:362).[6]

The need to be attentive to such dis/continuities returns us to the point Picchio makes about the possibility, despite the profound differences in women's experiences, that 'a focus on the specific question of reproduction might well facilitate new alliances' (1992: 114). This is still, I think, a question worth asking: can a focus on reproduction, the wage and alternative valorisation processes be of any analytical and political import today? Can it facilitate political alliances that do not end up universalising the category of 'woman'? It is certainly the case that we need to carefully trace the shifting gender/sexual, racial/ethnic and class articulations that make up the social reproductive sphere and that generate value, many of which present novel analytical and political challenges (see Adkins, 2009; Grabham, 2010; Arvidsson, 2012; Mezzadra and Neilson, 2013a and b; Bryan, Rafferty and Jefferis, 2015). However, this does not mean that the separation between production and reproduction under capitalism has become redundant. The contribution of 'Wages for/against Housework' scholars is significant in this respect: already in the 1970s they had highlighted the enormous pool of unwaged labour that sustains the life process, with the consequent problematisation of both the analytical and political privileging of wage labour. Whereas their initial focus was the situation of women in Fordist economies, particularly Italy and the US, their analyses soon became attentive to the spatial and temporal dis/continuities that made up the global economy and the racial, gender, sexual and class articulations of the social reproductive field within it. Federici's work in particular has insisted on the connections between the struggle of Black women in the US (the 'welfare mothers'), the youth movement and the anticolonial struggles, on the one hand; and the consequent reorganisation of socially reproductive labour on a global scale, on the other.

While producing different effects in different parts of the world, this reorganisation has relied on 'the state's disinvestment in the process of social reproduction', which has taken place through structural adjustment programmes, the dismantling of the welfare state (Federici, 2012:87,

101), the ascendancy of debt, and, more recently, through austerity measures. This has created a different situation from that analysed in the 1970s: as Federici points out, 'a shift has occurred in the temporal fix between reproduction and accumulation. As subsidies to healthcare, education, pensions, and public transport have all been cut, as high fees have been placed upon them, and workers have been forced to take on the cost of their reproduction, every articulation of the reproduction of labour power has been turned into an immediate point of accumulation' (2012:102). It is interesting, for instance, that the value of housework seems increasingly intertwined with, as it is being measured by, complex financial instruments (Adkins and Dever, 2014; Bryan, Rafferty and Jefferis, 2015). While it is important that we trace the connections between these processes of measurement and the social relations within and beyond the household – to understand in what way exactly these mechanisms are affecting the relationships they claim to be measuring – the work of 'Wages for/against Housework' scholars remains relevant in two respects. First, acknowledging that these processes take place, and some have 'performative' power, does not mean accepting their desirability. Indeed, the point of their work was not that capitalist value should be more accurately measured so as to take account of the value of domestic labour but, on the contrary, that those categories and measurement itself should be challenged from the perspective of the forms of labour they contribute to materialise. This is why their project was very different from that pursued by feminists within the UN, who argued for the inclusion of domestic labour in GDP measurement. Second, the analysis of the changes that have occurred within the social reproductive field and which have accompanied the shift from Fordism to post-Fordism acquire analytical and political relevance as long as we keep open the always incomplete process of tracing the connections that make up the world economy. This means acknowledging the political work done by the various separations that, as argued in Chapter 2, are productive of (capitalist) value, which in turn means recognising that material and immaterial production, productive and reproductive labour, and Fordist and post-Fordist production, to mention only a few, are always constituted by what they seem to exclude so that the divisions themselves explode as we delve deeper into the boundaries that are supposed to demarcate them.

As with the more general point about 'perspectival seeing', this process of tracing connections is always incomplete and therefore partial. However, there is one important advantage in pursuing it: recognising its incompleteness and partiality enables us to be both more open to new and different connections, connections we had not previously seen, and more aware of our own perspectival seeing, thereby opening the possibility of political alliances. Federici, for instance, recognises that the separation between production and reproduction is problematic, yet sees it as a very material process that needs to be analysed in order to be challenged. And she has specifically opted for retaining it because, despite the fact that the value of most reproductive activities is today 'immediately realized, rather than being made conditional on the performance of the workers they produce ... [t]he expansion of the service sector has by no means eliminated home-based, unpaid reproductive work', and to a large extent it has not done away with 'the sexual division of labour in which it is embedded, which still divides production and reproduction in terms of the subjects of these activities and the discriminating function of the wage and lack of it' (2012:100).

To be sure, it is important to recognise that the processes through which the boundaries between the two spheres are constantly redrawn take places differently in different parts of the world. In Europe, the trend towards privatisation had started before austerity, with social reproductive activities increasingly provided in the market by profit-making entities alongside unpaid labourers in the household or the community. This trend is exacerbated under conditions of austerity that see some parts of the population (those whose wages have been withdrawn or squeezed) having to provide more unpaid labour while others (those whose wealth is increasing) can afford to purchase more social reproductive labour. But as Bedford and Rai (2010:3) have importantly reminded us, this is in no way an exceptional situation, as around the world people 'have survived crises through everyday struggles, [while] feminists have analyzed and campaigned on economic crises for decades'. Concerns about this *crisis* should therefore not obfuscate the importance of both these struggles and the feminist analyses that have accompanied them, pointing to the dis/continuities in the global reorganisation of socially reproductive labour:

> Consumption in the North (fueled by accumulating debt) has transformed the economies of the developing world, where a new international division of labor has gone hand in hand with an increasing mobilization of female workers and the consolidation of a gendered division of labor ... The factories where women and men work (sometimes in terrible conditions) in China, India, South Korea, and Malaysia feed the appetite of Northern markets (Sen 1999), and care chains grow longer as migrant laborers provide the domestic and market-based caretaking work necessary to sustain Northern economies (Raijman, Schammah-Gesser, and Kemp 2003). At the same time, these modes of exchange deepen class divisions while creating new metropolises in the South that both cater to the consumer hunger of the North and attract migrant workers from elsewhere in the South in historic proportions. These migrations put incredible pressure on

creaking social infrastructures and can result in increased vulnerability and violence. All of these developments have important implications for everyday lives in both the global South and the global North.

Bedford and Rai (2010:3)

Indeed, the point that emerges from the analysis provided by 'Wages for/ against Housework' scholars in the past four decades is that the crisis of social reproduction can neither be viewed in isolation from processes of restructuring that takes place in other parts of the world, nor can it be considered a new or accidental phenomenon. As Federici (2012:104) has argued:

> Capitalism fosters a permanent reproduction crisis. If this has not been more apparent in our lifetimes, at least in many parts of the Global North, it is because the human catastrophes it has caused have been more often externalized, confined to the colonies, and rationalized as an effect of cultural backwardness or attachment to misguided traditions and 'tribalism'. For most of the '80s and '90s, moreover, the effects of the global restructuring in the North were hardly felt except in communities of color, or could appear in some cases (e.g., the flexibilization and precarization of work) as liberating alternatives to the regimentation of the 9-to-5 routine, if not anticipation of a workerless society.

This is not to deny the importance of those struggles which have expressed the desire for freedom from the 9-to-5 routine and from waged society, whose power Ferderici acknowledges, together with that of anticolonial and women's liberation movements, as having provoked the offensive of capital, a reaction which has taken in part the form of disinvestment from social reproduction. It is, however, to highlight the crucial role that the separation between production and reproduction plays in articulating the economy–society nexus. I am aware that positing the separation between the two spheres as representative of what goes on in the world – adopting, as I have done, the social provisioning approach to economics as my perspectival seeing – is highly problematic. Not only may production and reproduction be conceived of and practiced differently in different parts of the world, *re-presenting* the world in these terms may once again be a universalising move with profound epistemological and ontological consequences, one which reduces the heterogeneity of actual existing arrangements to a unity that makes sense of, while acting upon, them through this particular lens, thereby excluding other ways of conceiving of life and being together. While bearing in mind the existence of such heterogeneity and the dangers my own perspectival seeing poses, I turn to consider arrangements around the wage, such as the ELR, and in particular their potential to act as provocations, that is as specific instances that aim to instigate a different nexus between production and reproduction in post-Fordist societies. Whether, even understood as provocations, these demands can open up the possibility of political alliances beyond the specific context from which they originate is another question; however, in denaturalising and politicising such separation, in exposing its productiveness, they open up a space from which to pose this question.

The wage as a provocation?

'Wages for/against Housework' can help us think of the separation between production and reproduction as historical rather than natural; of current value making processes as contingent, although not without constraints, and therefore contestable; and of alternative valorisations as processes which have always existed and continue to exist alongside those privileged by a certain social enquiry – for instance, one that focuses exclusively on competition – and which can be brought to bear on the ways we organise our living together (Gibson-Graham, 1996; Bedford and Jakobsen, 2009). The question is how to enable and support alternative valorisation processes and in this respect I wonder whether one should read this body of work as warning us against current attempts to engage the state through macroeconomic proposals such as the ELR. As Wendy Brown put it in the 1990s, there is a tension between acknowledging, on the one hand, that the state is not a monolithic entity but a web of social powers and, on the other, thinking we can shape it through our intentions and actions (Brown, 1995). Brown was critical of positions which maintained the radical potential inherent in women's involvement with the state because these presuppose a transcendental subject who simply moves from isolated to collectivised conditions, as opposed to a subject who is produced by these respective conditions. As she puts it: '[t]his is because the state does not simply address private needs or issues but also configures, administers and actively produces them' (1995:195). She was writing at a particular point in the history of the feminist movement in the US when the faith in engaging with the state was at its highest. However, her argument takes us back to the question of how to view a macroeconomic programme such as the ELR. The fact that it remains an institution of wage labour is perhaps enough to guard us against engaging with such an intervention. Yet, I wonder whether thinking that the effect of an engagement at this level can only be the production of more disciplined workers does not assume the same transcendental subject Brown identifies in uncritical discourses supportive of women's engagement with the state. My point is that, unless we assume that we exist outside the capitalist relations that make us, then it is worth taking more seriously the complexity of a process which, although initially based on wage labour, also presents the opportunity to affect the concept of 'work' and productive activity.

How so? I think the potential for transformation has to be considered in relation to the changes in the system of (capitalist) valuation that the programme might instil over time. This is because whereas the profit motive is behind most economic activities, and it is certainly one of the most important drivers of private investment, the design of ELR jobs allows in principle for considerations other than the pursuit of profit. This process therefore introduces a system of remuneration other than pecuniary evaluation, which is particularly important in, but not limited to, the context of care activities, many of which are not subject to the profit motive and often remain performed in individual households because firms do not find investing in such activities profitable. The most evident instance is the provision of childcare services affordable to all income groups, but this is by no means the only case. The point is that, as a result of including them under the ELR programme, these investment decisions are lifted from the exclusive realm of pecuniary valuation that currently limits employment and output. It is certainly the case that this relocation concerns jobs which would not otherwise have been offered by the private sector. The reason for this requirement is that the nature of the programme is one of cooperation rather than competition with the private sector, and, therefore, ELR jobs are not supposed to displace private sector employment. However, as feminist economists who have engaged with the programme have pointed out, jobs could be designed in a way that applies to a vast and crucial array of activities that are now performed in an individualised manner or to new activities worth investing in, where worth is assessed in terms of their contribution to the sustenance and enhancement of life. And if private firms wished to provide them, they would need to offer more affordable services and/or better pay conditions, introducing values other than profit maximisation (Todorova, 2009).

Thus, despite the fact that the programme is based on a very contested premise, it opens up the possibility for other forms of valuation of economic activity, and thus for other meanings of work, to emerge. On this possibility, I think, rests the programme's potential: without the threat of exclusion from subsistence on which the wage society has relied for so long, and with meaningful and effective participation in the job design of the programme, which is one of its crucial challenges, the way in which we conceive of 'work', which includes but is not limited to caring labour, could be radically affected. In place of the old 'work as worth' ideology which has permeated both the welfare state and neoliberal welfare to work initiatives, we could start a discussion on how to organise the activities we value in life, which is the significant contribution made by the social provisioning approach to economics. In this discussion the boundaries between production and reproduction could be called into question and the meaning of socially reproductive labour could be rearticulated, delinked from the house, the family, the mother and possibly the 'woman'.

This is one of the crucial differences with the citizenship income movement, for which income needs to be decoupled from wage labour. Gorz, one of its major proponents, argued that efforts should concentrate on 'distributing all the socially necessary work and socially produced wealth' so that 'people will be able to divide their lives between a wide range of activities which will have neither payment nor profitability as their necessary condition or goal' (Gorz, 1999:46). A similar argument has been made more recently by Kathi Weeks (2011), who also draws on the 'Wages for/against Housework' campaign and presents citizenship income as its successor. The latter has, for Weeks, the advantage of doing away with the productivist logic 'Wages for/against Housework' unintentionally produced by focusing too much on 'work'. However, although they both point to the need for a political break, it is not really clear how this is to come about besides demanding that the state grants a citizenship income for the productive labour we are all engaged with. Although I appreciate their attempt to move beyond the work ideology, I think their position leaves a whole set of important questions about this process unanswered, for instance about the nature of our interaction with the state on which we place the demand for a citizenship income, which, as Brown has pointed out, is never unidirectional but shapes our very subjectivity as we make our demands; the parameters informing the revaluation of the different forms of labour we engage with or wish to foster; and the means through which the massive 'indigent' population can effectively participate in redefining 'work'. The ELR, on the other hand, does not introduce a political break overnight; in many respects this is a very conservative arrangement as it keeps intact, and indeed extends, the wage relation and the work ideology *to start with*. However, it provides the opportunity to get a socially desirable wage immediately, which enables participation in exactly such a complex process. Now the issue of participation is crucial here. As 'Wages for/against Housework' scholars pointed out in relation to the socialisation of social reproductive labour, this is not just a matter of accepting or refusing to engage with the state:

> It is one thing to set up a day care centre the way we want it, and then demand that the State pay for it. It is quite another thing to deliver our children to the State and then ask the state to control them not for five but for fifteen hours a day. It is one thing to organise communally the way we want to eat (by ourselves, in group) and then ask the State to pay for it, and it is the opposite thing to ask the State to organise our

meals. In one case we regain some control over our lives, in the other we extent the State's control over us.

(Federici, 1975 in Federici, 2012:21)

It is the quality of engagement that matters and this is the reason why feminist economists supporting the ELR have posed the question of whether and how effective participation can be enabled, taking also into account that participation will mean different things in different communities. This is an important point, although not something I fully address here. The question I am interested in exploring, however, is whether we should consider these two modes of feminist engagement with the state and wage labour in opposition to one another. I would like to suggest that rather than considering them as antithetical, it may make more sense to focus on what is at stake for both, that is, on the attempt to think of alternative processes of (non-capitalist) valorisation as well as of the arrangements, institutional and otherwise, which might be able to sustain them. As far as the ELR programme is concerned, one obvious objection is that insisting on the wage at a time when the role wage labour plays in productive processes is becoming increasingly marginal is anachronistic if not counterproductive. I take this argument seriously. The first point to make, however, is that wage labour has only ever been a dominant form of labour in some parts of the world, and even in Fordist economies it has not been the only one. As already mentioned, part of the contribution of 'Wages for/ against Housework' was to show how the 'worker' could not be identified exclusively or even principally with the waged labourer regulated by clock time and protected by unions; and, specifically, how the waged labourer required for its own productive existence, productive of capitalist value that is, the existence of the unwaged labourer.

If the centrality of the waged labourer in analyses of value creation and struggles over value making processes has been called into question, the powerful role the wage played in disciplining Fordist societies by making people's own sense of worth and subsistence conditions dependent on whether they had access to work cannot be underestimated. Has this normative role ceased to exist? This is the second point, and one which I think it is worth reflecting on. The role of the wage in providing access to the means of subsistence has certainly declined in post-Fordist economies. But what about its disciplinary role? Can we dismiss it at a time when ever more individual and societal 'worth' is produced through the ideology of work? Can we dismiss its political charge? And the fact that, contrary to claims that 'the number of "superfluous" workers would explode in the beginning of the twenty-first century', two to three billion workers have instead been added to the global workforce (Caffentzis, 2013:4)? As Mezzadra and Neilson (2013a:88–89) have agued, one of the most significant aspects of the shift to post-Fordistism is the proliferation and heterogeneisation of labour figures as well as of the regimes that attempt to regulate them. Hence, the extreme difficulty, and they would certainly argue the undesirability, of any attempt to streamline the plurality of these regimes, however problematic and exploitative they are, through a blanket programme such as the ELR, particularly as the latter remains predicated on fixed national borders that these labour figures and regimes call into question. Grabham (2010:1287) makes a similar point in relation to feminist labour lawyers' attempts to promote policies that balance 'work' and 'life'. 'Is it really possible', she asks, 'to improve the working lives of precarious workers, and others, in the new economy by seeking to limit or standardize working time?' The very premise this balance is based on is problematic for a series of reasons, including the positing of an arbitrary inside and outside of working time that ends up associating the latter with the realm of freedom from capital and capitalist value. And when not equated with 'the development of the individualized, ethical, spiritual, successful self' this freedom tends to coincide with the domain of the care and the family (Grabham, 2010:1290–1291). While I agree that we need to ask 'What other possibilities exist, for feminism agitation and activism, even for policy, outside of times-based labour demands?' (2010:1287), the point I make is that forms of engagement with the wage and the state such as the ELR programme can have the power of *provocation*. In the same way as 'Wages for/against Housework' never aimed to calculate value more accurately so as to extend the wage to domestic workers but rather aimed to expose and critique the political work that both value and the wage were doing, ELR may be used not to turn people into more docile workers but could offer the opportunity to reopen both the wage and the state, and the value relation that binds them across and beyond national borders, to political scrutiny.

Conclusion

To be clear, far be it from me to consider the ELR as a normative or universal plan for action, certainly no more than 'Wages for/against housework' was 'a thing rather than a perspective' (Federici, 1975 in 2012:15). Instead, borrowing from Weeks' reflection on the campaign, I consider it as both a perspective and a provocation. As a perspective, Weeks points out, 'Wages for Housework served to create critical distance from the dominant discourse of work and family … it was an attempt to demystify and deromanticize domestic labour, while simultaneously insisting on its necessity and value'; and its potential consisted precisely of its ability 'to open up the wage relation to new kinds of scrutiny by politicising estimations of skills and determinations of value' (Weeks, 2011:129). Such scrutiny I think is what programmes such as the ELR might enable. As a perspective it allows us to: focus on the wage to demystify its role, that is, to show how it operates by making people dependent on it for their survival while simultaneously denying access to it; and to reopen the conflict between the labouring population and its means of reproduction which the wage is supposed, but was never able, to mediate. As a provocation, Weeks continues, 'Wages for/against Housework' 'served also to elicit the subversive commitments, collective formations and political hopes that it appears only to reflect'. A provocation 'should [thus] be understood as an attempted claim and incitement of antagonism, collective power and desire'. Indeed, '[n]either the policy proposal, with its aura of neutrality, nor the plea, with its solicitousness, manages to capture the … belligerence with which this demand was routinely presented' (2011:131–132). In its performative dimension, therefore, the ELR might enable us to demand of the current system what the system promises but cannot deliver. In the process it might even allow us to reopen the conflict which we have kept hidden through notions of scarcity and economic imperatives as well as to call into question the way social provisioning is organised. Here is how Cox and Federici talked about the power of provocations in the 1970s:

> As for the financial aspects of Wages for Housework, they are 'highly problematical' … only if we take the viewpoint of capital – the view point of the Treasury Department – which always claims poverty when it is replying to the working class. Since we are not the Treasury Department *and have no aspiration to be*, we cannot see with their eyes, and we did not even conceive of planning for them systems of payment, wage differentials, productivity deals. It is not for us to put limits on our power, it is not for us to measure our value. It is only for us to organise a struggle to get all we want, for us all, and on our terms.
>
> (Cox and Federici, 1976:14; in Weeks, 2011:132)

In a similar fashion, and although this may seem too easy an exit from a complex political question, we may say that the immigration control aspects of the ELR programme are problematic only if we take the viewpoint of capital and the perspective of the nation state. Indeed, contrary to the latter's claims, one crucial aim of immigration controls is, and I would argue has always been, that of accomplishing the 'complex filtering, selecting and channelling' (rather than the simple inclusion and exclusion) of labour figures for the benefit of capital's productivity (Mezzadra and Neilson, 2013a:165–166). Echoing Federici and Cox then, it is not for us to participate in the inclusion/exclusion game we are drawn into through the phantom-like presence and appeal of the citizen worker; it is rather for us to open up to scrutiny the 'differential inclusion' to which labour and citizenship regimes contribute by exposing the massive amount of labour power and labour figures that participate in the production of value which continues to be extracted across national borders and precisely through these different regimes.

Can we then think of the state and the wage provocatively again? And can we conceive of provocative institutional arrangements such as the ELR as working in tandem with self-valorisation processes, those processes which Federici argues are unfolding around us?[7] If in 1975, like now, demanding a wage is not a 'struggle to enter capitalist relations, because we have never been out of them' (Federici, 1975; in Federici, 2012:19) but a struggle to enable alternative valorisations, then the two are not in opposition to one another. As Cooper (1995:141) has put it in another context: '[W]hile counter-hegemonic projects encourage the transformation of structures on the basis of an aspirational future, anti-hegemony reminds us that such a future can only remain a strategic narrative'. The concept of provocations might appear premised on the language of intentionality: it certainly is if by intention we mean owing our 'perspectival seeing', our desire to intervene in the economy–society nexus so to make it otherwise; it is not if it means disregarding that, however much we own our perspective and acknowledge that the tracing is always an incomplete process, the formatting will be different from the reality we envisage. Thus, provocations are a strategic part of struggles for different performations of markets, societies and their nexus.

Notes

1 This is not to say that social reproductive activities are not profitable. Indeed, services such as advanced health care and higher education have been, and are being, privatised for profit. Access to these services remains, however, dependent on income. At the same time, sectors which do not require high capital investment, mainly because labour cannot be easily replaced with capital and its productivity improved through technological development, will experience a different degree of privatisation. I thank Judy Fudge for raising this issue and pointing me in the direction of Himmelweit's work which has shown how, in relation to these sectors, an increase in wages will amount to an increase in the cost of care, with the likely result of 'inequality in access to affordable care becoming a major issue in many high income countries' (Himmelweit, 2013:12).

2 As feminist economists point out, it might also be able to affect the gender norms that are at the basis of the distinction between work and leisure, and public (market) and private (non-market) economic activities, norms which contribute to occupational segregation and

discrimination in terms of pay and benefits (Jennings 1992; Todorova, 2009:14).

3　Latour and Lepinay (2009) have shown how pervasive this problematic understandings of political economy is, despite the fact that, as Mirowski and Nik-Khah point out (2007), even neoclassical economists have come to acknowledge that markets are fabricated rather than natural, with the consequent awareness of the performative role their models play in shaping the economy–society nexus (see Chapter 3). Here I am drawing attention to the contribution 'Wage for/against Housework' scholars have made to this debate through their work on reproductive labour.

4　As Picchio (1992:17–18) argues: 'The share of output distributed to the labouring population as a whole cannot exceed the limits consistent with capitalist accumulation. The lower limit of that share is defined by the need to reproduce the labouring population, and the upper limit is defined by the needs of accumulation. In this double constraint lies the problem of the classical political economists'.

5　We have seen in Chapter 2 how it can be argued Smith attempted to naturalise the propensity to accumulate. However, if on the one hand he posits an accumulation drive, on the other he recognises, and indeed invokes, the role institutions play in crystallising such propensity, never losing sight of the fact that this is a political process.

6　Bryan, Rafferty and Jefferis (2015) have recently argued that, whereas the pre-crisis securitisation process was akin to primitive accumulation as it relied on households' defaults in order to extract value, the post-2008 securitisation of households assets can instead be conceptualised in terms of 'real subsumption' of labour to finance. This is, for them, an important shift in the way in which value is created as labour is increasingly being made productive within finance through the development of financial assets that give exposure to households and provide for the credible measurement of those risks. As they put it: 'The financial vision is to imagine the multiple dimensions of household wealth and expenditure that could be made profitable: to create a spectrum of liquid financial market assets built on the performance of (illiquid) household assets' (2015:320). Central to this process has been the creation of asset and mortgage backed securities that 'involve selling the liquid dimension of households' exposures: not the fixity (the house) but the mortgage *payments*, not the health care but the health insurance *payments*, and not the student learning experience but *payments* from post-student earnings' (2015:320) (emphasis added). Whereas these securities were developed before the crisis, what we have witnessed after 2008 is the movement of 'household payments into fixed-period contractual relations, to ensure locked-in future payments on which securities can be built and penalties for non- or even prepayment that disturbs the valuation of securities'. And the requirement on households is that they 'continue to make ever-more expenditures that are securitizable and that capital can know precisely the risks of each household's default on any of these payments' (2015:321). At issue, therefore, is not default but payment as evidenced by 'the growing emphasis in state policies of the "responsibilization" of households to their fixed payment commitments, via changes in bankruptcy laws and programs of financial literacy … and the invocation of the imperative of a morality of contractual compliance (that people *should* keep paying the mortgage, even when they have negative equity)' (2015:324) (emphasis added). Adopting the analytic of raciality on a par with gender and class remains crucial, however, if we are to understand how labour becomes productive *within* finance as individual households' attributes are dissected, defined and measured: indeed, 'for each type of security financialized capital needs households to be tranched (grouped together in terms of their risk characteristics) for the risk of a payment default, so that the securities built on household payments can be properly graded and priced (2015:321).

7 'What is needed', Federici argues, 'is the reopening of a collective struggle over reproduction, reclaiming control over the material conditions of our reproduction and creating new forms of cooperation around this work outside the logic of capital and the market. This is not a utopia, but a process already underway in many parts of the world … Governments are now attempting to use the crisis to impose stiff austerity regimes on us for years to come. But through land takeovers, urban farming, community-supported agriculture, through squats, the creation of various forms of barter, mutual aid, alternative forms of healthcare – to name some of the terrains on which this re-organisation of reproduction is more developed – a new economy is beginning to emerge that may turn reproductive work from a stifling, discriminatory activity into the most liberating and creative ground of experimentation in human relations' (Federici, 2012:111).

Conclusion

In a world obsessed with linking and networking, in practices of work and political organisation, it is important to remember the relations established in moments of disconnection, discontinuity, and confrontation with the untranslatable. While capital labours under the illusion of translating everything into its language of value, living labour is continuously crossed by discontinuities and differences.

(Mezzadra and Neilson, 2013a:273)

This book has attempted to think about the possibility of desirable instances of political economic action. It has been particularly concerned with the kind of arrangements that might enable alternative valorisation processes to affect the economy–society nexus, specifically in the realm of international economic law and regulation. At one level I have engaged with the post-crisis regulatory debate, showing how it remains premised on a conceptual separation between the real and the financial spheres of the economy – and between real and financial values – that is unhelpful for understanding how value is produced in today's financialised economies. The consequence is that forms of regulatory intervention such as those mentioned in Chapter 1 are unable to affect the value making process that takes place at the intersection between financial markets and the so-called real economy. If conceptually inadequate, such separation has been very productive: indeed, the willingness to hold on to it when devising policy responses has generated inaction at a time when international action seemed possible. In the context of the regulatory debate surrounding financial derivatives, for instance, the role that financial innovations play in value making processes has been left largely undisturbed thanks also to the fact that it has remained unacknowledged. How to account differently for these processes and whether a different understanding may enable more desirable instances of political economic action have been the questions this book has grappled with. To explore them, I have drawn on what I have grouped together as constructivist approaches to value, arguing that they present us with a much more analytically and politically salient understanding of value making. At another level, therefore, this book has been an attempt to think with constructivist scholars what it means to acknowledge value's contingency and contestability, and what possibilities this question opens for thinking more imaginatively about international economic action.

Both the performativity of the economics school and the post-Fordist work associated with the Italian autonomist literature have provided crucial resources for understanding how the real and the financial spheres of the economy are coproduced. Coproduction points to the entanglements that implicate one sphere with another, enabling us to see, for instance, how the technology of the financial derivative, supposed to pertain to the financial sphere, is in actual fact able to affect labour processes, thought instead to strictly pertain to the 'real' sphere of the economy. This is certainly not a unidirectional movement. As seen in Chapters 1 and 3, derivatives themselves have become successful financial innovations, that is, they can act as devices of commensuration of bits of capital across time and space, because of legitimatory in addition to linguistic and technological processes that have coalesced together, giving derivatives strength and therefore making them 'productive'. Performativity scholars acknowledge that there are constraints upon contingency, that not everything is possible or can be made to 'work' at any time (MacKenzie, 2008:20). Yet they refrain from thinking about such constraints in terms of capitalist processes and labour struggles. As Mezzadra and Neilson (2013b: 10) point out, referring to network and assemblage theorists more generally, there is a tendency with these approaches to avoid talking about subjectivity because of 'fear of falling into the subject-object relationship'. The subject is replaced with the actor or agent while the 'object emerges as the ontological orientation of the moment'. Thus:

> the rupture of social relations and established forms of subjectivity connected with the operations of capital are obscured by a logic that turns the subject into just another thing. However, the reproduction of capital as a social relation is predicated upon profound, violent and contested dynamics that reshape the subjectivity of the dominated and exploited. Fundamental dis-symmetry and antagonism are factors in the material constitution of any network or assemblage. Attention to the subjectivity of labour is crucial in this regard.
>
> (Mezzadra and Neilson, 2013b:10)

This attention, for instance, enables us to see that financialisation and labour struggles are deeply interrelated, as Marazzi (2010) does when he traces the links between the struggles of the working class within and beyond factory walls; the profit squeeze under Fordism; and the search of

capital for new profitable opportunities through the increasing financialisation of the economy and, as argued in Chapter 1, of life itself. Seeing the
productivity of financial innovations such as derivatives does not need to
exclude serious scrutiny of these processes, with which financial innovations are deeply imbricated. And we cannot understand financialisation
in terms of a unidirectional movement whereby financial processes shape
subjectivity either: as Allon (2010, 2015) has pointed out, such an account
does not appreciate the manifold ways in which desires and expectations
contribute to the emergence of financial practices. What is needed is a
much more nuanced understanding of the loops that articulate subjectivity
and financial practices. The need for widening the spectrum of analysis is
what is at stake in the 'thick' description of performativity scholars; labour
struggles, as well as the response by capital, however, are part of the phenomenon to be described, even when at issue is the description of financial
instruments.

   That is why I have argued that it is still possible, and indeed important,
to talk about the 'law' of value and, simultaneously, to take seriously the
role financial instruments play in value making processes. The analysis
of financial derivatives, for instance, points to how they are not only the
means through which firms and governments protect themselves against
the risk of price volatility, nor are they merely instruments of speculation
that affect the prices of commodities: they are all these things, and much
more, including the fact that they are able to affect labour and production
processes around the world. And this is the case even as we recognise that
the latter are characterised by deep heterogeneity and that the diversity
of labour figures, regimes and processes today cut across national borders
(Mezzadra and Neilson, 2013a:88). Indeed, it is this very heterogeneity
that derivatives deal with as they bridge, through the measurement they
enact, the spatio-temporal gaps in global accumulation, thereby giving
continuity to production on a global scale (Bryan and Rafferty, 2006). We
can recognise, and should take seriously, this diversity and heterogeneity,
while at the same time seeing how the measuring and comparison that
mechanisms such as derivatives enact allow for more value to be extracted,
for instance, by increasing competition among firms and governments on a
global scale – and not only by means of bringing down labour costs – or by
making households 'subject to the same risk/return calculations that apply
to capital's evaluation of itself' (Bryan, Rafferty and Jefferis, 2015:321).
The extraction of value is indeed the unity to which this diversity and
heterogeneity is reduced.

   This is what, in a different context, and drawing on the work of Deleuze
and Guattari, Mezzadra and Neilson (2013a:81) refer to as the 'axiomatic
of capital': the most diverse practices paradoxically exist alongside a
process that perpetuates unity. This denies nothing to the multiplicity,

heterogeneity and specificity of practices, but enables us to enquire further into the 'stickiness' of processes and institutions while we bear in mind that such diversity is what always exceeds this 'stickiness'. For example, it enables us to acknowledge the power that competition exerts within markets, and at the same time recognise, as argued in Chapter 3, that competition is not the only point of reference for action. This has nothing to do with finding an explanatory force of last instance: all measuring mechanisms, including the technology of the derivative I have referred to, are heterogeneous things themselves. Yet there is something that persists in the way in which new terrains are constantly open for capital valorisation around the world and this is what the 'law' of value points to. But how else can this something be thought of, and what is 'our' relation to 'it'?

Lazzarato (2014:220) has recently argued that capitalism's force does not lie in the objectivism '"of the laws of the market" but in the capacity to articulate economics (and communication, consumption, the welfare state, etc) with the production of subjectivity in various ways'. Indeed, production, of wealth as well as subjectivity, takes place at the intersection of what he calls 'social subjection' and 'machinic enslavement' (2014:24). While social subjection, following Marx, is the process 'by which capital relations become personified' and embodied (we embody competition as well as abstract labour, for instance), machinic enslavement, a concept Lazzarato borrows from Deleuze and Guattari's work, denotes instead the process through which the individual 'is no longer instituted as an "individuated subject", "economic subject" ... or "citizen" [but is instituted as] ... a gear, a cog, a component part in the "business" and "financial system" assemblages' (2014:25).[1] The individual becomes a 'dividual' who does not stand in opposition to, nor makes use of, the external object but is contiguous with it: 'human agents, like non-human agents, function as points of "connection, junction and disjunction" of flows and as the networks making up the corporate, collective assemblage, the communication systems and so on' (2014:27). 'Dividuation' is also what Bryan, Rafferty and Jefferis (2015:322) argue is at stake in the process they describe as the real subsumption of labour to finance, a process that sees households becoming productive *within* finance as assets, liabilities, incomes and expenditures are disassembled 'so as to identify household attributes that might be discretely risk-evaluated, securitized, and tranched by credit rating agencies'.

This is why, Lazzarato argues, capital is neither a 'mere relationship among "people"' nor 'an intersubjective relationship'. Rather, 'a power relation exists but one constituted by social machines and "assisted" by technical machines' (2014:28). His is a critique of approaches that see only subjection as much as of those that discard the power of the 'human', 'man' or the 'individual'. As he puts it in relation to Bruno Latour's work, for instance, we can only say 'we have never been modern' (in the sense that the modernist separation between society and nature, humans and non-humans, never really made much sense) if we take into account machinic enslavement. This is not the case, however, if we take seriously social subjection since 'Capitalist deterritorialisation continually reterritorializes itself on "man" and on the individualism of the subject, the individual, *homo economicus*, etc., which, systematically failing, falls back on the "collectivism" of nationalism, racism, fascism, Nazism, machinism, class exploitation, etc'. Thus, Lazzarato concludes, 'by neglecting the connection between enslavement and subjection, Latour takes major political risks, for he is incapable of accounting for the dramatic endpoint towards which capitalism tends' (2014:260). Indeed, as Federici's work has demonstrated, we cannot understand how new terrains are constantly open to capitalist valorisation without an appreciation of the historical role that capital has played, and continues to play, in generating divisions and separations for the extraction of value. These separations are the result of historical and political processes; they are constantly shifting and my argument throughout this book has been that it is this shifting that it is important to trace.

It is clear, for instance, that the sexual division of labour cannot be taken for granted and that the gender, sexual, racial and class articulations of the social reproductive field are never fixed, anywhere in the world. At the same time, there is something about the re-articulation of the production–reproduction nexus that speaks to both the constant extraction of value and the production of relations of social subjection, to stay a little longer with Lazzarato, and this something may well have to do, as seen in Chapter 2, with the ways in which these relations are (historically) embodied. Thus, Federici's work has shown how, as the site to be made productive (of value), the body was turned into a work machine detached, seen as other from the mind, will, self and reason, its labour power ultimately capable of being owned by the 'person'. This body was, and still is, deeply gendered and racialised rather than the bearer of pure potentiality. Thus, Ferreira da Silva's 'analytic of raciality' points to the persistence of the interiority/exteriority juxtaposition that continually allows for certain bodies and individuals to be written off. This juxtaposition has always been problematic, analytically and politically, even though, as Bhandar (2012:112–27) points out, its illusion is disintegrating before our eyes through the disaggregation and parcelling out that new technologies allow. Yet the (raced, gendered, sexed and classed) body remains a crucial site for the extraction of value, whether we refer to the biological body, the power or potentiality of which it is the bearer, or the 'dividual' which is part of machinic enslavement.

This is why authors like Federici, Fortunati and Picchio have retained the distinction between production and reproduction, not because of any essence pertaining to them but to highlight the specificity of reproductive labour as both the terrain on which the production and reproduction of life is made possible, and that on which capitalist value is extracted. This double and antagonistic character is what is lost in analyses of reproductive labour as the generic quality of post-Fordist work. As Federici (2011:70–71) puts it in the context of her critique of Hardt and Negri's concept of affectivity, by 'defining affectivity as primarily interactivity, self-organisation and cooperation' we lose sight of the antagonistic relations that are constitutive of reproductive work: it is only when we think of 'reproductive work in its double, contradictory function, as reproduction of human beings and reproduction labour-power, that we can imagine forms of struggles and refusal that empower rather than destroying those we care for'. This cannot happen, however, 'if this activity is presented not as work organised by and for capital, but an activity already exemplifying work in post-capitalist society'.

There is a difference, Lazzarato (2014:220) writes, between saying that political subjectivation cannot derive from capital and examining their 'paradoxical interdependence':

> In the first case you have the illusion of a 'pure' politics, since subjectivation left adrift, never attains the necessary consistency to exist. In the second, you open up sites of experimentation and construction since subjectivation must, if it is to exist, take on consistency, *retraverse* and *reconfigure* the social, the political, the economic, and so on. (original emphasis)

Now, while I have not engaged with political subjectivation in any meaningful way in this book, opening up sites of experimentation is what I consider to be at stake in thinking about institutional arrangements as provocations. And it is in this respect that I depart from Lazzarato's argument that sees the impossibility for institutions such as the wage to enable the generation of anything other than the reiteration of the same old politics in a spirit of conservation rather than creation; as he puts it, 'all income, every benefit, and every wage, are part of an "ethos" that prescribes and engages certain conduct, that is a way of doing and saying' (2014:228). The trouble for Lazzarato lies in the difficulty to accept that the social democratic model 'today represents a genuine obstacle to the emergence of new objects and new subjects of politics. The model is constitutionally incapable of including political subjects other than the state, unions and business associations' (2014:239).

I am not disputing the power of the 'ethos' through which the wage continues to prescribe a 'certain conduct'; yet there is something about the 'paradoxical interdependence' between the worker's subjectivation and the capitalist institution of the wage that is too easily discarded by seeing their relation as one dimensional. I have argued that, when conceived of as provocations, institutional arrangements such as the ELR can be concrete sites of experimentation exactly because they recognise this paradoxical interdependence. Institutional arrangements, not the social democratic model that has linked 'social' value to the proper gendered, raced and sexed subject through the differential access to labour and welfare, can become concrete sites of contestation, experimentation and what Lazzarato refers to as the 'transvaluation of values'.[2] This does not detract from the importance of his ethical project, one that refuses to accept demonstration, argumentation and interlocution as the only terms of political subjectivation. This was indeed the whole point of pursuing 'Wages for/ against Housework' alongside the promotion of self-valorisation processes. If today the machinic enslavements we are part of need to be taken more seriously into account, their refrain remains an important one: to denounce value making processes not in order to produce more accurate accounting but to generate different connectivities, different ways of being together, and perhaps different subjectivities, through experimentation. As seen in Chapter 4, demanding wages for and against housework cannot be reduced to the linguistic and political representation Lazzarato criticises since the point was never to be included and represented but to challenge the very language of value that reduces the heterogeneity of living practices to the unity of wage labour. ELR could provide a similar opportunity today if seen as a provocation, in much the same way as ALBA could challenge the unity and homogeneity of competition in trade relations and the RMA the individualisation of risks and uncertainty and the precarisation of life in financial relations. There is absolutely nothing foregone about this potential; these arrangements could result in strengthening and extending the ethos of which they are part, but this is in no way a predetermined outcome.

Seeing the law of value as I have done as a specific kind of connectivity, one which is the result of historic and political processes that are constantly and differently re-enacted, raises the question of whether value and measurement can do something other than reducing heterogeneity to sameness and unity. Graeber (2005) has argued that value is about meaning making, pointing to how for all classical thinkers it had to do with making sense of the relation between the parts and the whole. As seen in Chapter 2, the model that Smith advanced in accounting for the wealth of nations, and which Marx criticised by providing a different analysis of the workings of the capitalist system, can be seen as an attempt to think, and act upon, ie to actively shape, this relation. Should this conceptualisation be abandoned altogether or can the connectivity that value refers to be thought of in a way that does not perpetuate the analytically and politically problematic assumption of ever being able to account for totalities and their parts? In her exploration of agential realism, Barad (2007) draws on Bohr's philosophy-physics to argue that 'we are part of the nature we seek to understand'.[3] From this perspective, the juxtaposition of observer and observed collapses as no*thing* is the object or the subject to start with: these are not preexisting entities but they come into being as a result of what Barad calls 'intra-action'. What this means is that we can only ever know some of the parts that make the constant 're(con) figuration' of the world. As she puts it: 'since there is no outside to the universe, there is no way to describe the entire system ... description always occurs from within: *only parts of the world can be made intelligible to itself at a time, because the other part of the world has to be the part that it makes a difference to*' (2007:351) (original emphasis).

As the tracing of this connectivity is always a partial process, separations such as those between production and reproduction or economy and society may be needed to make sense of our actions, even though the more we zoom in the more we realise there is no essence pertaining to these spheres. However, it is important to keep in mind that these separations are always political and it is over their meaning, effects and redrawing that it is important to struggle, at least if we take seriously Barad's argument that description is what makes a difference to the part being described. This is what 'Wages for/against Housework' scholars have done by paying attention to the conceptual and political work that separations do while at the same time retaining a focus on our ability to contest value making processes. As seen in Chapter 2, this argument has a long history, one in which value's contingency has been thought together with its contestability. In certain respects Nietzsche's *Genealogy* is an invitation to think about action as the struggle over values, and I would argue that 'perspectival seeing' remains a crucial aspect of struggles even as we acknowledge that 'theorising and experimenting are not about intervening (from outside) but about intra-acting from within, and as part of, the phenomena produced' (Barad, 2007:56).

Thus, while the *agencement* of materials such as financial technologies and economic models is to be taken into account, action from a particular perspective does not need to be discarded. There is nothing particularly troubling about seeing from a certain perspective, one that, for instance, views as undesirable the privatisation of risks and uncertainty that currently invests the economy–finance nexus; and the precarisation of life that traverses the production–reproduction one. 'Perspectival seeing' can inform action and at the same time acknowledge that the world our action contributes to is not all of our making.[4] Similarly, there is nothing necessarily problematic in seeing 'measures' as mechanisms for orienting action if we take value to be about 'selecting out, comparing within a system of reference, and acting upon this comparison' (De Angelis, 2005:67). That is why I am inclined to agree with De Angelis that 'a measure is *always* a discoursive device that acts as point of reference, a benchmark, a typical norm, a standard' (2005:67). And this is also why I believe that, rather than focusing on the becoming immeasurable of value (as if value was once *within* measure), it makes more sense to ask: '*how* do we measure what we measure? Who or what sets the standard for the measurement? What forms of measurement are used in different discourses? What powers have been deployed and/or repressed with this or that measuring process? And what loops articulate human practices to practices of measures?' (De Angelis, 2005:69).

Institutional arrangements, conceived of as provocations, can be crucial sites where these questions can be posed and alternative valorisations promoted. And maintaining a focus on institutional arrangements as sites of struggles, alongside the many instances of self-valorisation practices that are conducted at a distance from the state, is important at a time when institutions, and the state in particular, have been relegated to a secondary place in struggles over power and knowledge (Chakravartty and Ferreira da Silva, 2012). I am aware that assuming a 'we' in talking about struggles over alternative political economic arrangements is problematic; and that the value making processes I have critiqued in this book may be seen as pertaining only to some economies. I hope that, however incomplete and limited the analysis of the dis/continuities that make up our global economy has been, this book has managed to give a sense of how deeply entangled spaces, places, processes (and subjectivities) are, not in the sense of being simply connected with, but as being made through, one another. Production and reproduction, the financial and the economic spheres, material and immaterial labour, Western and non-Western economies, financialisation and immiseration are only some examples touched upon in this book. I am aware, though, that much more work is needed if we are to engage in a 'politics of possibilities' that does not assume any easy common ground. What is crucial, Barad (2007:246) argues, referring to the work of Ruth Wilson Gilmore, is 'to trace the "frictions of distance", to do analyses that move through the range of scales of injustice, not by pointing out similarities between one place or event and another, but by understanding how these places or events are made through one another'.

Notes

1 As Lazzarato points out, Deleuze and Guatarri borrowed the term 'enslavement' from cybernetics where it is used to refer to the 'government' of the different parts of a system 'to ensure the cohesion and equilibrium of the functioning of the whole' and extended it to social machines such as the factory, business or the welfare system' (Lazzarato, 2014:26).

2 '[T]he issue is a "transvaluation" of all values, which also and especially concerns those with no part and their mode of subjectivation.
In transvaluation, equality combines with difference, political equality
with ethical differentiation' (Lazzarato, 2014:240). Lazzarato continues: 'if the paradoxical relations between equality and difference cannot
be inscribed in a constitution, in laws, if they can be neither learned
nor taught but only experimented, then the question of the modalities of acting together becomes fundamental ... How do we invent
and practice both equality and "ethical differentiation" (singularization)
while breaking with the machinic enslavements and social subjections
of modern-day capitalism that have a dual hold on our subjectivity?'
(2014:248–249).

3 Understanding the construction of the world as the inseparability of
matter and meaning, agential realism is 'an epistemological, ontological
and ethical framework' that puts the emphasis on intra, rather than inter,
action. Unlike interaction, 'which assumes that there are separate individual agencies that precede their interaction, the notion of intra-action
recognises that distinct agencies do not precede, but rather emerge
through, their intra-action'. 'It is important to note', Barad adds, 'that
the "distinct" agencies ... are only distinct in relation to their mutual
entanglement; they do not exist as individual elements' (2007:32–33).

4 Thus the question for Lazzarato (2014:36) is how 'we avoid the false
choice between being condemned to function like one component part
among others in the social machinery and being condemned to become
an individual subject, human capital (worker, consumer, user, debtor),
"man"'.

Bibliography

Adkins, Lisa (2015) 'What Are Post-Fordist Wages? Simmel, Labor Money, and the Problem of Value' 114:2 *South Atlantic Quarterly* 331–353.

Adkins, Lisa (2009) 'Feminism After Measure' 10:3 *Feminist Theory* 323–339.

Adkins L. and Dever M. (2014) 'Housework, Wages and Money: The Category of the Female Principal Breadwinner in Financial Capitalism' 29 *Australian Feminist Studies* 50–66.

Alessandrini, Donatella (2015) 'Financial Derivatives and the Challenge of Performation Where Contingency Meets Contestability' in E. Cloatre and M. Pickersgill (eds), *Knowledge, Technology and Law: At the Intersection of Socio-Legal and Science and Technology Studies* (Routledge, 2015) 154–170.

Alessandrini, Donatella (2013a) 'A Social Provisioning Employer of Last Resort: Post-Keynesianism Meets Feminist Economics' 4:2 *World Review of Political Economy* 230–254.

Alessandrini, Donatella (2013b) 'WTO at a Crossroads: The Crisis of Multilateral Trade and the Political Economy of the Flexibility Debate' 5:2 *Law, Trade and Development* 256–285

Alessandrini, Donatella (2012) 'Immaterial Labour and Alternative Valorisation Processes in Italian Feminist Debates: (Re)exploring the "Commons" of Re-production' 1:2 *feminists@law* 1–28.

Alessandrini, Donatella (2011) 'Regulating Financial Derivatives? Risks, Contested Values and Uncertain Futures' 20:4 *Social and Legal Studies* 1–22.

Alessandrini, Donatella (2010) *Developing Countries and the Multilateral Trade Regime: The Failure and Promise of the WTO's Development Mission* (Oxford: Hart Publishing).

Allon, Fiona (2015) 'Money, Debt, and the Business of "Free Stuff"' 114:2 *The South Atlantic Quarterly* 283–305.

Allon, Fiona (2011) '"Home Economics": The Management of the Household as an Enterprise' 68 *Journal of Australian Political Economy* 128–148.

Althusser, Louis and Balibar, Etienne (1970) *Reading Capital* (London and New York City: New Left Books).

Alviar Garcia, Helena (2014) 'Social Policy and the New Development State', in D. Trubek, H. Alviar, D. Coutinho and A. Santos (eds), *Law and the New Developmental State: The Brazilian Experience in Latin American Context* (Cambridge: Cambridge University Press).

Anghie, Antony (2007) *Imperialism, Sovereignty and the Making of International Law* (Cambridge: Cambridge University Press).

Antonopoulos, Rania (2007) 'The Right to a Job, the Right Types of Projects: Employment Guarantee Policies from a Gender Perspective', Working Paper No 516. Levy Economics Institute.

Arnoldi, Jakob (2004) 'Derivatives: Virtual Values and Real Risks' 20:6 *Theory, Culture and Society* 23–42.

Arrighi, Giovanni (2009) *Adam Smith in Beijing: Lineages of the Twenty-First Century* (London and New York: Verso).

Arthur, Brian W., Holland, John H., LeBaron, Blake, Palmer, Richard and Tayler, Paul (1996) 'Asset Pricing Under Endogenous Expectations in an Artificial Stock Market', Social Sciences Working Paper. Available at http://ssrn.com/abstract=2252 (accessed 24 April 2015).

Arvidsson, Adam (2012) 'General Sentiment: How Value and Affect Converge in the Information Economy' 59 *The Sociological Review* 39–59.

Asamblea Nacional (2009) Ley Orgánica del Régimen de Soberanía Alimentaria. Comisión Legislativa y de Fiscalización, Quito: Ecuador. Available at http://asambleanacional.gov.ec/blogs/soberania_alimen taria/files/2009/01/ley-soberaniaalimentaria.pdf (accessed 24 April 2015).

Bacallao-Pino, Lazaro (2014) 'Tensions and Challenges: Interrelationships between Social Movements and Progressive Institutional Politics in Latin America' 1 *Journal of Arts and Humanities* 84–97.

Backer, Larry and Molina, Augusto (2009–2010) 'Cuba and the Construction of Alternative Global Trade Systems: ALBA and Free Trade in the Americas' 31 *University of Pennsylvania Journal of International Law* 679–752.

Barad, Karen (2007) *Meeting the Universe Halfway: Quantum Physics and the Entanglement of Matter and Meaning* (Durham and London: Duke University Press).

Barrett, Michelle (1980) *Women's Oppression Today: Problems in Marxist Feminist Analysis* (London: Verso).

Bayliss, Kate (2014) 'Case Study: The Financialisation of Water in England and Wales', Working Paper Series No 52 (Leeds: FESSUD).

Beck, Ulrich (2006) 'Living in the World Risk Society' 35 *Economy and Society* 329–345.

Beckert, Jens and Aspers, Patrick (2011) *The Worth of Goods: Valuation and Pricing in the Economy* (Oxford: Oxford University Press).

Bedford, Kate (2009) *Developing Partnerships: Gender, Sexuality, and the Reformed World Bank* (Minneapolis: University of Minnesota Press).

Bedford, Kate and Jakobsen, Janet (2009) 'Towards a Vision of Sexual and Economic Justice', Report (New York: Barnard Center for Research on Women).

Bedford, Kate and Rai, Shirin (2010) 'Feminists Theorize International Political Economy – Introduction' 36:1 *Signs* 1–18.

Bellamy Foster, John and Magdoff, Fred (2009) *The Great Financial Crisis: Causes and Consequences* (New York: Monthly Review Press).

Beneria, Lourdes (2007) 'Gender and Social Construction of Markets', in Irene Staveren (ed), *Gender and the Social Construction of Markets* (London: Routledge).

Bhandar, Brenna (2015) 'Status as Property: Identity, Land and the Dispossession of First Nations Women in Canada', in B. Bhandar and D. Bhandar (eds), *Reflections on Dispossession: Critical Feminisms* (Living Commons Press). Forthcoming.

Bhandar, Brenna (2014) 'Property, Law and Race: Modes of Abstraction' 4 *UC Irvine Law Review* 203–218.

Bhandar, Brenna (2013) 'Race, Gender and Class: Some Reflections on Left Feminist Politics and Organising' 3:1 *feminists@law* 1–7.

Bhandar, Brenna (2012) 'Dis-Assembling Legal Form: Ownership and the Racial Body', in M. Stone, R.I. Wall and C. Douzinas (eds), *New Critical Legal Thinking* (London: Routledge).

Bijker Wiebe, Hughes, Thomas and Pinch, Trevor (2012) *The Social Construction of Technological Systems: New Directions in the Sociology and History of Technology* (Cambridge, Mass.: MIT Press).

BIS (2010) 'OTC Derivatives Market Activity in the Second Half of 2009', Report (Basel: Bank for International Settlement). Available at http://www.bis.org/press/p100511.htm (accessed 24 April 2015).

Bresser-Pereira, Luiz (2006) 'The New Developmentalism and Conventional Orthodoxy' 20 *Sao Paulo Em Perspectiva* 1–33.

Brown, Wendy (1995) *States of Injury: Power and Freedom in Late Modernity* (Princeton: Princeton University Press).

Bryan, Dick and Rafferty, Michael (2013) 'Fundamental Value: A Category in Transformation' 42:1 *Economy and Society* 130–153.

Bryan, Dick and Rafferty, Michael (2006) *Capitalism with Derivatives: A Political Economy of Financial Derivatives, Capital and Class* (London: Palgrave Macmillan).

Bryan, Dick, Martin, Randy and Rafferty, Michael (2009) 'Financialization and Marx: Giving Labor and Capital a Financial Makeover' 41:4 *Review of Radical Political Economics* 458–72.

Bryan, Dick, Rafferty, Michael and Jefferis, Chris (2015) 'Risk and Value: Finance, Labor, and Production' 114:2 *South Atlantic Quarterly* 307–329.

Bryan, Dick, Rafferty, Michael and Ackland, Neil (2000) 'Financial Derivatives and Marxist Value Theory', Working Paper ECOP2000–2 (Sydney: School of Economics and Political Science).

Burges, Sean (2007) 'Building a Global Southern Coalition: The Competing Approaches of Brazil's Lula and Venezuela's Chávez' 28:7 *Third World Quarterly* 1343–1358.

Caffentzis, George (2013) *In Letters of Blood and Fire: Work, Machines, and the Crisis of Capitalism* (Oakland: PM Press).

Caffentzis, George (2005) 'Immeasurable Value?: An Essay on Marx's Legacy' 10 *The Commoner* 87–114.

Caffentzis, George (1992) 'The Work/Energy Crisis and the Apocalypse', in Midnight Notes Collective (eds), *Midnight Oil: Work, Energy, War, 1973–1992* (Brooklyn NY: Autonomedia).

Callon, Michel (2008) 'What Does it Mean To Say That Economics is Performative?' in D. MacKenzie, F. Muniesa and L. Siv (eds), *Do Economics Make Markets: On the Performativity of Economics* (Woodstock, Oxfordshire: Princeton University Press).

Callon, Michel (1998) *The Laws of the Markets* (Oxford: Blackwell Publishers).

Callon, Michel and Caliskan, Koray (2005) 'New and Old Directions in the Anthropology of Markets', Paper presented to Wenner-Gren Foundation for Anthropological Research, New York, 9 April.

Chakravartty, Paula and Ferreira da Silva, Denise (2012) 'Accumulation, Dispossession, and Debt: The Racial Logic of Global Capitalism – An Introduction' 64:3 *American Quarterly* 361–385.

Chatrath, Arjun, Ramchander, Sanjay and Song, Frank (1996) 'The Role of Futures Trading Activity in Exchange Rate Volatility' 16:5 *The Journal of Futures Markets* 561–584.

Chimni, Bhupinder (2006) 'The World Trade Organization, Democracy and Development: A View from the South' 40:1 *Journal of Word Trade* 5–36.

Coase, Ronald (1976) 'Adam Smith's View of Man' 19:3 *Journal of Law and Economics* 529–546.

Codeluppi, Vanni (2008) *Il Biocapitalismo: Verso lo Sfuttamento Integrale di Corpi, Cervelli ed Emozioni* (Torino: Bollati Boringheri).

Collins, Harry and Evans, Robert (2002) 'The Third Wave of Science Studies: Studies of Expertise and Experience' 32:2 *Social Studies of Science* 235–296.

Cooper, Davina (1995) *Power in Struggle: Feminism, Sexuality and the State* (New York: New York University Press).

Cooper, Melinda (2008) 'Infrastructure and Event: Urbanism and the Accidents of Finance', Presentation at the Center for Place, Culture and Politics, CUNY.

Cooper, Melinda and Konings, Martijin (2015) 'Rethinking Money, Debt, and Finance after the Crisis' 114:2 *South Atlantic Quarterly* 239–423.

Costoya, Manuel (2011) 'Politics of Trade in Post-Neoliberal Latin America: the Case of Bolivia' 30:1 *Bulletin of Latin American Research* 80–96.

Cox, Nicole and Federici, Silvia (1976) *Counter-Planning from the Kitchen: Wages for Housework, A Perspective on Capital and the Left* (Brooklyn: New York Wages for Housework Committee).

Dalla Costa, Mariarosa (2002) 'The Door to the Garden: Feminism and Operaismo', Paper presented at the *Operaismo a Convegno* Conference, 1–2 June 2002. Rome. Available at http://libcom.org/library/the-door-to-the-garden-feminism-and-operaismo-mariarosa-dalla-costa (accessed 24 April 2015).

Dalla Costa, Mariarosa (1972) 'Quartiere, scuola e fabbrica dal punto di vista della donna' 1 *L'Offensiva*: *Quaderni di Lotta Femminista* 23–34.

Dalla Costa, Mariarosa and Fortunati, Leopoldina (1977) *Brutto Ciao* (Roma: Edizioni delle Donne).

Dalla Costa, Mariarosa and James, Selma (1972) *The Power of Women and the Subversion of the Community* (Bristol: Falling Wall).

Danby, Colin (2004) 'Toward a Gendered Post Keynesianism: Subjectivity and Time in a Non Modernist Framework' 10:3 *Feminist Economics* 55–75.

De Angelis, Massimo (2005) 'Value(s), Measure(s) and Disciplinary Markets' 10 *The Commoner* 66–86.

de Goede, Marieke (2015) 'Speculative Values and Courtroom Contestations' 114:2 *South Atlantic Quarterly* 355–375.

de Goede, Marieke (2005) *Virtue, Fortune, and Faith: A Genealogy of Finance* (Minneapolis: University of Minnesota Press).

Desai, Radhika (2011) 'The New Communists of the Commons: Twenty-First-Century Proudhonists' 1:2 *International Critical Thought* 204–223.

Dodd, Randall (2005) 'Derivatives Markets: Sources of Vulnerability in U.S. Financial Markets', in Gerald Epstein (ed), *Financialization and the World Economy* (London: Edward Elgar).

Dodd-Frank (2010) Wall Street Reform and Consumer Protection Act of 2010, H.R.4173, 111th Congress, 2009–2010.

Dowling, Emma and Harvie, David (2014) 'Harnessing the Social: State, Crisis and (Big) Society' 48:5 *Sociology* 869–886.

Ecuador, Permanent Mission to the United Nations (2008) *The Ecuadorian Proposal for a Crisis Response Agenda From the South* (New York: UN).

Elson, Diane (1979) 'The Value Theory of Labour', in D. Elson (ed), *Value: The Representation of Labour in Capitalism* (London: CSE Books).

Epstein, Gerard (2005) 'Introduction', in G. Epstein (ed), *Financialization and the World Economy* (Cheltenham: Edward Elgar).

Escobar, Arturo (2010) 'Latin America at a Crossroads' 34:1 *Cultural Studies* 1–65.

Escobar, Arturo (1995) *Encountering Development: The Making and Unmaking of the Third World* (Princeton: Princeton University Press).

Fama, Eugene (1970) 'Efficient Capital Markets: A Review of Theory and Empirical Work' 25 *Journal of Finance* 383–417

Fantone, Laura (2007) 'Precarious Changes: Gender and Generational Politics in Contemporary Italy' 87 *Feminist Review* 5–20.

Federici, Silvia (2012) *Revolution at Point Zero: Housework, Reproduction and Feminist Struggle* (Oakland: PM Press).

Federici, Silvia (2011) 'On Affective Labour', in M.A. Peters and E. Bulut (eds), *Cognitive Capitalism, Education and Digital Labour* (New York: Peter Lang).

Federici, Silvia (2010) 'The Reproduction of Labour-Power in the Global Economy, Marxist Theory and the Unfinished Feminist Revolution', Paper presented at the seminar held at University of California, Santa Cruz on 27 January 2010 on the Crisis of Social Reproduction and Feminist Struggle. Available at http://culturalstudies.ucsc.edu/EVENTS/Winter09/FedericiReading.pdf (accessed 24 April 2015)

Federici, Silvia (2008) 'Precarious Labour: A Feminist Perspective' 1 *The Journal of Aesthetics and Protest* 1–9.

Federici, Silvia (2004) *Caliban and the Witch: Women, the Body and Primitive Accumulation* (New York: Autonomedia).

Federici, Silvia (1980) 'Wages against Housework', in E. Malos (ed), *The Politics of Housework* (London: Allison and Busby).

Federici, Silvia (1975) *Wages Against Housework* (Bristol: Falling Wall Press).

Federici, Silvia and Fortunati, Leopoldina (1984) *Il Grande Calibano. Storia del corpo social ribelle nella prima fase del capitale* (Milano: FrancoAngeli Editore).

Ferreira da Silva, Denise (2007) *Towards a Global History of Race* (Minneapolis: University of Minnesota Press).

Folbre, Nancy and Nelson, Julie (2000) 'For Love and Money – or Both?' 14:4 *The Journal of Economic Perspectives* 123–140.

Forstater, Matthew (1999) 'Functional Finance and Full Employment: Lessons from Lerner for Today' 33:2 *Journal of Economic Issues* 475–482.

Fortunati, Leopoldina (2007) 'Immaterial Labour and its Machinization' 7:1 *Ephemera: Theory and Politics in Organisation* 139–157.

Fortunati, Leopoldina (2003) 'Real People, Artificial Bodies', in L.

Fortunati, J.E. Katz and R. Riccini (eds), *Mediating the Human Body: Technology, Communication and Fashion* (Mahwah, New Jersey: Erlbaum).

Fortunati, Leopoldina ([1981]1995) *The Arcane of Reproduction*, trans. H. Creek, J. Fleming (ed) (New York: Autonomedia).

Foucault, Michel ([1966]2002) *The Order of Things* (London: Routledge).

Fudge, Judy (2011) 'Labour as a "Fictive Commodity": Radically Reconceptualising Labour Law', in G. Davidov and B. Langville (eds), *The Idea of Labour Law* (Oxford: Oxford University Press).

Fumagalli, Andrea (2007) *Bioeconomia e Capitalismo Cognitivo: Verso un Nuovo Paradigm di Accumulazione* (Roma: Carocci Editore).

Fumagalli, Andrea and Mezzadra, Sandro (2009) *Crisi Dell'Economia Globale: Mercati Finanziari, Lotte Sociali e Nuovi Scenari Politici* (Verona: OmbreCorte–UniNomad).

Garbade, Kenneth and Silber, William (1983) 'Price Movements and Price Discovery in Futures and Cash Markets' 65:2 *Review of Economics and Statistics* 289–297.

Gibson-Graham, Julie-Katherine (1996) *The End of Capitalism (As We Knew It): A Feminist Critique of Political Economy* (Oxford: Blackwell).

Gordon, Gemmill (1986) *Futures and Options Trading in Commodity Markets* (Paris: ICC).

Gordon, Wendell (1997) 'Job Assurance: The Job Guarantee Revisited' 32:3 *Journal of Economic Issues* 826–834.

Gorz, Andre (1999) *Reclaiming Work: Beyond the Wage Based Society* (Cambridge: Polity Press).

Goss, Barry (1976) *The Economics of Futures Trading* (London: Macmillan).

Gowan, Peter (2009) 'Crisis in the Heartland: Consequences of the New Wall Street System' 55 *New Left Review* 5–29.

Grabham, Emily (2010) 'Dilemmas of Value in Post-Industrial Economies: Retrieving Clock Time Through the Four-Day Work Week?' 42:4 *Connecticut Law Review* 1285–1297.

Graeber, David (2005) 'Value as the Importance of Actions' 10 *The Commoner* 18–65.

Graham, Benjamin and Dodd, David (1940) *Security Analysis: Principles and Technique* (Columbus: McGraw-Hill)

Granovetter, Mark (1999) 'Coase Encounters and Formal Models: Taking Gibbons Seriously' 44 *Administrative Science Quarterly* 161–162.

Granovetter, Mark (1990) 'Interview', in Richard Swedberg, *Economics and Sociology* (Princeton: Princeton University Press).

Green, Andy, Mostafa, Tarek and Preston, John (2010) 'The Chimera of Competitiveness: Varieties of Capitalism and the Economic Crisis', Centre for Learning and Life Chances in Knowledge Economies and Societies. Available at http://www.llakes.org/wp-content/uploads/2010/08/R.-Chimera-of-Competitiveness.pdf (accessed 24 April 2015).

Gudynas, Eduardo, Guevara, Ruben and Roque, Francisco (2008) *Heterodoxos. Tensiones y posibilidades de las politicas sociales en los gobiernos progresistas de Americas del Sur* (Montevideo: CLAES y OXFAM). Available at http://www.democraciasur.com (accessed 24 April 2015).

Haraway, Donna (1985) 'Manifesto for Cyborgs: Science, Technology and Socialist Feminism in the 1980s' 90 *Socialist Review* 65–108.

Hardt, Michael and Negri, Antonio (2009) *Commonwealth* (Cambridge, Mass.: Harvard University Press).

Hardt, Michael and Negri, Antonio (2004) *Multitude: War and Democracy in the Age of Empire* (New York: Penguin).

Hardt, Michael and Negri, Antonio (2001) *Empire* (Cambridge, Mass. and London: Harvard University Press).

Hardt, Michael and Negri, Antonio (1994) *The Labour of Dionysus: A Critique of the State Form* (Minneapolis: University of Minnesota Press).

Hart-Landsberg, Martin (2009) 'Martin Learning from ALBA and the Bank of the South: Challenges and Possibilities' 61:4 *Monthly Review* 1–20.

Harvey, David (2010) *The Enigma of Capital: and the Crises of Capitalism* (London: Profile Books Ltd).

Harvey, John (2005) 'Post Keynesian versus Neoclassical Explanations of Exchange Rate Movements: A Short Look at the Long Run', Working Paper (Texas: Department of Economics, Texas Christian University).

Harvie, David (2005) 'All Labour is Productive and Unproductive' 10 *The Commoner* 132–171.

Hauserman, Bridget (2007) 'Exploring the New Frontiers of Law & Development. Reflections on Trubek/Santos eds., *The New Law and Economic Development*' 8 *German Law Journal* 533–547.

Hill Collins, Patricia (2000) *Black Feminist Thought: Knowledge, Consciousness and the Politics of the Women's Movement* (New York: Routledge).

Himmelweit, Susan (2013) 'Feminist Economic Theory and Policy Challenge' 16 *Journal of Gender Studies Ochanomizu University* 1–18.

Hirschman, Albert (1997) *The Passions and the Interests: Political Arguments for Capitalism before Its Triumph* (Princeton: Princeton University Press).

Hochschild, Arlie (1983) *The Managed Heart: Commercialization of Human Feeling* (Berkeley: University of California Press).

Ishikawa, Tetsuya (2009) 'Don't Kill Off Derivatives', *Guardian*, 1 February 2009.

Jabbour, George (1994) 'Prediction of the Future Currency Exchange Rates from Current Currency Futures Prices: The Case of the GM and JY' 14 *The Journal of Futures Markets* 25–36.

Jasanoff, Sheila (2003) 'Breaking the Waves in Science Studies: Comment on H.M. Collins and Robert Evans, The Third Wave of Science Studies' 33:3 *Social Studies of Science* 380–400.

Jenkins, Simon (2008) 'The End of Capitalism? No, Just Another Burst Bubble', *Guardian*, 15 October 2008.

Jennings, Ann (1992) 'Not the Economy', in William Dugger and William Waller (eds), *The Stratified State* (Armonk, New York: M.E. Sharpe Inc).

Johnson, Deborah and Wetmore, Jameson (2009) *Technology and Society: Building our Sociotechnical Future* (Cambridge, Mass.: MIT Press).

Kaboub, Fadhel (2007) 'Employment Guarantee Programs: A Survey of Theories and Policy Experiences', Working Paper No 498. (Levy Economics Institute).

Krippner, Greta (2005) 'The Financialization of the American Economy' 3 *Socio-Economic Review* 173–208.

Krugman, Paul (1983) 'New Theories of Trade among Industrial Countries' 73:2 *The American Economic Review* 343–347.

Krugman, Paul (1981) 'Intraindustry Specialization and the Gains from Trade' 89:5 *The Journal of Political Economy* 959–973.

Lang, Andrew (2011) *World Trade Law after Neo-liberalism: Re-Imagining the Global Economic Order* (Oxford: Oxford University Press).

Lang, Andrew (2009) 'Legal Regimes and Regimes of Knowledge: Governing Global Services Trade', Working Paper No 15 (London: LSE Legal Studies). Available at http://ssrn.com/abstract=1423538 (accessed 24 April 2015).

Latour, Bruno (2005) *The Politics of Nature: How to Bring the Sciences into Democracy* (Cambridge: Harvard University Press).

Latour, Bruno (1993) *We Have Never Been Modern* (Harvard: Harvard University Press).

Latour, Bruno and Lepinay, Vincent (2009) *The Science of Passionate Interests: an Introduction to Gabriel Tarde's Economic Anthropology* (Chicago: Prickly Paradigm Press).

Lazzarato, Maurizio (2014) *Signs and Machines: Capitalism and the Production of Subjectivity* (London: Semiotext(e)).

Lazzarato, Maurizio (1996) 'Immaterial Labor', trans. P. Colilli and E. Emery, in M. Hardt and P. Virno (eds), *Radical Thought in Italy: A Potential Politics* (Minneapolis: University of Minnesota Press).

Leon, Magdalena (2009) 'Changing the Economy in Order to Change Life', in A. Acosta and E. Martinez (eds), *El Buen Vivir: Una Via Para EL Desarollo* (Quito: Abya Yala).

Leon, Magdalena (2008) 'El Buen Vivir: Objetivo y Camino para Otro Modelo', in R. Borja (ed), *Analisis Nueva Constitucion* (Quito: ILDIS-La Tendencia).

Leon, Magdalena (1984) 'Measuring Women's Work: Methodological and Conceptual Issues in Latin America' 15:1 *IDS Bulletin* 12–17.

Levin, Lee (1995) 'Towards a Feminist, Post-Keynesian Theory of Investment', in E. Kuiper and J. Sap (eds), *Out of the Margin Feminist Perspectives on Economics* (London: Routledge).

Lipuma, Edward and Lee, Benjamin (2004) *Financial Derivatives and the Globalisation of Risks* (Durham and London: Duke University Press).

Lorente, S. (2004) 'Key issues regarding Domotic Applications' in Proceedings: 1st International Conference on Information and Communication Technologies: From Theory to Application, Damascus, Syria 19th–23rd April 2004.

Lothian, Tamara and Unger, Roberto (2011) 'Crisis, Slump, Superstition and Recover: Thinking and Acting beyond Vulgar Keynesianism', Working Paper series No 395 (New York: The Center for Law and Economic Studies, Columbia University School of Law).

Lysandrou, Photis (2011) 'Global inequality as one of the root causes of the financial crisis: a suggested explanation' 40:3 *Economy and Society* 323–394.

MacKenzie, Donald (2009) *Material Markets: How Economic Agents are Constructed* (Oxford: Oxford University Press).

MacKenzie, Donald (2008) *An Engine, Not a Camera: How Financial Models Shape Markets* (Cambridge, Mass.: MIT Press).

MacKenzie, Donald, Muniesa, Fabian and Siu, Lucia (2008) *Do Economists make Markets? On the Performativity of Economics* (Woodstock, Oxfordshire: Princeton University Press).

Macmillan, Fiona (2004) 'International Economic Law and Public International Law: Strangers in the Night' 6 *International Trade Law and Regulation* 115–124.

Majewski, Raymond (2004) 'Simulating an Employer of Last Resort Program', in George Argyrous, Mathew Forstater and Gari Mangiovi (eds), *Growth, Distribution and Effective Demand: Alternatives to Economic Orthodoxy, Essays in Honour of Edward J Nell* (Armonk, New York: M.E. Sharpe Inc).

Maldonado, Rita and Saunders, Anthony (1983) 'Foreign Exchange Futures and the Law of One Price' 12:1 *Financial Management* 19–23.

Mann, Geoff (2010) 'Value after Lehman' 18 *Historical Materialism* 72–188.

Marazzi, Christian (2010) *The Violence of Financial Capitalism* (London: The MIT Press).

Martin, Randy (2002) *Financialization of Daily Life* (Philadelphia, PA: Temple University Press).

Marx, Karl ([1884]1981) *Capital*, Vol 3 (London: Penguin Classics).

Marx, Karl ([1867]1990) *Capital*, Vol 1 (London: Penguin Classics).

Marx, Karl ([1863–1883]1992) *Capital*, Vol 2 (London: Penguin Classics).

Marx, Karl ([1857–1858]1973) *Grundrisse: Foundations of the Critique of Political Economy* (London: Vintage).

Maurer, Bill (2002) 'Repressed Futures: Financial Derivatives' Theological Unconscious' 31 *Economy and Society* 15–36.

McIntosh, Mary (1978) 'The State and the Oppression of Women', in A. Kuhn and A. Wolpe (eds), *Feminism and Materialism: Women and Modes of Production* (London and New York: Routledge and Kegan Paul).

McNally, David (2009) 'From Financial Crisis to World-Slump: Accumulation, Financialisation and the Global Slowdown' 17 *Historical Materialism* 35–83.

Merton, Robert (1968) *Social Theory and Social Structure* (New York: Free Press).

Mezzadra, Sandro and Neilson, Brett (2013a) *Border as Method: or, the Multiplication of Labour* (Durham and London: Duke University Press).

Mezzadra, Sandro and Neilson, Brett (2013b) 'Extraction, Logistics, Finance: Global Crisis and the Politics of Operations' 178 *Radical Philosophy* 8–18.

Mies, Maria (1986) *Patriarchy and Accumulation on a World Scale: Women in the International Division of Labour* (London: Zed Books).

Milberg, William (1994) 'Is Absolute Advantage Passe? Towards a Keynesian/Marxian theory of International Trade', in M. Glick (ed), *Competition, Technology and Money, Classical and Post-Keynesian Perspectives* (London: Edward Elgar).

Minsky, Hyman (1986) *Stabilizing an Unstable Economy* (New Haven, CT: Yale University Press).

Mirowski, Philip (1991) 'Postmodernism and the Social Theory of Value' 13:4 *Journal of Post-Keynesian Economics* 565–582.

Mirowski, Philip (1990) 'Learning the Meaning of a Dollar: Conservation Principles and the Social Theory of Value in Economic Theory' 57:3 *Social Research* 689–717.

Mirowski, Philip and Nik-Khah, Edward (2008) 'Markets Made Flesh: Performativity and a Problem in Science Studies, Augmented with the Consideration of the FCC Auctions', in D. MacKenzie, F. Muniesa and L. Siu (eds), *Do Economists Make Markets: On the Performativity of Economics* (Woodstock, Oxfordshire: Princeton University Press).

Mitchell, William and Watts, Martin (1997) 'The Path to Full Employment' 30:4 *Australian Economic Review* 433–435.

Mohun, Simon (2004) 'The Labour Theory of Value as Foundation for Empirical Investigations' 55:1 *Metroeconomica* 65–95.

Morini, Cristina (2007) 'The Feminization of Labour in Cognitive Capitalism' 87 *Feminist Review* 40–59.

Moya, Elena (2010) 'Brussels Proposes Tougher Regulation of Derivatives Market', *Guardian*, 15 September 2010.

Muhr, Thomas (2010) 'TINA go Home! Alba and Re-Theorising Resistance To Global Capitalism', Research Paper (Bristol: Centre for Globalisation, Education and Societies).

Muniesa, Fabian and Callon, Michel (2007) 'Economic Experiments and the Construction of Markets', in D. MacKenzie, F. Muniesa and L. Siu (eds), *Do Economists Make Markets? On the Performativity of Economics* (Woodstock, Oxfordshire: Princeton University Press).

Negri, Antonio ([2000]2003) 'Kairos, Alma Venus, Multitudo', in *Time for Revolution*, trans. M. Mandarini (London: Continuum).

Negri, Antonio (1968) *Keynes and the Capitalist Theory of the State*, reprinted in Negri (1994) *Labor of Dionysus: A Critique of the State Form* (Minneapolis: University of Minnesota Press).

Nelson, Julie (2003) 'Confronting the Science/Value Split: Notes on Feminist Economics, Institutionalism, Pragmatism and Process Thought' 27:1 *Cambridge Journal of Economics* 49–64.

Nietzsche, Friedrich ([1887]2008) *On the Genealogy of Morals* (Oxford: Oxford University Press).

Offer, Avner (2012) 'Self-interest, Sympathy and the Invisible Hand: From Adam Smith to Market Liberalism', Oxford University Economic and Social History Series, Paper No 101 (Oxford: Economics Group, Nuffield College, University of Oxford).

Pahuja, Sundhya (2013) *Decolonising International Law: Development, Economic Growth and the Politics of Universality* (Cambridge: Cambridge University Press).

Panzieri, Raniero (1994) 'Lotte Operaie Nello Sviluppo Capitalistico', in R. Panzieri, *Spontaneità e organizzazione. Gli anni dei 'Quaderni rossi' 1959–1964: Scritti scelti a cura di Stefano Merli* (Pisa: Franco Serantini).

Partnoy, Frank (2002) 'ISDA, NASD, CFMA, and SYNY: The Four Horsemen of Derivatives Regulation?', Working Paper 39 (San Diego: University of San Diego Law School).

Paulré, Bernard (2009) 'Capitalismo Cognitivo e Finanziarizzazione dei sistemi Economici', in A. Fumagalli and S. Mezzadra (eds), *Crisi Dell'Economia Globale: Mercati Finanziari, Lotte sociali e nuovi scenari politici* (Verona: OmbreCorte-UniNomade).

Pérez Caldentey, Esteban and Vernengo, Matias (2010) 'Modern Finance, Methodology and the Global Crisis' 52 *Real-World Economics Review* 69–81.

Picchio, Antonella (2009) 'Condiciones de Vida: Perspectivas, Analisis Economico y Politicas Publicas' 7 *Revista de Economia Critica* 27–54.

Picchio, Antonella (1992) *Social Reproduction: The Political Economy of the Labour Market* (Cambridge: Cambridge University Press).

Pickergill, Martyn (2012) 'The Co-production of science, ethics and emotion', 37:6 *Science, Technology & Human Values* 579–603.

Poovey, Mary (1998) *A History of the Modern Fact: Problems of Knowledge in the Science of Wealth and Society* (Chicago: Chicago University Press).

Power, Marilyn (2004) 'Social Provisioning as a Starting Point for Feminist Economics' 10:3 *Feminist Economics* 3–21.

Pryke, Michael (2007) 'Geomoney: An Option on Frost, Going Long on Clouds' 38 *Geoforum* 576–588.

Pryke, Michael (2006) 'Speculating on Geographies Finance' *CRESC Working Paper Series*, Working Paper no 24 (Centre for Socio-Cultural Change, Open University).

Rai, Shirin, Hoskyns, Catherine and Thomas, Dania (2010) 'Depletion and Social Reproduction', CSGR Working Paper 274/11, Centre for the Study of Globalisation and Regionalisation (Warwick: University of Warwick).

Ratton, Sanchez and Badin, Michelle (2011) 'Developmental Responses to the International Trade Legal Game: Examples of Intellectual Property and Export Credit Law Reforms in Brazil', Paper presented at the LANDS meeting, Sao Paulo, 12–13 May. Available at http://www.law.wisc.edu/gls/documents/developmental_responses_to_international_trade_michelle_badin.pdf (accessed 24 April 2013).

Republica del Ecuador (2009) 'Plan Nacional Para el Buen Vivir, 2009–2013: Construyendo un Estado Plurinacional e Intercultural', Report (Quito, Ecuador: SENPLADES).

Rifkin, Jeremy (2000) *L'era dell' accesso: La rivoluzione della new economy* (Milano: Mondadori).

Robinson, Joan (1972) 'The Second Crisis of Economic Theory' 62:1 *The American Economic Review* 1–10.

Robinson, Joan (1960) *Collected Economic Papers*, Vol 2 (Oxford: Basil Blackwell).

Rogoff, Kenneth (1996) 'The Purchasing Power Parity Puzzle' 34 *Journal of Economic Literature* 647–668.

Rosenberg, Jordana (2014) 'The Molecularization of Sexuality: on Some Primitivisms of the Present' 17:2 *Theory and Event* 1–19.

Rubin, Isaac (1972) *Essays on Marx's Theory of Value* (Detroit: Black and Red).

Safri, M. and Graham, J. (2010) 'The Global Household: Toward a Feminist Post-Capitalist International Political Economy' 36:1 *Signs: Journal of Women in Culture and Society* 99–125.

Santos, Alvaro (2012) 'Carving Out Policy Autonomy for Developing Countries in the World Trade Organization: the Experience of Brazil and Mexico' 52:3 *Virginia Journal of International Law* 551–632.

Schmidt, Vivien (2008) 'Discursive Institutionalism: The Explanatory Power of Ideas and Discourse' 11 *Annual Review of Political Science* 303–326.

Seguino, Stephanie (2010) 'The Global Economic Crisis, its Gender and

Ethnic Implications, and Policy Responses' 18:2 *Gender and Development* 179–199.

Shaikh, Anwar (2007) 'Globalization and the Myth of Free Trade', in A. Shaikh (ed), *Globalization and the Myth of Free Trade: History, Theory an Empirical Evidence* (London: Routledge).

Shaikh, Anwar (1996) 'Free Trade, Unemployment and Economic Policy', in J. Eatwell (ed), *Global Unemployment: Loss of Jobs in the 90s* (Armonk, NY and London: M.E. Sharpe).

Shaikh, Anwar (1980) 'The Law of International Exchange', in E. Nell (ed), *Growth, Profit and Property: Essays on the Revival of Political Economy* (Cambridge: Cambridge University Press).

Smith, Adam ([1776]2012) *An Inquiry into the Nature and Causes of the Wealth of Nations* (London: Wordsworth).

Smith, Adam ([1759]2009) *The Theory of Moral Sentiments* (London: Penguin Classics).

Smith, Adam ([1723–1790]1978) *Lectures on Jurisprudence* (Oxford: Oxford University Press).

Smith, Douglas (1966) 'Introduction', in Friedrich Nietzsche ([1887]1966) *On the Genealogy of Morals* (Oxford: Oxford University Press).

Spillman, Lyn (2012) *Solidarity in Strategy: Making Business Meaningful in American Trade Associations* (Chicago: University of Chicago Press).

Stoll, Hans and Whaley, Robert (1990) 'Stock Market Structure and Volatility' 3 *The Review of Financial Studies* 37–71.

Strange, Susan (1997) *Casino Capitalism* (Manchester: Manchester University Press).

Tarde, Gabriel (1902) *Psychologie Economique* (Paris: F. Alcan).

Terranova, Tiziana (2000) 'Free Labor: Producing Culture for the Digital Economy' 63:18 *Social Text* 33–58.

Todorova, Zdravka (2009) 'Employer of Last Resort Policy and Feminist Economics: Social Provisioning and Socialization of Investment', MPRA Paper 16240 (Munich: University Library of Munich, Germany).

Tong, Rosemarie (1998) *Feminist Thought: A More Comprehensive Introduction* (Boulder, CO: Westview Press).

Trebilcock, Michael and Howse, Robert (2005) *The Regulation of International Trade* (London: Routledge).

Trebilcock, Michael, Howse, Robert and Eliason, Antonia (2012) *The Regulation of International Trade* (London: Routledge).

Tronti, Mario (1966) *Operai e Capitale* (Turin: Einaudi).

Trubek, David (2014) 'Law and the "New Developmentalism"', in D. Trubek, H. Alviar Garcia, D. Coutinho and A. Santos (2014), *Law and the New Developmental State: The Brazilian Experience in Latin American Context* (Cambridge: Cambridge University Press).

Trubek, David (2012) 'Reversal of Fortune? International Economic

Governance, Alternative Development Strategies and the Rise of the BRICS', Paper presented at the European University Institute, Florence, Italy. Available at http://www.eui.eu/Events/download.jsp?FILE_ ID=3062 (accessed 24 April 2015).

Trubek, David (2008) 'Developmental States and the Legal Order: Towards a New Political Economy of Development and Law', University of Wisconsin Legal Studies, Research Paper. Available at http://ssrn.com/ abstract=1349163 (accessed 24 April 2015).

Trubek, David (2007) 'The Owl and the Pussy-Cat: Is there a future for "Law and Development?"', University of Wisconsin Legal Studies, Research Paper (Madison: University of Wisconsin Law School). Available at http://hosted.law.wisc.edu/wordpress/wilj/files/2012/02/ trubek.pdf (accessed 22 April 2015).

Trubek, David and Santos, Alvaro (2006) *The New Law and Economic Development: an Appraisal* (Cambridge: Cambridge University Press).

Trubek, David, Alviar Garcia, Helena, Coutinho, Diogo and Santos, Alvaro (2014) *Law and the New Developmental State: The Brazilian Experience in Latin American Context* (Cambridge: Cambridge University Press).

Van Staveren, Irene and Danby, Colin (2010) 'Forum: Introduction to the Symposium on Post-Keynesian and Feminist Economics' 34:6 *Cambridge Journal of Economics* 1105–1172.

Vercellone, Carlo (2009) 'Crisi della Legge di Valore e Divenire Rendita del Profitto. Appunti Sulla Crisi Sistemica del Capitalismo Cognitivo', in A. Fumagalli and S. Mezzadra (eds), *Crisi Dell'Economia Globale: Mercati Finanziari, Lotte sociali e nuovi scenari politici* (Verona: OmbreCorte-UniNomade).

Vercellone, Carlo (2006) *Capitalismo Cognitivo: Conoscenza e Finanza nell'epoca postfordista* (Roma: Manifestolibri).

Vickrey, William (1993) 'The Other Side of the Coin' 37:2 *The American Economist* 5–16.

Virno, Paolo (2004) *A Grammar of the Multitude: for an Analysis of Contemporary Forms of Life* (New York: Semiotex(e)).

Vrolijk, Coenraad (1997) 'Derivatives Effect on Monetary Policy Transmission', Working Paper WP-97-121 (Washington: IMF Monetary and Exchange Department).

Weeks, John (1982) *Capital and Exploitation* (Princeton: Princeton University Press).

Weeks, Kathi (2011) *The Problem with Work: Feminism, Marxism, Antiwork Politics and Post Work Imaginaries* (Durham, NC: Duke University Press).

Williams, Toni (2013) 'Who Wants to Watch? A Comment on the New International Paradigm of Financial Consumer Market Regulation' 36 *Seattle University Law Review* 1187–1217.

Williams, Toni (2007) 'Empowerment of Whom and for What? Financial Literacy Education and the New Regulation of Consumer Financial Services' 29 *Law and Policy* 226–256.

Women's Budget Group (2013) 'The Impact on Women of the Coalition Government's Spending Round 2013' (London: WBG). Available at http://wbg.org.uk/pdfs/WBG-Analysis-June-2013-Spending-Round.pdf (accessed 22 April 2015).

Women's Budget Group (2011) 'The Impact on Women of the Budget'. London: WBG. Available at http://www.wbg.org.uk/index_7_282363355.pdf (accessed 22 April 2015).

Women's Budget Group (2010) 'The Impact on Women of the Coalition Spending Review 2010' (London: WBG). Available at http://www.wbg.org.uk/RRB_Reports_2_1887146139.pdf (accessed 22 April 2015).

Wray, Randall (2008) 'The Commodities Market Bubble: Money Manager Capitalism and the Financialisation of Commodities', Economics Public Policy Brief Archive (New York: The Levy Economics Institute).

Wray, Randall (2007) 'The Employer of Last Resort Programme: Could it Work for Developing Countries?' Economic and Labour Markets Paper 2007/5. Geneva: International Labour Office.

Wray, Randall (1998) *Understanding Modern Money: The Key to Full Employment and Price Stability* (Northampton, Mass.: Edward Elgar).

Wynne, Brian (2003) 'Seasick on the Third Wave? Subverting the Hegemony of Propositionalism' 33:3 *Social Studies of Science* 401–417.

Yamey, Basil S., Sandor, Richard L. and Hundley, Brian (1985) *How Commodity Futures Market Work* (London: Trade Policy Research Centre).

Yi Kang, Laura (2012) 'The Uses of Asianization: Figuring Crises, 1997–98 and 2007–?' 64:3 *American Quarterly* 361–494.

Zelizer, Viviana (2011) 'How I Became a Relational Economic Sociologist and What Does that Mean?', Working Paper No 5 (Princeton: Center for the Study of Social Organization).

Zelizer, Viviana (2010) *Economic Lives: How Culture Shapes the Economy* (Princeton: Princeton University Press).

Zelizer, Viviana (2005) *The Purchase of Intimacy* (Princeton: Princeton University Press).

Zelizer, Viviana (1994) *The Social Meaning of Money: Pin Money, Paychecks, Poor Relief, and Other Currencies* (Princeton: Princeton University Press).

Index

accumulation of stock 56–8, 62
'affective' workers 38
affectivity, concept of 151
agencements, concept of 92, 93–4, 153
agriculture: and commerce/manufacturing 55; and derivatives 20
Allon, F. 33, 148
alternative valorisation processes: institutions and 9–11, 154; wage as provocation 137–41, 142, 143
Althusser, L. and Balibar, E. 61
Anatonopoulos, R. 128
Arrighi, G. 26, 60, 109–11, 115
Arthur, B.W. et al. 25
austerity 1–2, 3–4, 135

Backer, L. and Molina, A. 116–17
Barad, K. 153, 154
Beckert, J. and Aspers, P. 5
Bedford, K. and Rai, S. 76, 135–6
Beneria, L. 114
Bhandar, B. 73–4, 131–2, 150
Black-Scholes-Merton model of option pricing 25, 91–3, 94, 96–7
blending and binding function of derivatives 22–3, 26, 43
body and Self/Reason split 72–3
Bolivian Alternative for Our Peoples of the Americas (ALBA) 115–17
Bretton Woods, collapse of of 23, 33, 96
Brown, W. 137, 139
Bryan, D.: et al. 17, 23, 27, 33–4, 75–6, 134, 148, 149; and Rafferty, M. 21–3, 33, 42, 148

Caffentzis, G. 32–3, 38
Caliban and the Witch (Federici) 69–73

Callon, M. 90, 94
capitalism: 'casino capitalism' 21; and labour theories 28–42; subjection/subjectivation 149–50, 151–2
Chakravartty, P. and Ferreira da Silva, D. 132–3, 154
classical political economy (Smith) 53–61
Coarse, R. 112–13
'cognitive' workforce and 'affective' workers 38
colonialism: Latin America 101, 102; and race 69, 73–4, 131–3, 150
commerce see trade/commerce
commodities: agricultural 20; exchangeability of 58–9; production and value of 63–8
competition: comparative and competitive advantage 106–8; global competitiveness 109–15
complementarity: competition and 109–15; and cooperation 115–17
contestability and contingency of values 4–9, 50–3; derivatives 18–19, 23, 42–4; Federici: *Caliban and the Witch* and 'misfortune' of reproduction 69–76; Marx: critical reading strategy 61–9, 75, 76; Nietzsche 76–80; Smith: economic 'model' 53–61
Cooper, M. 143
Cox, N. and Federici, S. 142
crisis: feminist and global perspective 135–6; of value measurement 27; see also financial crisis
critical reading strategy (Marx) 61–9, 75, 76

Dalla Costa, M. et al. 7–8, 35
Danby, C. 122, 123

For Product Safety Concerns and Information please contact our
EU representative GPSR@taylorandfrancis.com or Taylor & Francis
Verlag GmbH, Kaufingerstraße 24, 80331 München, Germany.